Hiccups

Hiccups

A Pediatrician Mom's Guide to Surviving Your First Year of Parenthood

Diane Arnaout, MD, FAAP

BLOOMSBURY ACADEMIC
NEW YORK • LONDON • OXFORD • NEW DELHI • SYDNEY

BLOOMSBURY ACADEMIC

Bloomsbury Publishing Inc, 1359 Broadway, 12th Floor, New York, NY 10018, USA
Bloomsbury Publishing Plc, 50 Bedford Square, London, WC1B 3DP, UK
Bloomsbury Publishing Ireland, 29 Earlsfort Terrace, Dublin 2, D02 AY28, Ireland

BLOOMSBURY, BLOOMSBURY ACADEMIC and the Diana logo are trademarks of
Bloomsbury Publishing Plc

First published in the United States of America 2026

Copyright © Diane Arnaout, 2026

Cover design: Dustin Watson
Cover image © istock/id-work

All rights reserved. No part of this publication may be: i) reproduced or transmitted in any form, electronic or mechanical, including photocopying, recording or by means of any information storage or retrieval system without prior permission in writing from the publishers; or ii) used or reproduced in any way for the training, development or operation of artificial intelligence (AI) technologies, including generative AI technologies. The rights holders expressly reserve this publication from the text and data mining exception as per Article 4(3) of the Digital Single Market Directive (EU) 2019/790.

Bloomsbury Publishing Inc does not have any control over, or responsibility for, any third-party websites referred to or in this book. All internet addresses given in this book were correct at the time of going to press. The author and publisher regret any inconvenience caused if addresses have changed or sites have ceased to exist, but can accept no responsibility for any such changes.

A catalog record for this book is available from the Library of Congress.

ISBN: HB: 979-8-8818-0609-5
ePDF: 979-8-2163-7397-1
eBook: 979-8-8818-0610-1

Typeset by Deanta Global Publishing Services, Chennai, India
Printed and bound in the United States of America

For product safety related questions contact productsafety@bloomsbury.com.

To find out more about our authors and books visit www.bloomsbury.com and sign up for our newsletters.

For my children, Jack and Abby.
You have taught me more than any book ever could,
and I love you.
Thank you for understanding why I wrote about
your butt rashes online.

Contents

Introduction 1
1 The First Few Days 9
    A Few Vital Just-Got-Home Pointers 9
    How Much Should My Baby Be Eating in the Beginning? 11
    When Do I Let People Visit? 12
    When Can I Go Out with the Baby? 13
    Safe Sleep! 15
    What Should My Baby Wear to Sleep? Should I Swaddle My Baby? 18
    How Do I Start Good Sleep Practices as Soon as We Get Home from the Hospital? 18
    How Often Do I Need to Wake My Baby to Eat? 19
    A Straight-from-My-Office Handout 20
        Newborn Notes from a Pediatrician 20

2 Newborns: They Dislike Not Being Inside of a Uterus 23
    Learn Your Baby's Personality 24
    What to Expect When It Comes to Crying 25
    Causes of Fussiness in Young Babies 25
    For Fussiness: Mimic the Womb 27
    Get Creative 28
    Technology Can Help! 29

How Often Do I Bathe My Baby? 30
So, What Do I Do with My Baby at This Age? How Do I Entertain Them? 31

3 The Newborn Body Is Weird 33
Head 33
Hair 35
Eyes/Ears/Mouth 35
Skin 37
Neck and Chest 40
Belly 41
Hips 42
Penises and Vaginas 42
Arms, Hands, Legs, and Feet 44
Fingers and Toes 45

4 Breastfeeding Can Be a Real B*tch 47
Breastfeeding and Data 49
Learning to Breastfeed Ain't a Simple Task 51
The First Few Days of Breastfeeding 52
How Do You Know When Your Milk Is "In"? 53
Holding Your Baby While Nursing 54
Getting a Good Latch 55
Your Poor Nips (and Other Breastfeeding Pains) 56
Pumping 58
Can I Mix Formula and Breast Milk? 59
How Long Should You Breastfeed? 59
Can You Breastfeed When You've Been Drinking Alcohol? 60
Do Pacifiers Ruin Breastfeeding? 60
What's the Deal with Tongue Ties? 61
Why Do I Sometimes Feel Suddenly Sad or Anxious When I Nurse? 62

Can I Breastfeed If I Didn't Physically Give Birth to My Child? 64
What's the Deal with Vitamin D Drops? 64
Help! My Breastfed Baby Won't Take a Bottle! 65

5 Formula Facts and Fibs 67
Which Formula Should I Choose? 67
Quick Dr. Diane Formula Tips 70
How Do I Mix Formula? What Type of Water Do I Use? 71
Cleaning? Sterilizing? 73
What Temperature Does the Formula Need to Be? 73
How Do I Transition from Breast Milk to Formula? 74
How Long Does My Baby Need to Be on Formula? 74
Should I Order My Formula from Europe? 74
Should I Use Toddler Formula? 75

6 The Period of PURPLE Crying: Why Weeks 3–12 May Drive You Absolutely Bonkers 77
What Causes the Period of PURPLE Crying? 79
What Are Some Typical Things I May See During This Phase? 80
What Helps? 80
When Should I Worry? When Is It Too Much? 81
Milk and Soy Protein Intolerance (MSPI) 82

7 Reflux and Other Problems: The Reason Your Baby May Sometimes Puke Like That Kid in *The Exorcist* 85
What Is Reflux? 86
How Many Babies Experience Reflux? How Long Does It Last? 86
What Causes Reflux? 86
What Are Some Signs of Reflux? 87
What Should I Do About My Baby's Reflux? 87
Should We Try a Medication for My Baby's Reflux? 88

It Seems Like So Much Milk Is Coming Up. When Do I
  Worry? 89
What Is Milk and Soy Protein Intolerance and How Does It
  Relate to Reflux? 90
Do I Elevate My Baby at Night So They Won't Spit Up? 90

8   Solids, Liquids, and Gases 93
Why Are My Newborn's Poops So Dark and Sticky? 94
How Often Should My Baby Poop and Pee? 94
What Are Newborn Poops Supposed to Look Like? 95
What Poop Colors Should I Worry About? 95
Why Does My Baby Look Like She's in Pain When She
  Poops? 95
What Do I Do for Constipation? 96
What Do I Do for Diarrhea? 97
What Are These Orange or Pink Spots in My Newborn's
  Diaper? 98
What Is the Best Way to Burp a Baby? How Often Do I Need to
  Burp Her? 98
My Baby Farts a Lot. Is This Normal? 99

9   Four to Seven Months: The Happy Potato Stage 101
What Is a Happy Potato? 101
What Are Some Changes I May See at This Age? 103
What Do I Do with My Baby at This Age? How Do I Entertain
  Them? 104
What About Going Outside? Can I Use Sunscreen? DEET? 105
Which Toys Are Worth the Money? 106

10   "Sleep Is for the Weak."—Most Babies 109
Why Is Sleep Important for Babies? 111
Is It Normal for My Baby to Make Noises While She
  Sleeps? 111
What Are Wake Times? 112

What Does It Look Like When My Baby Is Overtired? 113
How Soon Can I Start a Schedule? 113
How Many Naps Should My Kid Be Taking? 114
So, How Do I Set My Baby Up for Nighttime Sleep
    Success? 114
What Is the Eat-Play-Sleep Routine? 116
What Is Sleep Training? 117
Does Sleep Training Even Work? 118
It's So Hard for Me to Hear My Baby Fuss! Is Sleep Training Safe
    for Babies? 119
Quick Tips by Age 120
    Six Weeks to Three Months 120
    *Four Months: The Dreaded Four-Month Sleep
        Regression* 121
    Six Months and Older 122
What About "Sleep Hiccups"? 123
When Can My Baby Sleep in Her Own Room? 123

11 Sight, Hearing, and Baby Squeaks 125
How Much Can My Baby See? 125
What Are Red Flags for Vision Problems? 126
Is It Normal for My Baby to Be Cross-Eyed? 126
What Is a "Lazy Eye"? 127
When Will I Know My Baby's Eye Color? 127
How Do I Know If My Baby Can Hear? 128
When and How Do I Protect My Baby's Hearing? 128
What Sounds Should My Baby Be Making During Their First
    Year? 129
How Do I Promote Language Development in the First
    Year? 129
Should I Expose My Baby to More Than One Language? 130

12 Teething Is Horrific (and Other Myths) 131
What Is Teething? When Does It Happen? 131
Babies Can Be Born with Teeth?! 132
Why Are My Baby's Hands in His Mouth, and Why Is He
    Constantly Drooling? 132
What Symptoms Does Teething Actually Cause? 133
What Symptoms Does Teething Not Cause? 134
What Should I Do for My Child's Teething Symptoms? 135
Are Those Amber Teething Necklaces Helpful? 136

13 FOOD! 139
When Do I Start Introducing Foods to My Baby? 140
Recommendations for Starting New Foods (By Age) 140
   Four to Five Months: Zero to One Meal a Day 140
   Six to Seven Months: One to Two Meals a Day 141
   Eight to Twelve Months: Three Meals a Day 143
Should I Make My Baby's Food or Buy It? 143
Gagging and Barfing and Coughing: Oh My! 144
What's the Deal with Peanuts? 145
Is Baby-Led Weaning Really Better? 146
What About Water? Juice? 148
When Do I Start Sippy Cups? 148
Are There Gonna Be Poop Changes? 148

14 When Food Goes Wrong 151
Food Allergies 152
What Are the Most Common Foods That Kids Are Allergic
    to? 154
FPIES 154
Lactose Intolerance 155
Troubles with Swallowing 156
Choking 157
Why Is My Kid's Skin Turning Yellow? 158

15 Scroll, Cry, Repeat: How to Spot Online Garbage and Save Your Sanity 161

16 The Absolute Brilliance of Your Kid's Immune System 167
Does My Baby Have a Strong Immune System When She's Born? 168
Is My Baby's Immune System Able to Handle More Than One Germ at a Time? 169
What Are Lymph Nodes and What Do They Do? 170
What Happens When My Kid Spikes a Fever? 170
Are There Any Vitamins or Supplements That Can "Boost" My Baby's Immune System? 172
How Much Sickness Is Too Sick? How Do I Know If My Baby Has an Immune System Problem? 172

17 Vaccines. Vaccines. Vaccines! 175
What Are Vaccines and How Do They Work? 177
Are There Any Harmful Ingredients in Vaccines? 178
What Are the Diseases We Vaccinate Against? 179
Should I "Spread Out" Vaccines? 184
Do Vaccines Cause Autism? 185
What Are Some Side Effects of Vaccines I May See in My Baby? Are There Any Serious Adverse Effects? 186
But What About "Vaccine Injuries"? 187
Dr. Diane, Do You Vaccinate Your Kids? 188

18 What Could Go Wrong?: Common Medical Ailments That May Come Up 189
Eye Goo/Pink Eye 189
Flat Head (Plagiocephaly) 191
Baby Acne 192
Cradle Cap 193
Diaper Rashes 193

Fever 195
> Under Three Months Old 195
> Three Months and Older 196

Belly Button Stuff 197

Eczema 198

Drool Rashes 200

Common Colds 200
> When Do I Worry? 202

Ear Infections 203

Viral Rashes 204

Hives 205

RSV 206

Tummy Bugs (Throwing Up and Diarrhea) 208

The Flu 209

Covid 211

Roseola 212

Hand, Foot, and Mouth Disease 213

Croup 214

19 Movin' and Groovin' 217

What Types of Big Movements Should My Baby Start Doing? 218

Is There Some Variability in How and When Babies Start to Move? 219

What Are Some Ways I Can Encourage My Baby to Start Sitting and Moving More? 220

Bouncers and Walkers (A Personal Story) 221

When Will Walking Happen? 223

20 Baby-Proofing, A to Z 225

21 Taking Care of Teeth 229

Is There Any Mouth or Gum Care I Need to Do Before the First Tooth Comes In? 229

When Will the First Tooth Come In? Which One Will It Be? 230
Do I Need to Brush My Baby's First Teeth? 230
Which Toothpaste Should I Use? 230
When Should My Baby See a Dentist? 231
What Is "Bottle Rot"? 231

22 The Top 10 Weirdest Baby Things That Parents (Understandably) Worry About 233

10. Snot Color 233
9. Earwax Color/Texture/Amount 234
8. Teeth Grinding 235
7. Popping Joints ("Things Crack When I Pick Her Up!") 235
6. Wonky Crawling 235
5. Bow Leggedness in Newborns 236
4. Ear Pulling 236
3. Poop Smell 237
2. Toenails 237
1. Penis Color 238
Honorable Mention: Belly Button Color 238

23 Moving into Toddlerhood (Good Luck and Godspeed) 239

Development Roll Call 243
Acknowledgments 250
Notes 252
Further Reading 270
Index 273
About the Author 281

Introduction

The stars were out, and the nighttime October air was cool.

. . . not that I noticed any of that.

I paced our driveway, tears streaming down my face. I was doing that ugly type of gasp-crying, where the snot puddled on my top lip and dripped down into my mouth.

What the hell kind of mother was I?

My new baby lay in his crib, screaming for the entire neighborhood to hear. I had to put him down to take a minute to breathe, to pace, and to ruminate in the closest quiet area I could find (something I tell my patients' parents to do when they're feeling overwhelmed). Because this was NOT what I expected when I came home from the hospital. Because I was *so* damned frustrated with being a new parent. Because I was really confused about what I was feeling. Where were the feelings of joy, of love, and accomplishment I was supposed to have?

Going outside at 3:00 a.m. seemed like the right thing to do at the wrongest of moments.

Thirty Minutes Earlier

"What do I do? Why won't he calm down? I can't do this."

My husband was half asleep on his side of the bed as I whimpered to myself that I had made the *biggest mistake of my life*. My new baby, Jack, was a robust and voracious boy who weighed in at over nine pounds and had to be cut out of my body three days prior. The day they plopped him on the warming table, suddenly, there was an elephant in the room. Everyone in the surgery suite cooed with adoration. I, meanwhile, stared at the ceiling, wondering if my intestines had been placed back inside my body yet. And was it normal not to feel incredibly in love within five minutes of meeting my kid?

Two nights later, that elephant was being quite demanding.

Demanding, as in . . . *screaming all night.*

I was so confused. I latched him to my breast (not without wincing and tearing up—given that my nipples now resembled roast beef) and he stopped yelling at me. Then, he'd immediately fall asleep, and I'd take him off my breast. And then he'd start screaming again. And then I'd cry.

My C-sectioned belly hurt like hell. I didn't know how to hold the baby without being in pain. Jack and I were a total sobbing mess. The sleeping and screaming and sleeping and screaming pattern? Rinse, repeat. About thirty-five times from 10 p.m. to 4 a.m.. And my husband, bless him, was blissfully unaware of my life falling apart a mere three feet away.

I couldn't understand what the baby wanted. Why did he insist on screaming for hours? Why didn't he realize he was getting exactly what he was asking for—to be fed? If he was hungry, why was he fighting me when I tried to put him on the breast?

Looking back on that night, it's obvious to me now that my newborn was cluster feeding in order to get my body to make breast milk. It's actually a beautiful and very effective process that most babies go through at some point in the first few days of their life. Retrospect is always 20/20, isn't it? It was hard for me to understand this during my waking nightmare.

Unfortunately, through all the hazy exhaustion, all I could think about was my raging anxiety. Not to mention my hurting body. My sense of everything being . . . not real anymore. So much had changed overnight. My fierce independence had been stripped away from me.

My free time was completely gone. My body was a sagging shell of what it used to be. I swore I'd never understand why people did this, and I cried a few hundred tears that night because my life, as I knew it, was over.

When I had my first child, I'd been a board-certified pediatrician for two years. I thought I knew it all. I mean, people sat in my rooms, listening intently to my advice about their children daily. I totally knew what was coming . . . right?

Obviously, I had read, like, a lot about the health of children. The science books, the human body books, the research articles, the parenting books—all had been crammed into my head over the past decade. After college, I spent four grueling years in medical school (where I called my mom crying from the library bathroom no less than a dozen times a year), and then three years in pediatric residency at the Texas Medical Center in Houston (where I spent so many nights in the hospital, I often forgot what my apartment looked like). I basically poured the entirety of my twenties into learning about little humans. More than twenty-four years of education under my belt—and now I carried a nine-pound screaming potato who assured me I didn't know jack.

> Nothing could have prepared me for The Great Humbling.
>
> So, I paced the driveway while my kid screamed in his crib.
>
> I wondered why no one ever told me about this part: why has no book ever mentioned the realities of being a new parent?
>
> I wondered if I'd ever feel like myself again.
>
> I wondered if I'd ever feel the overwhelming love that everyone told me I'd feel when I had a baby.
>
> Spoiler: it gets better. It gets so much better.
>
> Hiccups are normal for babies. And having a few hundred hiccups along the way is totally normal for you, too.

Raising a kid these days is somehow both the easiest and most difficult it has ever been. Your cell phone searches attempt to give you the answers to everything you could ever wonder about. How much spit up is normal spit up? Why are my baby's feet sometimes purple? Is this teething gel safe? Are baby heads supposed to smell like parmesan cheese?

Dr. Google is there to let you know that problem—that minor issue—is probably deadly. Social media is there to tell you that whatever you're doing, you're doing it so wrong. But sometimes—let's be real—neither Instagram nor Google is gonna give you the same quality of advice and experience that an experienced doctor or parent might be able to share.

It's okay to fumble things once in a while—you may not have the warm reassurance of experience. As a pediatrician with thousands of patients, I have found a pretty solid foundation in seeing many of the same things every day. But that doesn't necessarily help with the emotions of being a new parent, as I learned while sobbing in that driveway. So . . . I'm hoping to hold your hand here.

It's Going to Get Better.

As a pediatrician, I'm supposed to be an expert on *flails hands in the air* all the things. That's my job. But my job as a new mom was to become an expert on *one* baby. All babies are different. You'll learn what is best for yours—and how to make the best decisions—with time, experience, good advice, and your own stellar, built-in intuition.

That screaming baby? The one that made me pace the driveway in tears? Very soon after that first difficult night at home, my love for that little guy grew and grew and *grew*. I gradually started to feel more like myself again, started to sleep again, started to get the hang of it all, and I realized how that all-encompassing love that parents feel for their children really *is* as powerful as everyone says it is. That screaming baby is now the sweetest, kindest, most low-maintenance eleven-year-old you'll ever meet, and he's currently sitting next to me reading a book as I type this (funnily enough, in the same bedroom that was soaked in my tears a decade ago). What a whirlwind this has been. What joys this room has seen since then!

My kids are now in middle school. I still have a lot of learning to do, and I swear, I sometimes still can't believe I'm someone's mom. Why does no one talk about *Parent* Imposter Syndrome? But my husband and I have reached that pinnacle—that Everest—that ultimate point in parenting where on weekend mornings our kids can wake up, pour themselves a bowl of cereal, and turn on a TV show. And *oh man*, I can sleep *in* a little! Life is gonna get good, just you wait. You'll be sleeping in, too, before you know it. Screen time rules be damned on Saturday mornings.

How to Use This Book

First off: please understand that I'm not your kid's doctor (if I am—hi!!). I need you to remember that what I write here *is not a replacement for the advice given to you by your pediatrician.* That person, who has examined your child and learned about what works best for you all as a team, is the person who is gonna give you the best advice for your particular baby. This book is for entertainment purposes only and should only be used to "fill in the blanks" from time to time when you need more guidance.

That being said, this book's goal is to guide you through the most common questions I get in my clinic rooms regarding some of the most common topics parents wonder about. It starts with the moment you bring your baby through your front door and ends—*splat*—on that first birthday smash cake.

There's a lot of information here. That was probably the hardest part I experienced in writing it—figuring out how to fit it all in, and then how to organize it in a way that is seamless as you move chronologically through your first year. But please know that you may find it useful to jump around sometimes.

For example, the sleep chapter could hold some useful information for you earlier in your baby's life than where it lies in this book. The discussion about vaccines in Chapter 16 could be something helpful to read before your baby's first set of shots. I'd scan the chapter subtitles in the Table of Contents to navigate easily.

Use this book as a quick reference, or as a long talk with a friend—it'll work both ways. You can read it from beginning to end, or flip it open to absorb a chapter and throw it back on the shelf for another day. It's here for you whenever you need it.

When I give you advice in this book, it'll be a culmination of (1) good data and evidence, (2) my observations as a practicing doctor who has cared for thousands of kids (and thousands of parents), and (3) my experiences as a mom.

I'll be sure to try and cite any new or controversial information sources in either endnotes or the back of the book. As a physician, I have had a lot of training on how to figure out what is good research and what is pretty much garbage, so I'll focus on only the solid stuff.

This isn't going to be a textbook. I will not—I cannot—bore you with the mundane details and the big medical words. There are plenty of other resources out there for that. I'm here to help you decide when to worry and when to hunker down, grab a drink, and ride it out.

One thing that can be hard for new parents to figure out is whether their baby is following normal development patterns. That's why I've included a section at the end, the Appendix called "Developmental Roll Call," dedicated to the normal developmental steps I typically see each month. Use it as a quick reference, but please know it is not by any means complete—and that each baby follows their own path.

In this book, I will write to you the same words, verbatim, that I speak to parents daily in my exam rooms. One of the best parts of being a pediatrician is meeting and knowing parents: biological parents, adoptive parents, foster parents, grandparents, guardians—*all* types of parents. And I gotta tell you, my favorite parents are the new ones. The first baby's parents. They roll in twenty minutes late, having no idea how long it takes to get out of the house with a newborn, sweating with all the baby gear on their backs, faces painted with looks of exhaustion and fear. I want to hug each of them. I want to buy each of them either a coffee or a beer. I swear, if I had a nickel for the number of times I've thought about opening up a bar in room sixteen.

Instead, I keep a fat and permanent box of Kleenex in each room. Because this is really hard. It justifiably may be the hardest time in any parent's life (maybe until their teenager starts slamming those doors). And it feels important to me to be a part of your village and help guide you through the muck. Consider me the Yoda to your Luke. And as Master Yoda says, "The greatest teacher, failure is."

We joke in pediatrics that our real patients are the parents. Parents are the ones we are typically reassuring, calming, and teaching—and the babies are actually the easy part of our job. But I wouldn't trade it for the world. What an honor it is to hold your hand. How cool is it to help people step into one of the most vulnerable times in their lives, and to aid in pulling them through to the other side? I'm so happy to be here and to guide you through one of the biggest years of your life.

Allow me to give you a big ol' warm hug with this book. You got this.

Pull up a cup of coffee. Or wine.

Let's go.

1

The First Few Days

So, the white cheesy stuff was wiped off the baby. The lactation consultants squeezed and prodded. The nurses came and went from the room all night long. Someone slept on an uncomfortable hospital chair. The car seat was fumbled over what seemed like a dozen times.

Huzzah! You and your newly changed family are ready to go home!

You walk through your front door. The dog sniffs the baby's head for about half an hour. *Greetings, new human. Welcome to the family. You smell strange.*

What now?

A Few Vital Just-Got-Home Pointers

- Take that giant water jug with a handle and straw they gave you at the hospital and keep it full of water. Hydration is easily forgotten, but it is so important for you in those first few weeks.

- Take a hot shower whenever you can. It's a great reset button.

- If you had a C-section, set yourself up somewhere you can sleep with your upper body propped up and have all your stuff easily accessible. Constantly getting up from laying down all night is really hard to do when your entire abdominal wall has been sliced open.

- Consider setting up some temporary diaper-changing stations around the home. It's kind of a pain to have to get up from the living room and go upstairs or across the house to the nursery every time the baby sharts (and trust me, at first, it's like fifteen sharts a day).

- Allow people to bring you snacks and meals. People will want to, I promise. Let them. And it's completely acceptable to say, "Oh my gosh! You made me food! Thank you so much! But we are asking for no visitors right now in this quiet time." People will understand. Stockpile the food in the freezer so you can easily defrost it when needed. Cooking is not a priority right now.

- Set up a napping/sitting area for the baby in the most active, brightest, and loudest part of the house, like the living room. A portable bassinet is great here. If the baby is awake and you're awake, they can sit in an inclined baby chair or swing. Letting them spend the day in the living room during the first month will help their bodies figure out when it is daytime versus nighttime. And don't worry about being quiet around the baby! More on this later.

- No need to keep the house warm. It's okay to keep the house at a cool 68–72 degrees Fahrenheit. This temperature range is actually safest for babies.

- Start to look into baby-wearing options. Sometimes, if your baby wants to be on you constantly, having two hands free is such a huge relief. I highly recommend the easy ones that just involve a large piece of cloth and a single belt loop (Ring Sling© and the like).

As you settle in with your new little person, set things up in a way that makes feedings, naps, and diaper changes convenient and easy for a post-birth body to get to quickly. It's okay if this leads to your house looking a little chaotic—if it works, it works. Think mini fridges in the bedroom and bottle warmers in the bathroom.

Best to put the baby's bassinet or crib in your bedroom at first because the baby will need to eat frequently through the night. Generally, at least at first, you will want them close by. My husband and I switched things up with the second kid. When we decided to divide and conquer, I set my second baby up in her crib in her own room and slept on a twin bed in the same room. He slept in our bedroom to deal with the toddler in the morning. This was temporary, but it really worked for us. Do what works for you.

How Much Should My Baby Be Eating in the Beginning?

New babies have tiny tummies and very little body fat to keep their energy levels up. They need to eat small meals frequently. We generally allow them to lose 10 percent of their birthweight in those first few days as they figure out the challenges of eating. We want them to gain this back roughly around the two-week mark. The problem is, sometimes they're super sleepy (this is especially common if they're born prematurely). So sleepy that they may not have the energy to eat vigorously and frequently. This is why you usually visit with your doctor soon after birth and again around the two-week mark to see how things are going and how much weight they're gaining.

If you're nursing, you can expect them to want to eat at least every one to two hours in those first few days, sometimes more frequently. I promise this is temporary! And it's a good way to get your breasts to start making more milk. Most babies want to nurse twenty to thirty minutes at a time, but this can change from feed to feed. For my pumped milk and formula-feeding babies, I expect them to take anywhere from a half ounce to three ounces per bottle in those first fourteen days, and I'd wake your baby at the three-hour mark to eat if they haven't woken on their own (this changes later).

(Something to keep in mind throughout the first year: you're going to find a lot of conflicting information about feeding babies online. Lots of confusing charts, volume ranges, and feeding information that may not make sense for your particular kid. This is why I ask parents to read their baby, not the "book." If your baby is making frequent urine and poops, seems content throughout the day, and is gaining good weight at the doctor's office, I think you're doing a great job at reading your baby's hunger cues!)

When Do I Let People Visit?

A little background on this (and I promise there is a point): when an infant under two months of age gets a fever (a rectal temperature above 100.4 degrees Fahrenheit), they have to go straight to the Emergency Room for blood work and evaluation. They also typically have to be admitted into the hospital for at least two days to make sure no bacteria grow in the blood, urine, and sometimes spinal fluid tests. All of this happens even if the baby probably just has a cold! The reasoning behind the aggressive approach is that a newborn's immune system is brand new, and somewhat "borrowed" from mom for a few weeks. So, in general, the zero-to-eight-week-old newborn is more susceptible to scary stuff like bloodstream infections, kidney and urinary tract infections, and brain lining infections (meningitis).

That being said, I think it makes a lot of sense to limit the number of people your baby meets in the first eight weeks of her life. If she gets sick, she's almost guaranteed to need a hospital stay. Not to mention that newborns often have a harder time with common viruses like colds and the flu. I'd let a limited number of close adults—people who will mean a lot in the baby's life early on—come on over and say hello! Most folks these days have a little common sense about this, but just in case, I'd ask them to avoid visiting if they're not feeling well or have "allergies." You might even consider asking them to wear a mask if they're visiting in the winter months. Keeping a little container of hand sanitizer close by for people to use is helpful, too.

It was also a requirement in my house that anyone who wanted to see the baby had to have recent flu and pertussis boosters (also known as Tdap). I was pretty strict about this. No vaccines? No baby time.

And, I hate to say it, but it is best to avoid kids who don't live in your home during those fragile first few weeks. Kids are huge germ vectors, especially in the winter. Does your baby have siblings at home? Ask them to only kiss baby's feet or the top of her head if they're feeling the love! Only a select few close healthy adults should be kissing the baby in that first month. And lots of handwashing and practicing the covering of coughs and sneezes goes without saying.

Things feel a lot less fragile after the eight-week mark passes. Infants get their first set of vaccines around this time, and they have a nicely formed immune system that can handle germs a little better. Get on out and see more people if you want!

When Can I Go Out with the Baby?

Getting out of the house with your new baby is really important. Why? Because if you ask any new parent, having a baby makes life feel a little weird and surreal for a while. You might feel pretty isolated—I did. You tend to lose track of what day or time it is. Schedules and routines get a bit blurry for a few weeks. Sometimes it feels like a never-ending, perpetual cycle of feedings, napping, and diaper changes. Going out and doing the things you did pre-baby is important to feel more like a human again. And . . . you need to feel like a human again.

I personally took it pretty slow. At first, I used to have my spouse or a family member come over to hold or watch the baby so I could have a little break away from the house. I'd go sit in the drive-thru line at the coffee shop or stare at the different yogurt options at the grocery store or look at ugly nursing bra options. These were small and sometimes silly outings, but I really needed them to keep in touch with reality.

Up next? Take a walk in the neighborhood. When the weather was tolerable and I wasn't horribly sleep-deprived, my baby and I took daily walks. It felt nice to get some fresh air, and during the fussy phases, my kiddo would get a quiet nap no matter how hard he fought it when we were home. Dress your baby in the same manner you are dressed—with the same number of layers and perhaps one blanket more. If it's warm out, it's fine to use one of those small fans that attach to the stroller. If babies feel too hot or too cold on these walks, they will generally let you know by crying.

Next, after scrounging up some courage, I attempted short treks to places on my own with the baby. Listen, just try it. You need to get out, and well, frankly—you need to experience a poop blowout in Target. You need to deal with a crying fit in the department store. You need to deal with barf at the post office. Trust me on this. It will be challenging at first, but you'll totally get the hang of it. And you'll figure out what stuff needs to go with you and what can stay home. It will soon become second nature and should get easier and more enjoyable with time. When I went on outings to grocery stores or the library, I'd just put my baby in his car seat and cover the seat itself with a light breathable muslin blanket to avoid him getting coughed and sneezed on by the general public. I'd also keep a little bottle of sanitizer attached to it to use as needed when I was picking him up or touching him. Running all my usual errands with my baby soon became second nature.

Some families I see in my practice skip all these steps and just *dive right into it*! Restaurants, shopping, road trips—ventures all taken in the first few weeks of life! I'm always envious of these folks. And I think it's totally awesome that they work so hard to make sure they still do and feel the same things they did pre-baby. They tell me, "Our baby needs to get used to our way of life; not the other way around!" More power to ya! We usually chat about the best ways to keep it safe, and off they go.

If you do go out right away with your baby, I'd avoid large crowds for the first two months and, in particular, would avoid big groups of children. Again, children tend to be much more infectious than adults, just given their general hygiene and behavior. Your niece is having her thirtieth-kid birthday party at the trampoline park? Your response: "My doctor told me it's best not to be around a lot of kids at this time" (I'm always happy to be your "doctor" in this scenario, and your safety wing-woman)!

Safe Sleep!

When you first bring your baby home, it's best to have their crib or bassinet set up in your room and close to your bed. You can even find some bassinets that attach to your bed—keeping the baby close but in their own sleep space. The American Academy of Pediatrics (AAP) recommends babies be in their parents' rooms for at least the first six months of life. The data shows this may reduce SIDS death by 50 percent[1]. I think there's definitely some flexibility here depending on the scenario. I know many families who slowly moved their children to their own rooms before this time (mine included) in a safe manner, so it's okay to talk about this with your pediatrician after the first two or three months. I do think *room-sharing is a LOT safer than bed-sharing*.

Babies have brand-new brains. Breathing can be a pretty complex process. These baby brains are still figuring out the whole breathing—carbon dioxide—oxygen balance thing. Put super simply, when the carbon dioxide levels in our blood build up, our brain tells us to breathe more. When our carbon dioxide levels go down, our brain tells us to breathe slower. Because of this delicate balance, we theorize that sleeping in certain positions or on certain surfaces can be really dangerous for babies, whose brains haven't quite figured this out yet. They also have very floppy heads that are heavy and hard to lift or move to a position that helps them breathe. The dangers associated with sleeping mostly apply to the first four months of life, because after this age, they start to build more strength in their neck and torso and their brains have matured. Creating a safe sleep environment is really important in those first few months, no matter what social media tells you (and hoo-boy, does social media have opinions).

The most important things to remember for safe sleep:

- *Babies need to sleep alone, in their own sleep space.* I need to take a minute to be really serious here: I have personally done CPR on three dead babies who were found unconscious in their parents' bed. I am super aware of what social media, friends, or family may tell you about bed-sharing. I have heard *all* the arguments but remain unchanged in my opinion here. As an experienced physician, I can tell you that *sleeping with your baby in your bed increases the chance that your baby will die.* That's it. That's the fact. I know—it's so hard. I know we pediatricians seem heartless when we tell you not to co-sleep in the same bed. I swear to you I thought about doing it too, the nights my kids wouldn't stop screaming. Please do not sleep with your baby in your bed. We really have seen babies die because of it. We have held the mothers who are screaming in the ER after losing their child. We never, ever want that to happen to you and your baby. If you absolutely must, and there are zero other safer options, *please* talk to your pediatrician about how to do this most safely (knowing that, again—this process will increase risk no matter what).

- *Babies need a flat, firm surface to sleep on.* No thick mattresses or soft cushions.
- *Babies always need to be put to sleep on their backs.* There's been a significant decline in sudden infant crib death since the 1990s thanks to the "Back to Sleep" campaign! If they eventually wiggle over to their side, that's okay. In a few months, if they eventually get strong enough to flip themselves onto their tummy, that's okay too, and you don't need to keep repositioning them—as long as they get into the position by themselves.
- *No blankets or pillows or bumpers or stuffed animals* in their sleep space. Remember that carbon dioxide-oxygen balance problem I mentioned earlier? When their face is pressed up against fabric, we theorize that their carbon dioxide levels can build and build, and as they re-breathe that carbon dioxide trapped in these areas, there is a risk of death.
- *Avoid Dock-A-Tots and other "sleep nests"*—they're not safe and babies can suffocate in them.
- *If your baby falls asleep in the car seat, try to transfer them to a flat surface as soon as possible.* If their floppy head falls forward, there is a risk of cutting off their breathing. Once you're out of the car, transfer baby to a flat surface!
- *Make sure the baby isn't too hot.* As mentioned earlier, around 68 to 72 degrees Fahrenheit (20–22 degrees Celsius) is safest for infants[2]. More on this in the next section.
- *Maintain a smoke-free environment.* Babies die in cribs more often in homes where they are exposed to second-hand smoke[3].

Random side note: the Consumer Product and Safety Commission Recall Search Page is a great way to assure whatever baby sleep product you've purchased is safe and hasn't been recalled for some reason. You can find this search bar at https://www.cpsc.gov/recalls.

What Should My Baby Wear to Sleep? Should I Swaddle My Baby?

In those first few weeks, most babies will sleep in just about anything. "I slept like a baby" is a famous line for a reason—newborns sleep pretty hard. But keeping them safe and warm (or cool) is important since their internal temperature regulation kind of sucks at first.

Again, keeping the house at 68 to 72 degrees Fahrenheit seems to be the safest temperature for infants. Most babies do well in a single layer of clothing, like a short or long-sleeved onesie, and then a swaddle around that. I think that layering your baby in the same number of layers *you* are wearing, along with a thin blanket as needed, is a good general rule.

Swaddles mimic the way babies feel in the womb (more on this in Chapter 2) and help compress all the wild, wobbly movements of the arms and legs at this age, including the startle reflex. They're safe to use as long as the baby isn't trying to roll over. This usually happens around three to four months of age. Keep the hips loose—we want the legs to be able to crunch up and move and bend easily, so no tightness around the hips and no straight legs.

There are lots of types of swaddles, including Velcro and zipper varieties. Make sure the top part of the swaddle isn't covering the baby's mouth or face in any way. And I'd avoid the weighted swaddles—they're not safe and pose an increased risk of suffocation or injury.

How Do I Start Good Sleep Practices as Soon as We Get Home from the Hospital?

Your baby was in a dark womb for a really long time. When they're born, it makes sense that many of them will have no idea when they're experiencing day and night. So, we're going to teach them.

The first thing to do is keep your baby in a well-lit, active room throughout the day. In the evening, start dimming the lights and eventually at bedtime, put him in a dark, quiet room. Light has a huge influence on human circadian rhythms (the internal clock that regulates when and how we sleep). Light can even penetrate through eyelids to affect circadian rhythms!

Open the windows, make all the noises. Vacuum. Turn on the TV. Talk with visitors. There is no need to tiptoe around in the first month of life. Daytime is the time we want him to eventually be more awake. Don't worry—even if he sleeps through most of the day, the light and noise are slowly causing changes inside his brain.

At night, make it a point not to stimulate the baby too much. Don't do a lot of talking or make a lot of noise. I liked to use a little night light to keep things dim and peaceful. Unswaddle, change the diaper, feed, burp a little, back down. All business.

One technique I used with both of my newborns was to start waking them up at the same time every day, and setting my "day" and "night" modes to go from 7 a.m. to 7 p.m. So no matter how the night went, I'd wake them to start their day and routine at 7:00 a.m. And at 7 p.m., I started the darker room/quieter room process. Over time, I really think this helped their little bodies start following a routine.

After four to six weeks, I usually recommend that parents put their baby in their crib for daytime naps. This is an age when they're starting to see better and be more aware of their surroundings, and going to the same sleep area over and over helps the baby start to learn, "hey, when I put you here, it's time to sleep." They get used to the same feelings, sounds, and smells of the room and the crib. Go with a dim or dark room, and consider a quiet sound machine.

How Often Do I Need to Wake My Baby to Eat?

During the first three months of life, I tell all families to wake their baby at the three-hour mark to eat during the day. This means that if they started the last meal at 9:00 a.m., and then they take a monster nap, and 12:00 p.m. rolls around and they're still sleeping, I would wake them up to eat. This is because I want babies to get most of their calories *during the day*. Many newborn babies will wake themselves up to eat at the two- or two-and-a-half-hour mark, but this is just the plan if they seem to be having a sleepy day.

As for nighttime sleep, you might need to follow your doctor's advice. In the first few weeks of life, I generally want parents to wake their baby up around the three-to-four-hour mark if he hasn't woken up on his own, but some newborns may need to be woken more often than this. Once babies see me at the two-week appointment and have proven they can gain weight appropriately, there is generally no more need for scheduling these wake-ups.

Twins are a special case for night wake-ups—if one wakes up and the other doesn't, I'd wake the sleepy one for a feed, too. I also tend to tread more carefully with premature babies. Again, it's best to ask your doc for specific info here.

A Straight-from-My-Office Handout

Newborn Notes from a Pediatrician

It's wild how connected we all are online now. One Saturday morning a few years ago, during the Covid lockdown, I was sitting with my kids eating Cheerios and thinking about the questions that newborn parents ask me every day. I felt so strongly for the sweet families who just had a new baby, but who were in lockdown so couldn't see the friends and family who would typically provide support. So, I wrote out some of my most common answers and posted the ramblings on one of my social media pages.

Two million viral online reads later, that post—which I called *Newborn Notes from a Pediatrician*—has now made it to official handout status in my office. Everybody gets a copy. It helps parents to take a deep breath, I think, and realize it's all normal-ish? And okay.

So, to give you the best chance possible of human-ing when you first get home, here are some brief and immediate words of survival:

---

1. *The hiccups are normal.*
2. *The sneezing is normal. It's not allergies.*
3. *The booty is going to get red (baby's, not yours). This is from the constant wiping and moisture. If ulcers start to form, be gentler with the wiping, or even run that tushy under some warm water in the sink rather than wiping, and apply a barrier cream with each diaper change (Desitin, A&D, Boudreaux). Air dry the booty often.*
4. *No amount of lotion will help that peeling, flaky skin in the first few weeks. Babies are like snakes—they shed that first layer after birth.*
5. *No need for lotion unless your pediatrician tells you so.*
6. *After they lay down for a while, babies often sound congested. This is usually because of reflux, which all infants experience at some point or another* (more on this later).
7. *If you've chosen to breastfeed—congratulations on a great way to feed and nourish your child!*
8. *If you've chosen to formula feed—congratulations on a great way to feed and nourish your child!*
9. *Spitting up is normal now and then. Sometimes it comes out of the nose, yes. That's okay. It's just another hole in the head.*
10. *Putting the baby on a schedule is hard at first. They really need to eat as much as their brains are telling them to—and that often seems sporadic and chaotic, but it needs to happen. You can start some simple sleep training steps from day one, though. Start waking your baby at the same time every morning. And put her in the living room during the day for the first month—make sure there's lots of light and noise in the area. Even if she's sleeping through it, this will start to "set" the circadian rhythms— which tell her when to be awake and when to sleep. At the same time each night, turn the lights low and put the baby in a quiet room.*
11. *During the day, feed your baby at least every three hours. They'll want to eat more often than that sometimes, and that's okay. But if it's been 3 hours, go ahead and wake her up. We want to get as many "daytime calories" in them as possible!*

12. There is a very common, very gassy/grumpy phase they start around week 3. It is called the Period of PURPLE Crying. Often, during a certain part of the day (i.e., evening), they will cry, grunt, and generally look uncomfortable (more on this in Chapter 6).
13. Some babies poop after every meal. Some babies poop once a week. Both are normal.
14. It's common for the hands and feet to be purple sometimes, especially if their legs are squeezed or they're cold. This is called acrocyanosis and goes away with time. Always call an ambulance if you notice any difficulty in breathing, or if the baby's tongue or gums look dusky or purple—this is different.
15. You don't have to use clippers on the fingernails and toenails. You can peel or file them down.
16. Belly buttons are weird. Umbilical cords are weird. They ooze a little now and then, and sometimes there's a spot of blood on the diaper as they're drying up and falling off. Let your pediatrician know if the skin around the cord is red and if that redness is spreading. Or if you notice yellow goo oozing from it is excessive or soaks into clothes.

I know you feel alone, but know that you're not alone in your isolation these days, and there are still ways to connect. Create a safe "pod" of help and support and if you're my patient, know that I am in it with you.

It's okay to feel weird and "off" those first few weeks or months—I did.

It's okay if you don't feel connected to your baby at first—I didn't. It was like a loud elephant was suddenly in the room.

If your feelings overwhelm you or worry you, PLEASE ask for help.

I remember the night my first baby was born. I was anxious, scared, exhausted, in pain, and I had no idea what I was in for.

Book smarts are nothing compared to experience, my friends. You will know more every minute, hour, and day.

2

Newborns: They Dislike Not Being Inside of a Uterus

The sweet mom sitting across from me in the exam room looked exhausted. Disheveled, missing an earring, hunched over, and with deep purple circles under her eyes, she tried so hard not to burst into tears. The transition from womb to world had not been an easy one for her baby, she told me. The little one was really struggling to sleep without constantly being held. The baby cried—a lot. This fussiness, as a result, left two very tired parents at their wit's end.

They eventually started practicing sleep habits that were pretty unsafe. Grabbing an hour of sleep while holding the baby on the couch, or laying the baby on her stomach in between them in the bed, seemed to be the only way they could get some rest. I didn't judge—I never do—because let's face it, we are all just trying to survive in a situation like this.

Every single parent I know has a breaking point, me included, and the "fourth trimester" can be hard as hell. Not going to sugarcoat it—the first three months were *not* my jam as a new parent. But let's dive into some of the same advice I gave these sweet parents to help their baby learn how to transition into the outside world a little easier, soothe their fussy moments, and help encourage good (and safe) sleep for all parties.

Learn Your Baby's Personality

My personality differs from my husband's. I'm more sensitive, and he's more relaxed. I fall asleep really easily, and he struggles. I thrive on a routine; he's more go-with-the-flow. Why do we expect babies to all be the same, when we adults are nothing alike?

Babies have different personalities, too. My son loved pacifiers; my daughter hated them. My son self-soothed easily, and my daughter raised pure hell if we dared to lay her down awake. Some babies are high maintenance, and some are chill. Some don't care that their diaper is full of poop, and some act like the world has ended when a shart pops out. Let's give them the benefit of knowing that what works for one may not work for another. Get to know your kid. And know that it may take some time to figure it out.

Please give yourself some grace in those first few months—all babies have bad days, no matter what their personality type is. I think that this was one of the most frustrating things for me to understand as a new, Type A mom. I'd do the same thing every day, but each day would look so different!

Some days were sleepy days.

Some days all the baby wanted to do was eat.

Some days the kid just stared at me, awake for ridiculous amounts of time.

Some days were super fussy days (for absolutely no obvious reason).

Please know that this is all so totally normal at this age. But I get it—it's frustrating as hell.

What to Expect When It Comes to Crying

All babies cry. Crying is how they communicate with us.

If babies tinkled like quiet little fairies whenever they needed food or warmth or help, our species would have died out a long time ago.

They cry—and that crying *hurts our damn ears*. This is important! Ugh! We want that sound to stop! We need to tend to that baby! We need to find some way to make it stop: feeding, soothing, tending to the diaper, helping the fart get out. Thus, the survival of the species. Thank you, screaming banshee child.

You will quickly learn that your kid cries differently for different needs. It's pretty cool. But it takes time to get comfortable with this idea that you can be capable of understanding which cry means what. Crying also changes as babies get older. "Fake" crying is a thing, too—ha! That's a fun phase.

Did you know that during the first six weeks, the average baby cries on an average for about two to three hours per day? And much of it may go unexplained.

After the first couple of weeks, you may realize that your baby tends to be the fussiest in the evenings. We aren't sure why this is. I have theories. Perhaps the gas bubbles build up throughout the day as they swallow air while eating and crying (a normal process)? Maybe they cry more often in the evenings in order to be fed more, so they can "tank up" for longer and longer sleep sessions at night? Perhaps they experience existential crises in the evenings? Nighttime is when I do most of *my* worrying . . . anyway, I'll talk to you more about this evening crying in the *Period of PURPLE Crying* chapter.

Causes of Fussiness in Young Babies

I once went to a concert when my second child was only three months old. It was a hot mess all around (this isn't the first time this night will be mentioned in this book).

I was planning to have a blissful child-free three hours. But my husband was nervous, as baby Abby was a notoriously opinionated and fussy infant. And this was my first time being away for so long. So, I actually whipped out a large piece of paper and a marker, and made him a flow chart of things to try if the going got rough ('cause I'd be damned if a fussy baby was going to keep me from seeing Taylor Swift's *1989* tour):

- **Hunger**: probably the number one cause of fussiness in the first month. They've got these tiny bellies and not much room for food—so they need repetitive, small meals every one to three hours. They cry often to let you know it's time to reload. On cluster-feeding days, this may happen as soon as thirty to forty-five minutes after the last meal! The more fat they build on their bodies, the longer they can start to go between feeds.

- **Fatigue:** babies cry when they're tired. I remember many moments involving staring at my wailing kid, thinking to myself, *c'mon, turkey. If you're tired, just sleep. I wish I could sleep. I certainly wouldn't cry about it.* Newborns can hardly stay awake thirty to forty-five minutes after their last nap. One-to-two-month-olds? sixty to ninety minutes. Learn your kiddo's sleepy signs, and know that crying and fussiness are often one of those signs.

- **Poop or pee in the diaper**: some babies care. Some babies don't.

- **Wanting to be held**: some babies really like the feeling of being held (a lot). Some don't.

- **Too hot or too cold:** babies generally are most comfortable (and most safe) between 68 and 72 degrees Fahrenheit. Despite the urge to protect, try not to layer them up too much. I usually recommend dressing them in the same number of layers you're dressed in, with possibly one more, like a swaddle.

- **They're in pain:** a less common cause of daily infant fussiness, but present nonetheless. Gas bubbles, reflux, a hair twirled around a toe, and illness can all commonly cause crying. If it's a really bad day, check the rectal temperature and do a head-to-toe exam of your kiddo. Call or see the pediatrician if you're worried it's gone on longer than usual or seems more intense.
- **For no reason at all:** isn't parenting fun?!

For Fussiness: Mimic the Womb

When a baby is in a womb, there are a lot of different stimuli that we can assume the fetus grows very accustomed to. When they join us in the outside world, the harsh reality is that many babies don't like the change. It's helpful to mimic the uterus as much as possible in the first few months of an infant's life.

You've probably heard of Dr. Harvey Karp's "Five S's" to calm babies. I think they're a lovely set of tools to try. Swaddling, Side/Stomach Position, Shushing, Swinging, Sucking—all great ideas to mimic the environment inside the uterus. You can read more about this in his book, *The Happiest Baby on the Block*[1]. My tips are pretty similar ideas to put in your toolbox.

First thing to think about: they're smushed. Compression is all they know for that last trimester in utero. Some ribs above, a pelvis below, and a tight muscle wraps around them. So, it makes sense that they get used to this feeling, and mimicking it can calm babies after birth. This is where swaddles help. There are so many different types out there these days, which is great. In the hospital, they'll often teach you how to swaddle with a large blanket. There are some easier options on the market that involve zippers and Velcro. Try to swaddle the baby with their arms down, and with looseness around the hips. My first baby got so pissed when I put his arms down—he wanted his little hands around his face, just like in utero—but it really does help them sleep to put them downward. It muffles the startle reflex, and prevents those hands from flailing out and hitting themselves in the face. The legs need to be looser when swaddled—and the hips need to be able to bend to at least a 90-degree angle. If the legs are stuck tight, or completely straight, this may lead to a medical problem called hip dysplasia.

Next up: the womb is a loud place. Arteries pumping blood everywhere, a steady heartbeat mere inches away, the booming aorta, the constant gurgle of the intestines—babies get used to this shushing, thrumming environment. So, try to emulate this in the outside world. Saying "shhhh" over and over quietly can be helpful when you're trying to calm little Grumpy. There are also some great sound machines on the market that make similar white noise. Try to keep the sound machine at 50–60 decibels or lower to protect their little ears. There are some decent phone apps if you'd like to figure out how loud you can set the machine, but the internet tells me that 50 decibels is likened to a "quiet refrigerator."

Swinging and rocking your baby can mimic what it feels like inside a busy uterus. Pregnant moms are walking, going up stairs, turning, and swiveling in office chairs. It makes sense that many infants miss this movement in the outside world. Swinging in your arms, walking around the room, rocking in a chair—all can help mimic these movements. There are many electric swings that are available for infants, too, but proceed with caution. We really don't like babies sleeping in these unattended, as rarely the airway can occasionally be blocked off if the head tips forward while inclined. I also worry that babies who are put in swings for all naps will get so dependent on them that napping or any sleep in a crib may eventually become difficult. But they're fine for occasional use!

Get Creative

Positioning plays a decent role in calming a fussy baby. Many fussy babies with gas pains feel better if they are swung gently while on their stomach. Some babies do better with fussiness if they're held on their side in their parents' arms, or in something called the "reverse football hold." The over-the-shoulder position really helped my first baby with tough evenings. Get creative with position as you gently rock your little grump.

Pacifiers are a great tool for soothing as well. They're called "pacifiers" for a reason! And I think for a majority of babies it's totally fine to use pacis from day one. I like the little green/teal newborn pacis at first, but many older babies like the larger and different shapes to suck on as they grow. Many parents worry about their baby growing dependent on pacifiers, but given how useful and typically low-risk they are, I don't think this is too big of a deal in the long-run. There is also some data that shows that pacifiers may reduce SIDS deaths[2]! I tend to start talking about getting rid of pacifiers around twelve to fifteen months, so that their teeth and speech aren't affected in the long-term.

Both my babies really soothed with *butt pops* when I would hold them. This is basically just clapping/patting a palm on the baby's bottom. A gentle sway back and forth, with firm butt pops? Chef's kiss for some of the worse nights. Back pats are also super helpful for some kiddos. Also—go outside if you're desperate. Being outside can calm some of the angriest little people. Works almost 100 percent of the time.

Technology Can Help!

- **Bottle warmers** and **Formula mixing machines** can be a great way to get food to that screaming baby quickly.
- **Sound machines** for the win. Now your kid might have a fighting chance to stay asleep in a home with a barking dog or a loud air conditioner.

- **Vibrating baby chairs** were a great way to keep my baby in the living room with all of us, while offering calm and gentle rocking/vibrations for the fussy evenings. Some also have songs and dangling toys for them to gaze at. Remember: no unsupervised naps in these.
- **Smart Bassinets** are (often expensive) sleeping bassinets that have sensors that detect infant movement and crying, and automatically gently rock the baby. They can be a real game-changer for babies who struggle to soothe themselves back to sleep. You can rent and borrow these pretty easily if the cost is too high.

Please remember, if you're frustrated with how fussy your baby is, or how much of a struggle the day has been, it is *always okay* to put her in her crib or bassinet or hand her to someone else and walk away for a few minutes. Remember the introduction to this book? When this pediatrician paced and cried in her driveway while her kid wailed in his crib? Yep, pediatricians do it, too.

Take a minute. Breathe. Absorb the quiet. Walk back in refreshed and ready to try something new. We *all* get frustrated at some point when we have a baby, and it's important not to let those big feelings create a situation that might be harmful to either of you. No matter how frustrated you are, please don't shake or hit your baby. It may seem preposterous for me to even bring it up—but it happens over and over and every single day in this world. It's important to know your limits, and take a step back when you need it. You're not a bad parent if you try to create some space for your mental health. You got this.

How Often Do I Bathe My Baby?

Throwing this here because I really found that putting my baby in a bathtub often helped the evening grumpies.

You can bathe your baby as often or as little as you want. They honestly don't get too "dirty" in those first months other than the typical sweat, spit-ups, and diaper deposits. I'd say, on average, most families bathe their baby two to three times a week.

Most young infants don't *need* a bath daily, but it's *okay* to do one each evening if you'd like to start a routine. My second baby had such fussy evenings; I found the bath to be a nice break from all the burping and bouncing. Soaking a warm washcloth and laying it on her little chest and belly were very soothing for her (and my ears). If you do bathe your baby nightly, use gentle baby washes, and watch to make sure the skin isn't getting too dry. This is no big deal, just apply a nice, clear emollient like Vaseline afterward if it seems to happen.

So, What Do I Do with My Baby at This Age? How Do I Entertain Them?

Navigating the first few months is hard enough with the burden of just, you know, trying to keep them alive and happy. But what do you *do* with the baby between all the eating, crying, sleeping, and pooping in order to help them develop new skills? Well,

1. Prop them up on your legs and talk to him. Just talk. If you don't know what to talk about, read books to him. Or discuss nineteenth-century European art. Whatever.
2. Sing songs. Play music. Missy Elliott is just as educational as Mozart.
3. Put him on the floor, on his tummy, for ten to fifteen minutes at a time. There's no standard protocol for tummy time. Just try to do a little bit daily.
4. Put him on a playmat that has high-contrast toys or pictures for his viewing pleasure. High-contrast books and cards are nice

to use here. They also focus on human faces, so mirrors and pictures of parents are fun, too.

5. Put something noisy near his legs or on his feet so he can kick and hear sounds—auditory feedback is lovely for learning how to use his legs!

6. Cuddle. Touch. Give him little massages. Skin-on-skin is so important.

7. Dangle toys in front of him to encourage grasping. I like the ones with bells on them so the baby gets an auditory cue that what they're doing is working!

8. Take him outside. Let the wind blow through the fourteen hairs on his head.

9. Babywear him while you do things around the house.

10. Run errands together. Babies love to snooze in the car and when pushed around in a grocery cart, and the new sights and sounds are a nice break from the daily views!

3

The Newborn Body Is Weird

"Oh my God. Oh my God, I can feel the baby's heartbeat in his skull. What do I do? What do I dooooo?"—*quoth* my husband, who was walking into the bathroom with our newborn as I attempted to take my first post-hospital shower.

I took a brief moment (out of the nineteen minutes I had spent under the spray of hot water staring at the wall) to assure him, "it's normal. Get out."

He, along with many other parents, realized very quickly that the newborn body is *weird* and *very different* from adult bodies. Baby bodies consist of different anatomy, physiology, smells, sounds, solids, liquids, and sights. During the few weeks after birth, babies look kind of strange. They've seen some things. They are cute, balding, rashy, grunty little tree frogs. Let's do a fast breakdown of what the hell is going on from head to toe.

Head

The baby head is a dome of tectonic plates. There are five bones in the newborn skull, and they're separated by dividing lines called *sutures*.

The skull bones are relatively soft and move around—if they didn't, babies wouldn't be able to fit through the birth canal! They meet together in places called *fontanelles*. There are two fontanelles on the newborn's head. The one on the back of the skull closes soon after birth. The fontanelle in the front third of the head is often called the "soft spot," and sometimes you can see a baby's heartbeat bumping up and down in it. Yes—it's weird, but totally not a reason to interrupt a mother's sacred shower.

The soft spot generally closes between the first and second years of life. It can give us clues sometimes when a baby is sick. Soft spot bulging out? The baby might have increased pressure in the brain for some reason. I also see this when a baby is crying hard. Get in to see your doctor or go to the ER if this is persistent or the baby isn't acting normally. Soft spot sunken in? The baby may be dehydrated. If she seems sick, head in to see your doc.

After a particularly cumbersome march down the birth canal, a baby's head may have a strange shape to it, and/or a soft squishy scalp lump on it for a bit. These are little collections of fluid and blood under the skin called *cephalohematomas*. They're soft, pliant, and sometimes even a little bruised-looking. I see cephalohematomas often with big babies who needed big squeezes to come out, and deliveries that needed the assistance of forceps or vacuum.

The head can come out a bit wonky—or change shape over time—if babies lay on the pelvic bone in utero, or lay on the same side of the head over and over after they're born. They can get flat spots in these areas, since their little heads are relatively "softer" than ours. This flat spot is called *plagiocephaly*, or sometimes *brachycephaly* depending on the shape. Rarely, if it gets severe enough and is affecting the symmetry and features of the face, physical therapy or cranial helmets can help to gently guide the head to grow in a certain way. These helmets are sometimes a controversial topic, so we'll talk more on it later in Chapter 9.

Sometimes, parents find small, movable bumps under the skin on the back of the skull—toward the back and bottom, sometimes behind the ears. These are tiny little *lymph nodes* that you can easily feel at this age. No need to worry about them unless they are rapidly growing larger, or the area is suddenly red and warm.

Hair

Newborns come out with all sorts of hair types: dark, light, strawberry blonde, thick, thin, curly, straight, bald—I see it all. Chances are excellent that the hair may change within the first few months. And a lot of babies, both boys and girls, get a little front-scalp-male-pattern baldness over the first few months. Some kids even have color changes soon after birth as new hair grows in.

A skin issue I see on nearly every newborn's head is varying degrees of *cradle cap*. Cradle cap is more annoying than anything else. We think it's caused by hormones causing lots of oil excretion on the skin. When this oil meets up with normal dead sloughing skin cells, cradle cap is born. The scalp may slowly start to develop crusts or flakes, and sometimes it's thick and yellow or light brown. Cradle cap can be on the eyebrow area, too, or behind the ears. It doesn't seem itchy or painful at all. Depending on how bad the cradle cap is, there are many ways to approach it. You can certainly just leave it alone; most cradle cap goes away on its own with time. You can also use a special cradle cap brush along with baby oil or coconut oil to loosen the scales up and brush them off. Sometimes, if it's really thick, we will try antifungal creams or shampoos. Sometimes steroid creams help (like over-the-counter hydrocortisone).

Eyes/Ears/Mouth

Baby faces can come out looking strange sometimes. In utero, mama's pelvic bones can smush the face for a bit, and kids sometimes come out with an ear folded over, or even an asymmetrical-looking nose. Newborns also typically look puffy for a few days after birth. This will all change with time. It's pretty interesting to look at your baby's birth photos and compare them to photos taken even a week later!

The newborn's eyes are brand spankin' new, and they don't work very well for the first few months. They may come out bruised and with red spots on them after birth. Initially, all that babies can see are lights and dark contrasts. It's common for the eyes to cross once in a while or dart back and forth as they test out their focusing muscles.

Jaundice is commonly seen in newborn eyes: the whites may look a little yellow for the first few days (or even months if your baby just gets breast milk).

You may see discharge or crustiness on the inner parts of the eye. This is usually due to a problematic tear duct located on the inner part of that lower eyelid. Pull down your lower eyelid in front of a mirror—see it there? That little hole toward your nose? When tears wash over the eye throughout the day, they end up going down that duct into the nasal cavity. Sometimes, that duct doesn't work very well in babies. We call this *lacrimal duct stenosis*.

Since the tears aren't very good at draining down that duct yet, they'll just sit in the eye and eventually start drying up. And since there are lots of cells in tears, when they dry, it can look like yellow or green goo. Let your pediatrician know if the white parts of the eye are getting pinker or more irritated. Otherwise, it's okay to just wipe the eyes as needed. A good firm massage with a warm washcloth on the inner part of the eye toward the nose can help this duct work a little better. This is called *lacrimal duct massage*. Lacrimal duct stenosis may take a few months to improve on its own.

The newborn nose often has little harmless white or yellow spots called *milia* on it. These will go away with time. Milia are common all over the body, actually.

There are also sometimes red stain-looking patches on eyelids, forehead, neck, or nose. These are called *nevus simplex* and will usually fade with time (also called "salmon patches," "angel kisses" on the face, and "stork bites," if located on the back of the neck).

Congestion sounds are common in the newborn nose. Those nostrils are teeny tiny passageways for air—and one booger lodged in there is gonna make a lot of noise. Colds often cause congestion as well, as does reflux. Reflux is probably the most common cause of congestion I see in those first few weeks. More on this later!

The ears may sometimes have *cerumen*, or earwax in them. Wax comes in all kinds of colors, like yellow, orange, brown, and black. Earwax is super helpful. It protects the ear canal and prevents infection. We pediatricians will remove some if there's enough to block the ear canal—otherwise I recommend just leaving earwax alone for the most part.

In the newborn mouth, you may notice little white spots on the gums or on the roof. These are called *Epstein pearls* and are totally okay. Sometimes they even look like teeth busting through the gum! They're caused by a normal substance our body makes called keratin, and they're completely harmless. They usually go away in a few weeks to months.

There are also normal skin latches under the tongue and the top lip called *frenulums*. The internet calls these "tongue ties" and "lip ties," and they are completely normal to see. They are usually unproblematic in the majority of babies. Rarely, if a child struggles with latching to a breast or bottle, clipping a restrictive tongue-tie can be helpful. Lip and tongue ties are somewhat controversial issues in the world of newborn health. Folks have *strong* opinions about them, and it's a bit controversial how often they should be clipped. I dabbled on this a bit in Chapter 3.

Skin

This is where things get really weird.

One thing to know about baby skin is that it's pretty sensitive in general. It's gonna break out in pink bumps for days if the baby gets a little sweaty or warm here and there. The skin is going to scrape and welt up easily from the nails of those flailing, wild fingers.

Whenever you're worried about your baby's new rash, try to look at the big picture: Does the baby seem okay? Is she drinking well and calm? Is she breathing easily and urinating at least every six to eight hours? Is she fever-free? If this is the case, it's probably ok to call your pediatrician's office in the morning.

Another thing that differs from our adult skin is how thin, and sometimes transparent, baby skin can be. It's very normal to see the veins running under the skin of the eyelids or nose bridge, for example. And newborn skin may get something called a *mottled* look to it—that is, a blotchy, pale, red, or purple spider-web-type look to it—when cold or sick.

Many babies are born with *lanugo* on their skin—this is a soft, downy hair all over the back, arms, and shoulders. Nope, she's not morphing into a werewolf. This will go away with time.

Jaundice is pretty common early on, and almost all babies experience some level of it. Jaundice is the word for the yellow coloring of the eyes and skin that usually starts up on day 2 or 3. This happens because the new liver is trying to figure out how to filter, process and get rid of something called *bilirubin* from the blood. The babies will eventually poop out the bilirubin (fun fact: bilirubin is partly the reason your poop is brown) and the number will start to slowly come down. However, while we're waiting for this to happen, sometimes the levels get too high in the blood. And if they stay too high, the bilirubin can make it into the fluid around the brain. This can cause some pretty scary stuff like cerebral palsy, hearing loss, or intellectual disabilities. This is why we keep poking and checking your kid those first few days—we have to make sure we watch these numbers closely! If the number gets too high (it usually likes to peak around day 3 to 5), there's an easy fix: UV light treatment called phototherapy.

As mentioned in my *Newborn Notes* (Chapter 1), the peeling and flaking skin is completely normal. These dry-looking areas will move around in the first few weeks after birth. No amount of lotion is going to make this better. It's kinda like a snake shedding its first layer of skin.

"My kid is covered in flea bites!"—a true quote from a panicked parent at my office. Some babies quickly start to show a rash called *erythema toxicum*. This looks a lot like bug bites—little pink or red splotches with a white "head" occasionally. They come and go and can move around for days to weeks after a child is born. This is a really common immune system rash that will go away on its own.

Another common thing I see starting around week two is *neonatal acne*. These are pink spots that look like zits, basically, and are usually on the infant's face. Neonatal acne is caused by hormones and wacky oil production in the skin around this time. It can last a few weeks and doesn't hurt the kiddo at all; just wash the face gently with a mild soap. Try not to pop them or squeeze them. They'll go away on their own!

Again, *milia* are tiny white spots or bumps that are occasionally found on the nose and chin—or really anywhere on the body. I'll even see them on a nipple or penis every now and then. This is just a bit of normal skin cells and oil that got trapped under the skin and should disappear on its own.

Hemangiomas are super-red birthmarks that can be found anywhere on the baby's body, and they may or may not protrude from the skin. They're tumors. Isn't that a fun word to hear in regard to your child? Don't worry, they're benign tumors (ah, that's better) made out of clusters of tiny blood vessels. They tend to grow larger in the first few months of life—or some appear for the first time in this phase. Then, between six and twelve months, they slow down or completely halt their growth. Over the next few years, they slowly shrink and go away. I was trained in residency that "30% are gone by age 3, 50% by age 5, 70% by age 7" and so on. Rarely, if a hemangioma seems to be located in an area that may cause future issues (like an eyelid or ear canal) or seems to cause scabbing and frequent bleeding, it can be treated with certain medications. Talk to your doc about whether or not this is an option.

Neck and Chest

The newborn neck is a cute little skinny thing compared to that big dome of a head. Think about the proportions of your kid's head versus his body size—and then compare that to yours. It'd be like your head being the size of one of those giant beach balls. Oof. The newborn neck has a hard job to do in those first few months, lifting that big ole brain, which is already 25 percent of its adult size. This is why we recommend "tummy time" here and there each day to help the child start to strengthen the neck and back and coordinate head-lifting as the nerves mature. There's no strict schedule of tummy time you need to follow—just make room for fifteen minutes of it two to three times in your day. And yep, it can be on your chest.

Speaking of the chest, one thing many parents notice in the newborn's chest is the little bump at the bottom of the breastbone. It looks to be at the very top of the tummy and the bottom midline of the chest. This is called the *xiphoid process*, and it can stick out pretty impressively in babies. You sometimes see this because of body proportions; the newborn rib cage is tiny and angled, and the newborn belly is big. So, when the child breathes, you'll occasionally see this little bump move up and down with the chest. No worries about this; it's common and will slowly not be as obvious as the child grows.

Ever notice that the baby stops breathing altogether for a few seconds, then pants really fast, and then breathes at a normal regular rate again? This is called *periodic breathing* and is totally normal in babies even up to age four months old. That new baby brain is still trying to figure out how all this works, so sometimes you'll see a few minutes of this funny breathing here and there. It's completely normal and as long as a regular breathing rate eventually comes back around (about thirty to fifty times a minute), you're good.

The newborn heart is faster than ours—much faster. Their heart rate at rest can sit in the 170s to 180s (for reference, our resting heart rate as adults is fifty-five to eighty-five on average).

Belly

The newborn belly is a rotund beast. Given the teeny ribcage and the spindly arms and legs, that stomach looks enormous. And at the end of the day, it can be normal for the belly to look nine months pregnant as it fills up with food and gas. As long as the baby isn't acting extra fussy, no need to worry about it—some farts are gonna pop out and flatten it out eventually. And yes—those constant *very loud* farts are completely normal. I lovingly refer to them as "trucker farts audible across the house." Perhaps I'll copyright that phrase one day.

The umbilical cord and belly button area, also known as the *umbilicus*, understandably stresses parents out. Mystery nubbins are not something we encounter much in the adult body, are they? Try not to worry too much about it. It's surprisingly good at taking care of itself with very few complications. Most umbilical cords fall off anytime between a few days to one month after birth. Maintenance is pretty easy. You don't need to tug at it; just try to keep it dry and clean. And if you want to clean the area (because poop or pee *will* make it up there at some point), use a warm washcloth soaked with water. Avoid dunking the baby in a bath before it falls off —while rare, we don't want the umbilical area to get infected. Washcloth wipe-downs are totally fine, though. When it does fall off, have at it! Also, head's up: it's very normal to see a little mild yellow, pink, or red discharge from the umbilical area for a few days after the cord falls off.

Belly button issues that may warrant a call to your doctor:

- The cord doesn't fall off by the age one month;
- You frequently have to wipe blood from the cord for more than one to two days, or if it's oozing constantly;
- Redness seems to be spreading from the belly button outwards (this could be a sign of a rare umbilical infection).

Hips

One joint you might notice we pay special attention to is the hips. Sometimes, rarely, hip joints don't form correctly in utero. This is a condition called *developmental dysplasia of the hip*, and you might see us roll and press on the hips throughout the first year to rule this out. Let your pediatrician know if you feel the hips pop, if the leg fat folds look asymmetrical, or if you feel that one leg is longer than the other.

Penises and Vaginas

Ah, the private parts. This region is confusing from day one, isn't it? Whether you've got a boy or a girl, folks often have lots of questions about the mysteries of the genitals.

Let's start with newborn boys.

Circumcised or not (and I am truly neutral on the matter, by the way—I am 100 percent circumcision Switzerland), the penis can look different from baby to baby. They vary a tiny bit in size and color. I see penis colors range anywhere from peach to pink to bluish-purple (and if the baby seems fine and content, that bluish color can be totally normal).

The *scrotum*, or ball sack, can also look different from kid to kid. Sometimes, they look huge and swollen when they're first born (new fathers are particularly proud of this) because of something common called a *hydrocele*. This is when there is some leftover fluid in the sack. I can put my flashlight up to the balls and the sack fluid will illuminate! Merry Christmas! Hydroceles can be pretty common. They usually get better on their own, and the sack will slowly shrink over time. If there's still fluid in there by the one-year birthday, or if it seems to be getting firmer or larger, we'll send you to see a surgeon or urologist (not an emergency, just something that needs to be addressed).

If you choose to get your son circumcised, the follow-up hygiene is pretty simple. Whether the foreskin was taken off with a blade or clamp, or was tied off with a piece of string (a common method used currently called the Plastibell method), the main goals are just to keep the area as clean as possible and watch for any bleeding. Use wipes on the area with diaper changes and look for bleeding that doesn't seem to want to stop (most docs watch for bleeding closely for a while after they have completed the procedure, so this is a pretty rare occurrence). That Plastibell method I mentioned earlier will leave a ring around the head of the penis when your little boy is brought home, and you may see the white string tucked around it. This will peel itself off slowly as the area heals—and may take up to three or four weeks to come off completely. Try not to tug at it.

If you opted out of circumcision, again, try not to fuss too much over the penis. It's very, very normal for you not to be able to pull the foreskin all the way back over the penis head—if you explore this area, please don't use any force here! Use wipes to clean as needed and don't worry if you find a little white bit of cheesy stuff here and there in the folds of the groin and privates—this is called *smegma* and is normal in both boys and girls in this area! Could we have named it anything cuter?

Girl parts are no less confusing sometimes. First of all, soon after she is born, it's very normal to see some white mucous discharge or even blood come out of the vagina. This is because leaving the hormone-rich environment of the mother's body causes baby girls to have basically a "mini period." Weird, I know.

About 10 percent of newborn girls have a tiny fleshy tag sticking out of the vaginal opening. This is called a *hymenal tag* and is not worrisome. It should disappear within a few weeks—though some girls may still have one even into adulthood.

Hygiene of baby girl parts can sometimes be perplexing. My first kid was a boy, so when my girl came next, she posed a bit of a challenge to my husband during that first diaper change. "Um, the poop is *everywhere*." First off—it's okay if poop gets inside the vaginal area. The vagina is not meant to be a sterile environment. Just clean it out gently as best you can with wipes. Again, you may see *smegma* here and there in the folds of the labia and groin. This cheesy white stuff is totally normal; just clean it out if it seems to be building up.

Arms, Hands, Legs, and Feet

Newborns have very little control over their upper limbs. They'll flail and startle a lot, and occasionally even scratch themselves with their fingernails.

The startle reflex, or *Moro reflex*, is something you may see for the first four months of your baby's life. This reflex sort of looks like their arms suddenly shooting outwards and giving you "jazz hands." We'll check this reflex during the checkup as it is a great sign that the brain and spine are working normally. If the Moro looks different in one arm versus the other, sometimes it makes me wonder if the nerves in the arm or shoulder are inflamed or damaged. This can happen with a traumatic birth.

It's very common for newborn hands and feet to look quite purple for a while after they are born. This is called *acrocyanosis* and generally has to do with lousy newborn circulation in this area. When they're cold, or you've smushed a leg or arm firmly against you as you're holding them, they'll look even more impressively dusky. As long as your baby isn't screaming in pain, showing purple tongue or gums, or having issues with breathing (possibly indicating a heart problem), this is no big deal. It slowly improves within a few months. I see many toddlers in my cold exam rooms who still occasionally have purple feet! The gums and tongue are where I typically look to see if a child is truly *cyanotic*, which means experiencing low oxygen levels. Cyanosis is a true emergency, and if you feel like your baby is not acting right, is breathing abnormally, and/or has darker-looking tongue or gums, you need to get to the emergency room ASAP.

One concern people seem to have a lot about the lower body is the shape and curve of the legs and feet. It's totally normal for their shins to have a bit of a bend in them, almost like a "C" shape. Most babies look a little bow-legged. These legs are crunched up and cross over each other in the uterus, and so it makes sense that they come out a little bendy-looking. They may stay this way for a while, even until they start walking. It's normal for some kids to hold on to a mild "pigeon-toed" look for a while. A foot deformity called *clubfoot* is worth mentioning here. If you feel one or both of the feet are really curved inwards—where the bottom always faces the side or even upward, and cannot be corrected downward—best to talk to your doctor.

Fingers and Toes

Fingers and toes may come out looking weirdly purple or blue (that *acrocyanosis* I mentioned earlier). And they will move and flail and slap and scratch with absolutely zero control. And the nails—oh, the nails. I get tons of questions about newborn finger and toenails. They look pretty weird compared to ours. By the way, they may come out of the womb freakishly long (at least, my own kid's freaked me the hell out. Wtf, those things were inside me?!).

Baby nail shape is different, and the texture is softer than ours (they're often easy to just peel off as needed), and they grow much faster than adult nails. Try not to stress too much over them. Just peel or file them if you're nervous about the clippers and watch for redness, swelling, or pus showing itself around the nail bed.

Baby toenails may have wings on them or seem to sit very deep in the toe flesh. Try to trim these straight across and not too terribly short, to prevent ingrown toenails. It happens though, and again, as long as it's not looking infected, spreading redness, or leaking pus, it's ok to just leave these be.

Some babies are born with extra fingers or toes (*polydactyly*). This is actually one of the more common birth defects we see in pediatrics and isn't usually a sign of anything dangerous. Talk to your pediatrician about the pros and cons and options for treatment of polydactyly.

After learning about the very different body your new roommate possesses, is it any wonder their parts are sometimes confusing? Cut yourself a little slack here and don't be afraid to ask your baby's doctor about anything you deem weird. I promise, we've heard the question before, and we'll never judge you for asking.

4

*Breastfeeding Can Be a Real B*tch*

My husband gaped at my exposed nipples. I had just pulled off the breast pump flanges, and they were purple. They were *purple*.

"Um, are they . . . supposed to look like that?"

Purple, my own personal color of failure. Purple is what happens when your breast pump's suction setting is too high. Or the flange size is too small for your nipple. Purple is something I know now to be . . . not good. My whole pumping situation was a hot mess. Producing and extracting breast milk wasn't something they taught me about in pediatric residency. This was new territory, and I obviously didn't know what the hell I was doing.

I once posed a question on my Facebook page: "What part of parenthood made you cry *ugly* tears?" Over a hundred parents commented, and man, a huge portion involved breastfeeding. Amen. I hear you guys. I think I cried more about breastfeeding than any other part of my parenting experience (thus far). I dealt with a lot of fear and insecurities with nursing my first baby and battled a low supply. The stress of being a new mom and raging postpartum anxiety contributed heavily to my body saying "oh *hell* no" to producing a lot of milk. That's something to think about, isn't it? Emotional stress can *absolutely* contribute to how much breast milk some women produce.

So, I gave my first baby some formula after the first few weeks, and guess what? He survived. And thrived. But my guilt—*I was a pediatrician who couldn't exclusively breastfeed!?*—ate away at me. When the second baby came around two years later, I dropped the guilt, prepped for the stress, and packed my closet full of formula. And guess what? I had a successful and pretty much stress-free exclusive breastfeeding journey with her. Each experience with your kids may be really different for you, too.

Let me be clear—some women absolutely thrive at breastfeeding, and I celebrate this with them. If it comes naturally to both mom and baby, it is immediately rewarding and a generally adored activity by both parties. It warms my heart to know that for many of the moms I see, producing breast milk for their child is a much-loved and eventually much-missed part of having a baby. For some women, it is their *favorite* part of having a baby.

But for other moms, breastfeeding can be a huge source of stress, physical pain, and mental anguish. It is the number one reason I reach for the Kleenex box at the newborn check-ups. The nursing journey often doesn't look like what some may have expected, and the "failures" can weigh heavily on a mother's heart. I just want you to know I'm holding your hand here, sweet friend. You're doing awesome no matter *what* you choose to do, and you're not alone. This shit is *definitely* not as easy as that Mother Earth Mommy on Instagram makes it seem.

Breastfeeding is a topic that could fill an entire book all on its own. And while I'm a seasoned mother and doctor, I am by no means as knowledgeable as our dear friends the lactation consultants when it comes to the details and the troubleshooting of the entire process. For that reason, I asked a colleague and dear friend, Dr. Andrea Wadley, a pediatrician and board-certified breastfeeding medicine specialist and lactation consultant, to review this in its entirety for accuracy.

In this chapter, I'm hopeful you will gain some support and insight, understand the data behind the benefits, and learn a few simple tips and tricks for breastfeeding and pumping (based on my own and thousands of patient family experiences).

Breastfeeding and Data

As a new mom, you're kind of bombarded with the idea that "Breast is Best." So . . . is it? Well, in this pediatrician's opinion, yes . . . to a certain extent. I do believe breast milk is the most healthful and biologically beneficial option for feeding an infant prior to age twelve months. I think breastfeeding and/or offering pumped breast milk is an excellent way to protect your baby from severe infections before the first birthday. Do I think it's the only way for infants to thrive and do awesome? Nope. Do I think the *long-term* benefits could possibly be over-hyped based on existing data? Yep. More on this later. I'm gonna keep this brief given the broad scope of this book, but there's lots of credible information out there on nationally-accredited data search engines like the National Institute of Health, the Cochrane Library, and PubMed.

Breastfeeding offers a lot of protection for babies, especially in the first twelve months of life. There is pretty good data out there that shows that babies are less likely to suffer tummy problems like infectious diarrhea, or a severe intestinal infection (that usually affects preterm babies) called necrotizing enterocolitis.[1] Babies who breastfeed in the first six months of life also seem to need fewer hospitalizations in general, and experience less severe illnesses.[2,3] Does this mean if your baby is breastfed, they'll never get diarrheal infections or be in the hospital? No. There's a reduced chance for it, though. There is also some evidence that ingesting breast milk over time can prevent eczema, asthma,[4,5] severe respiratory infections, and otitis media (a.k.a. ear infections). There is pretty compelling data that the longer babies breastfeed, the less likely they are to die of SIDS (Sudden Infant Death Syndrome, or death of unknown cause under age twelve months).[6]

While I'm not a fan of anecdotes in comparison to the large, randomized double-blind studies and systematic reviews I like to cite, I will tell you that in my practice, I often see what I can only assume is the "protective" nature of breast milk in action. I have had many mothers call my office worried about their newborn becoming ill while they or one of the baby's very close siblings suddenly seem pretty sick.

I remember one mom in particular who had been burning with a 104 degree Fahrenheit fever and had a positive flu test who called me asking if she should stop nursing. My advice was: heck no. Give that baby those antibodies. When the mother's body is ill and fighting off an infection, it produces a huge amount of these fighter cells in order to detect and kill the germs. Those antibodies are passed through the breast milk to the infant, and then line the gut with a "standing army" of protection. Flu mama's baby never had a single symptom of illness that week, which, given the natural constant closeness of mother and child, is pretty impressive to me. And I have experienced this story on repeat throughout my practice years.

We also should give credit where credit is due and bring up the less-discussed benefits of breastfeeding—the benefits for mothers. Cost-wise, breast milk is generally the cheaper feeding alternative (though we could really dive into the costs of breast pumps, pumping supplies, nursing pillows, and nursing supplements if we wanted to argue this claim). Some women find that breastfeeding helps them naturally lose the postpartum baby weight (though not all women experience this). Breastfeeding has also been a strong force in reducing certain types of cancer[7-9] in mothers later on down the line—particularly breast, endometrial, and ovarian cancers.

When you start looking at the data about long-term benefits for babies who breastfeed for an extended period of time, however, things get a little foggier in my opinion. There are many claims that breastfeeding directly contributes to the prevention of obesity and hypertension, reduction in Type 2 diabetes, and increased IQ scores. These are topics that can be a lot harder to study because of the old adage, *correlation does not always equal causation.* This, in essence, questions the idea that it is the ingestion of breast milk that is the *sole* cause of these benefits.

Could it also be that mothers who breastfeed tend to have higher IQ's, thus leading to children with higher IQ's? Could it be that breastfeeding has been proven to be more commonly practiced in women with higher education levels and higher socioeconomic statuses?[10,11] Could environmental factors be a higher contributing force to these babies growing up to be "healthier" adults? I think these factors do play a role, though exactly how much is questionable. And that's why you'll often see phrases online like "this is suggested as a possible cause" rather than "this *is* the cause." It's just harder to prove the cause-and-effect relationship here, in my opinion. Dr. Emily Oster's excellent data-driven book, *Cribsheet,* dives into this concept more extensively should you want to do some extended reading here.

Learning to Breastfeed Ain't a Simple Task

One thing that no one seems to talk about is that learning how to breastfeed is *not* just about putting your baby's mouth on your nipple and crossing your fingers. Breastfeeding is a whole system that may take a lot of study and time to master. You have to learn how to:

- Hold the baby effectively while nursing.
- Position a baby's head in a way that allows for great milk transfer.
- Sit properly in a chair for long periods of time, allowing for the best breast access and the least pain.

- Eat, drink, and support your own physically-stressed body so that it can produce milk.
- Potentially use a complicated tool called a breast pump.
- Understand how to store milk.
- Build up a small stash of milk if needed in the future.
- Learn the nature of breast milk production—supply and demand.
- Potentially learn how to do all the things in very public settings.

It's just . . . so much. So please know that if you feel overwhelmed, it makes sense. You couldn't understand how to put together a car in a single day, right? Learning large amounts of information takes time.

Let's dive into some tips and tricks for all of this, and more.

The First Few Days of Breastfeeding

The first few days of breastfeeding can be really challenging. But there are a lot of people around to help! In hospitals and birthing centers, one thing staff will try to do (if your birth situation allows) is to ensure some skin-to-skin time immediately after your baby is born. Skin-to-skin contact in the first hour of life seems to be related to more success with breastfeeding long-term.[12,13] The data here seems pretty compelling, so I think it's worth it to do skin-to-skin for the first hour of life if you can (and if you had C-sections like me, or your baby had to go to the NICU right away, guess what? Successful breastfeeding relationships have happened easily in both situations!).

For some folks, the hardest part of those first few days may be getting used to people seeing and touching your boobs. Gone are the days of modesty—in those first few postpartum days, your doula or lactation consultant or delivery nurse is probably going to need to show you how to do things after the excitement of birth has died down. Sometimes it can feel new and almost aggressive—but I think I personally learned the most about the brute mechanics of nursing from these wonderful folks the few days I was in the hospital.

Don't hesitate to reach out to lactation consultants after you have gone home. I have spoken with many moms who do this even weeks or months after their baby is born. LCs are endless pools of knowledge and can really help you in your breastfeeding journey. You can typically find one in person and/or virtually online, and many communities and hospital systems have their own local breastfeeding programs and resources.

How Do You Know When Your Milk Is "In"?

Milk takes time to start being plentifully made. With your first baby, it may take as long as five to six days for the "big volume" of milk to come in. I'd say most women experience it around day three or four after birth. With your subsequent babies, this process should get faster.

When I became a mom, people kept asking me, was my milk in? Was my milk in? How the hell was I supposed to know? I had never been a human dairy dispenser prior to this. What was it supposed to feel like?

Some clues your milk may be coming in:

- Your boobs may feel like two bags of rocks strapped to your chest (ow): more firm, more tender, more warm
- Your breasts may leak, and the milk may be changing to a lighter color (the initial milk you make is important stuff called "colostrum," and it is thicker and more yellow than later milk)
- Your baby will start to gulp, and milk may leak from the side of his mouth.

- Your baby's poops will slowly transition from the thick tarry stuff (meconium) to brown, green, and eventually yellow. Breastfed baby stools look a lot like seedy French's mustard.

Holding Your Baby While Nursing

Every baby is a different size and shape, and every breast is a different size and shape. Holding a baby to the breast is pretty different when the infant is 9 lbs versus 4.5 lbs, or when mom is a G-cup versus an A-cup, right? What about a mother who has had a C-section and is struggling with a fresh and painfully healing abdominal wound? Or a mom who cannot use one of her arms due to a medical condition? Or a baby who requires a nasal oxygen cannula or a feeding tube? The physical process here is a dynamic spectrum, folks. There are *vast differences* in what may be effective for one mom versus another.

Do you have larger breasts and/or a larger baby? Are you post C-section? Consider the *side-lying position*, where you and baby lay down on the bed facing each other. You also may want to look into something called the *football hold*. Smaller breasts? Consider the *laid-back position*, where you lay down on the bed on your back, and your baby lays face-downward on you, face parallel with your breast. *Cradle* and *cross-cradle* holds can also be a very comfortable position for any of these scenarios, with lots of support.

Some of the best general advice I can give you about positioning is to use the objects and props around you to aid you in your success. Use the hell out of pillows and cushions for yourself while you nurse. Use two, four, or eighteen while also trying to keep the skin-on-skin action going. Support your lower back, neck, and shoulders with whatever configuration works for you. The goal is to get the baby's head level with the nipple without you needing to hunch over. Look into different breastfeeding pillows, of which there are many, and know that there may need to be a layer of pillows *under* them to lift that baby up to the level that works best for you.

And as for nursing in public? Let's revisit the hot mess that was this pediatrician's first breastfeeding experience: I had a huge baby and huge boobs. I remember looking enviously at moms in restaurants who could easily hold their infant to the breast while they used the other hand to stab their salad and continue easy conversation. For me, nursing in those circumstances was like using one hand to wrestle an angry, sweaty, vicious warthog while my other hand attempted to support a breast that was not unlike a giant bag of rocks. The situation always tended to always end up in tears (both baby's and mine), and inevitably failed. So, guess what? I used bottles when my baby needed to feed in public. Everyone was happier and fed. And you're allowed to adjust each and every situation into one that gets your baby fed and you both happy.

Getting a Good Latch

A good nursing latch can be a tough thing to obtain at first. Some babies get it right away, and some babies may take *weeks* to figure it out. I remember putting my nipple in my first newborn's mouth on the first day of his life (because that's all it took, right? Just putting the boob in the baby's mouth?) and all he'd do was pant, whine, sniff, erratically wiggle and flail his head around, and eventually start screaming at me. An angry warthog. The boob was *right there.* The nipple was *riiiiiiggght theerrrrrree.* Why did he hate me so much?

Some tips when trying to latch your baby:

1. Make sure there's a cool, calm vibe in the room. Get both of you comfortable.
2. Try to ensure your baby's face is facing your nipple.
3. Make sure the baby's stomach is facing your stomach (skin-on-skin is awesome here).
4. Tickle the baby's nose with your nipple. This will encourage a *wide* mouth opening, which is super important right now.

5. One vivid instructional method my lactation consultant gave me was: "mash your nipple into a sandwich, and point the sandwich deep and upward in the baby's mouth." I swear I thought of a PB&J every single time I latched my kid for the first couple of weeks.
6. Bring the baby's head toward your breast, rather than the breast to the baby.
7. Make sure your baby can breathe comfortably through the nose while nursing. If this is difficult, try a different hold.
8. Make the baby's lips are pointed outwards like a duck (think about when a Kardashian takes a selfie), and not "tucked in." Use your finger to flip that lip outwards if needed.

Your Poor Nips (and Other Breastfeeding Pains)

Another thing that blew my mind when I became a new mom: no one tells you how much breastfeeding can *hurt*.

The moment my first baby latched onto my breast, (and every time he did so for the next two weeks), my eyes welled up with tears due to the pain. I also experienced a lot of pain in my upper back, arms, and shoulders due to all the hunching over and readjusting of my large newborn and my large breasts. Holy cow, was this supposed to be a joyful and tender activity I was going to enjoy with my baby?

Don't fear. It usually gets better. And the pain with latch should not last longer than one minute or so at the beginning of nursing—please talk to your doctor if it does. Within two to three weeks, I don't want moms to be experiencing any more nursing pain at all. If it's still pretty painful after this point, I usually ask moms to talk with a lactation consultant for some troubleshooting, and/or have a baby's mouth evaluated for a tight/short tongue-tie (more on this later). Sometimes the trouble lies with other anatomic issues, like the size of mom's nipples versus the size of baby's mouth, mom having inverted nipples, or the shape and size of the baby's jaw or palate (roof of mouth).

Lanolin can help sore, cracked nipples, as can rubbing breast milk on the nipples themselves. If you're in pretty severe pain, your nipples are red or rashy, itchy, or slow to heal, you may want to bring it up with your doctor. Sometimes yeast infections can occur, though this is somewhat rare.

One thing that can help nipple pain is nipple shields. These are thin plastic nipple-shaped covers with holes in them. You put them over your nipples, and they can help the baby latch. Nipple shields are typically a useful accessory for a temporary amount of time—like a few weeks. There are some studies that show that over time, nipple shields may slowly reduce supply or prevent babies from transferring milk effectively, but I find the data mixed. Many moms find that they can remove the shields and have successful nursing sessions after those first few weeks. Some moms find they're helpful for months—and if you can keep up your supply, go for it.

If a specific part of one of your breasts is in a lot of pain, and you feel warmth or a lump in that part of the breast, you may have a *plugged duct*. Most plugged ducts improve on their own in twenty-four to forty-eight hours, and nursing helps a lot! If you have a warm red part of the breast along with pain, body aches, chills, and a new fever, you may need to call your doctor, as this may be mastitis.

Mastitis is inflammation in the breast tissue that can cause a lot of discomfort. It is often caused by an oversupply or poor milk discharge. Sometimes severe mastitis may require antibiotics, but not always (see "Further Reading" sources for an interesting read about how antibiotics may be sometimes overused for mastitis).

Pumping

After a week or so of struggling to nurse my first kid (the very cute, very angry warthog), I decided to exclusively pump my breast milk for him. I think this was mostly due to my personality type—type A, that is—and I wanted to know how much my kiddo was drinking. I did this because he *always* seemed hungry, and often didn't seem satisfied. Looking back, I think given his good weight gain at the pediatrician, his frequent pees and poops, and the understanding I now have about how cluster feeding works, I probably should have just trusted the nursing process a bit more. Forgive my stream of consciousness here—hindsight is always 20/20—but maybe it will help you with this decision as well, because exclusive pumping can be a hard journey.

Whether you are pumping exclusively or building a supply, no matter what type of pump you choose to use, how often you choose to use it, where you use it, etc.—the most important thing to understand when pumping is that after the first week of life, breast milk tends to be made in a "*supply and demand*" manner. If you pump out a certain amount of breast milk each and every day, you should continue to make this amount daily. If you need more breast milk, you need to add a consistent pump at the same time and for the same length each day. Over time, more demand will lead to more milk production.

A lot of moms ask me about "starting a stash" of breast milk before they start back at work. I usually don't recommend getting the pump out until after two weeks after the baby's birth, to establish nursing. After that, I recommend moms start pumping in the mornings once a day at the same time each day. Over time, you'll start to make extra ounces of milk at that time. You don't need a gigantic stash before you go back—honestly, just one to two days' worth of milk should be fine. When you start back at work, if you maintain a regular pumping schedule, you should continue to make the days' worth of milk your baby needs.

Can I Mix Formula and Breast Milk?

Well, sure. Humans eat meat and potatoes in the same meal, right? A baby's digestive system does just fine with both at the same time. Some moms give breast milk first, and then "top off" with any formula (and I have zero formula preference here—more in the next chapter). Some moms mix it together, though I think if you have a limited stash, try to offer the breast milk first so it isn't wasted if baby doesn't finish the bottle.

How Long Should You Breastfeed?

In general, the longer you breastfeed, the better. Our acronym friends, the World Health Organization (WHO) and the American Academy of Pediatrics (AAP), both recommend breastfeeding for at least two years. They recommend that a baby should *only* get breast milk for the first six months of life (though I believe there are some exceptions for food allergy prevention here, which I will discuss more later on in the food chapters).

Do most of the mothers I see in my office breastfeed for two years? No. Everyone's situation is different, and their babies are different. Breastfeeding should continue past a year if both parties involved are willing and still want it to happen.

If you can breastfeed for at least eight weeks after your baby is born, I think it offers such beautiful protection for babies when their immune systems are the most vulnerable. So, for moms who are on the fence, that's usually my recommended goal.

If you hate breastfeeding, or your baby hates breastfeeding, or making breast milk has been really hard for you? Take this day-by-day. It's okay to say your goal is "one month" or "until next week" or "until tomorrow." Sometimes smaller goals feel a lot more achievable.

Can You Breastfeed When You've Been Drinking Alcohol?

The short answer: yes, as long as you do not feel "buzzed" or drunk at the moment.

The long answer: think of your breast milk just like you think of your bloodstream. Things are constantly moving into it and dissolving out of it. When you start your drink, the breast milk initially is booze-free. Then, slowly, the alcohol contents increase as you continue your libations. If you feel "buzzed," the milk in your breasts at that moment is "buzzed milk." So—not okay for baby. If you feel drunk—well, please don't breastfeed—your milk at that moment is drunk! If, however, after your two glasses of wine, you decide to drink water, relax, and wait until the giddiness goes away (and you feel completely normal again), you can nurse or pump at that time. Please don't "pump and dump"—just wait it out. Instead of "pump and dump" can we change the saying to "wait and hydrate"? Ha.

Do Pacifiers Ruin Breastfeeding?

Parents tend to worry that using a pacifier will cause something called "nipple confusion" in the first few weeks of life, while struggling with a baby who wants nothing more than to suck on something 24/7. While I do think new moms could use the first three to four days of breastfeeding to learn their baby's hunger cues and solidify that good latch, I'm not sure that I see much real nipple confusion beyond the first few days of life. Newborn babies are smarter than we give them credit for. And I think a majority of breastfed kids learn how to nurse regardless of whether pacifiers are used occasionally or not. To be honest with you, I took pacifiers to the hospital when I delivered both of my babies.

I'm not a huge fan of restricting pacifier use for weeks after a baby is born because I think so many babies and their families can benefit from paci use. Pacifiers are excellent for soothing fussy babies and helping them sleep. A pretty convincing review of two large trials involving 1,302 breastfed infants showed that "pacifier use in healthy breastfeeding infants had no significant effect on the proportion of infants exclusively breastfed at three months"[14] Pacis also can reduce the risk for SIDS death (more on this later). So . . . I wouldn't stress about pacis.

What's the Deal with Tongue Ties?

Oh, Lordy. Tongue ties.

A "tongue tie," or ankyloglossia, is what it's called when the tongue frenulum (band of tissue that connects the tongue to the floor of the mouth) is short or tight and affects the functions and movements of the tongue. Most of us have tongue frenulum. Many of us have short ones. The majority of the time, these frenula cause no issues whatsoever.

Most of us pediatricians were very perplexed about twelve years ago when parents started marching into our offices demanding their baby's tongue frenulum be cut. We all collectively scratched our heads—as this was not something recognized or promoted by the most up-to-date research (and it still isn't). This was a movement gently pushed by lactation specialists and dentists.

Tongue tie treatment can be a controversial topic in medicine. Depending on whom you talk to, the advice you receive will change. That's because we're still lacking large, sweeping studies that prove one way or another that the procedure helps more than harms (though there are some small ones).[15,16] Also, a gentle reminder that the folks who perform these procedures generally make a significant amount of money because of it—thus creating biased advice from some avenues, I think.

I generally recommend tongue ties be cut for two reasons, and two reasons only. First, if a child struggles to transfer milk from a breast or a bottle. This can be evidenced by poor weight gain in the first few weeks of life, frequent unlatching, and fussiness during the feed, or weighted feeds (where you weigh a baby before they nurse, let them nurse, and then weigh them again afterward) where very little is gained.

Second, I recommend a tongue-tie evaluation if a mother is in a significant amount of pain when nursing. Remember, initial pain with latching can be *normal* in the first two weeks of a baby's life. However, the pain should slowly improve. And if the pain extends beyond one or two minutes of nursing, or the pain is occurring beyond the two-week mark, it might help to get the mouth anatomy checked out.

I'm not trying to dissuade you from getting your child's tongue-tie released by any means—we physicians just realize that with any procedure, even the simple ones, there is the rare chance of problems or complications. This could include bleeding, pain, scarring, or damage to the tongue muscle or salivary glands. I've even had some babies experience enough pain after the procedure that it discourages them from breastfeeding further. Thankfully, this is rare.

As far as speech goes, there isn't really much evidence that a tight tongue-tie affects how we talk later on, if you can believe it.[17] There is no hard evidence that tongue ties cause speech delays, or speech disorders. Again—you'll find conflicting conversations of this online.

Why Do I Sometimes Feel Suddenly Sad or Anxious When I Nurse?

Okay—this is a rare thing, but a real thing. Nursing was never easy for me, but to make it worse, I started noticing all these "bad feelings"

I had when I breastfed my second baby. I'd latch her on to the boob, and within one to two minutes I'd suddenly have a huge rush of negative feelings. I mostly felt panicked, anxious, and scared. Then, in another few minutes ... boom. Gone. It was the weirdest thing. And I thought I was maybe going a little crazy. But the feelings felt so real, and strong—even if they did go away just as suddenly as they came. I started to dread nursing because of it.

After some research, I learned that *many* women experience something similar to what I did, and the majority suffer alone with it. *Dysphoric Milk Ejection Reflex (D-MER)* is a sudden emotional "drop" that occurs in some women just before milk release and continues for a few minutes after nursing begins. The brief negative feelings range in severity from anxiousness to wistfulness to extreme sadness to maybe even self-hatred. It's bizarre, I know. Most theories about D-MER suggest that it is an abrupt drop in dopamine that occurs when milk release is triggered, resulting in a real but quick dopamine deficit for a few minutes.

To be clear, we still aren't sure what causes it. But the dopamine theory seems pretty solid. Dopamine has to go down for prolactin (the breast milk-making hormone) to rise.

It felt so good to read this to finally affirm that I wasn't going crazy, and over the years I've met more women who have suffered from it.

Women who have D-MER all feel differently. Some feel anxious (like I did). Some feel depressed or hopeless. Some feel anger. Some just feel uneasy. The intensity is different from woman to woman. It definitely discourages some women from breastfeeding. I'm hopeful if this is shared, women will know they are not alone—and that it's just a pesky and temporary thing!

My D-MER symptoms were strong and consistent for about two months, then slowly started to happen less and less until they finally went away around month four. For many women, it goes away sooner. For some, it continues the entirety of their nursing experience. Know that there are medications out there—mostly low-dose antidepressants—that can help if things are feeling severe. And please remember that D-MER only happens during milk let-down. If you are feeling these big negative feelings at other times, please consider talking to your ob-gyn, your pediatrician, or your PCP about it.

Can I Breastfeed If I Didn't Physically Give Birth to My Child?

Yes! Did you know that you can breastfeed even if you have never been pregnant? This is called *induced breastfeeding*, and it's an option for adoptive, surrogacy, or other parenting situations. It requires the help of a breastfeeding medicine doctor, or an obstetrician who is familiar with the protocol. You will need the help of hormone therapy, which your doctor can prescribe, in order to mimic the hormone changes that happen in pregnancy. Frequent pumping with a breast pump for weeks prior to the baby's birth, can help you start to produce milk and can help you start to stash a supply!

What's the Deal with Vitamin D Drops?

Vitamin D is a lovely vitamin that helps strengthen our bones. Most of us get it from sunlight and foods like fatty fish, egg yolks, and milk. Babies have really sensitive skin that burns easily, so we don't recommend much direct sunlight in those first six months—at least not enough to get all the Vitamin D they need. There isn't much Vitamin D in breast milk, and if they get less than 32 ounces of formula a day, you will need to supplement your baby with a little Vitamin D (400 IU) each day until they're eating more foods. You can find Vitamin D drops for infants online and in most grocery stores!

Help! My Breastfed Baby Won't Take a Bottle!

Omigosh, this can be so stressful. My second baby, who was exclusively breastfed before I went back to work at ten weeks, absolutely *refused* to take a bottle from our nanny. It was a constant source of worry for me. Would I have to be up all night nursing to make up for the lost calories?

Here are some things to try that have helped me and my patients' moms:

- Don't do what I did and wait until it was too late—start introducing a bottle feed here and there after the two-week mark so the baby gets used to the feeling! Make sure she can not only take it from you, but someone who is not you as well.

- Switch back and forth between breast and bottle *during the same feed*. This sort of reassures the baby, "see? You can get the same milk from *both* of these sources!"

- Let the person feeding the baby lay a T-shirt with your scent on it over their chest (sleep in in a few nights and get it good and funky).

- Don't be afraid to switch things up, position-wise. Babies may not be comfortable taking a bottle the exact same way they drink from the breast. A completely different method, sitting elevation, and environment may be needed! The more chill and quieter the vibe in the room, the better. Some people swear that facing the baby *away* from the bottle-giver is helpful.

- Try different bottles. Try different nipples. Try different nipple speeds. Give each one a few days to feel it out. Lots of changes at once may confuse your little one.

- Dip the nipple in warm breast milk so the baby tastes it right away. It may be encouraging!

- Angle the bottle nipple upward toward the roof of the baby's mouth. This stimulates the suck reflex.
- If desperate, it's totally okay to try open or sippy cup feeding or syringe feeding!
- Remember: this transition takes time and it is totally normal for things to be miserable for at least a few days. 99 percent of babies will absolutely get it down within a few weeks. If it's not working, reach out to a lactation consultant or your pediatrician for help!

5

Formula Facts and Fibs

"Well, Doc, we've tried four different formulas this week, and all of them seem to make her want to fart."

Spoiler: babies swallow air when they drink, sleep, and cry. They all burp and they all fart many times a day. If it doesn't come out the top, it's gonna come out the bottom, and the type of formula you use may have nothing to do with it. But, yes—sometimes it does. The first two months are really and truly a *super gassy and fussy* time, and sometimes feels like nothing you're doing is right.

I went on to explain this to these sweet parents, who were battling what I call formula fatigue—the way you feel when you try a bazillion formulas and you aren't sure if any of them are the right fit. I also let them know that *all babies have bad days* regardless of what formula they're drinking—and one to two days usually isn't enough time to figure out if a formula is a good match for a baby. I think it may actually take more like two or three weeks to know if it's a winner.

Which Formula Should I Choose?

This is the question I get asked the most: "which formula is the best one?" This answer is both simple and complicated, depending on the baby.

Chances are great that your term, healthy baby, is going to be happy and thrive on whichever can of infant formula you grab off the shelf. There is no one perfect formula for all babies. Some babies do awesome on the exact same type of formula that others may suffer on. Your neighbor's kid may be all smiles on Enfamil Gentlease, for example, while your little nugget is spewing anger from every orifice on it. Let me walk you through the process of how formula is regulated, and how to make the best choice for your baby.

In the United States, if a company decides to create and market an infant formula and labels it as such, the FDA requires that they:

1. Notify them that they are doing so.
2. Use ingredients that are safe for babies.
3. Include thirty essential nutrients (with minimum and maximum amounts in the said formula).
4. Establish a system of controls to assure that their formula will not become contaminated with germs.
5. Establish a testing system for both the formula and the water used to assure that no germs will contaminate it.
6. Allow the FDA to inspect their facilities yearly.
7. Have labels that are FDA inspected and approved.

All this to say—if it says "infant formula" on it in the United States, it's probably been vetted as being safe and nutritious for your baby.

Don't even get me started on formula can labels. Could they *be* any busier and more confusing? I completely understand why you might feel overwhelmed while standing in the formula aisle at the store.

Cow's milk-based infant formulas are the most common types of formula out there. These use a cow's milk base to provide the protein part of the baby's nutrition. Examples include Similac Advance, Enfamil Infant, Earth's Best, Bobbie Organic, Gerber GoodStart, and many, many others.

If your baby is on a regular infant formula and seems to be gassy or grumpy on it, you can try the "gentle" versions of these same formulas. These milk proteins are *partially hydrolyzed formulas* and are partially broken down so they're easier to digest. The cans will often say "gentle" on them. Examples of these are Similac Pro-Total Comfort and Enfamil Gentlease.

Goat milk formulas are great and nutritionally complete. In these, goat milk derivatives serve as the protein base. Goat's milk-based formula is pretty similar to cow's milk-based formula as far as tolerance and nutrition. They're becoming easier to find in the United States and many of my patient families have been happy with them. One systematic review of the nutrition and benefits of goat milk formula found that babies grow well on it, but that parent-reported benefits, like softer stools or less crying time, might be overexaggerated[1].

Soy formulas use soybeans as the main source of protein. I generally only recommend soy formulas for vegan families who are looking to avoid the use of animal proteins. There is a lot of cross-reactivity between dairy and soy proteins, so I don't recommend soy formulas for kids who have *milk protein intolerance* or "milk allergy."

Fully hydrolyzed, or *hypoallergenic formulas* are made with milk proteins that are completely broken down, so that many babies with cow's milk protein intolerance can drink them. Examples of these are Similac Alimentum, Gerber Extensive HA, or Enfamil Nutramigen. I wouldn't expect parents to know on their own if their baby needs these formulas—most of the time, your pediatrician will help you know if this is something you should try with your baby.

Some babies have such severe milk and soy protein intolerances that they need to be on *amino acid-based formulas* like Neocate, PurAmino, or Elecare. I definitely would not expect parents to know if their baby needs these—pediatricians do a lot of the guidance here—but most of the time I recommend it if a baby with milk and soy protein intolerance does not do well on a hypoallergenic formula after a two-to-four-week trial.

Reflux formulas deserve a mention—they are dairy-based options for babies who struggle with reflux. Examples are Enfamil AR and Similac for Spit-Up. If your baby spits up but seems happy and is growing well, you don't necessarily need to use these (I dive more into reflux in Chapter 7). However, if the spit-up or silent reflux seems to be painful, using these formulas, which are typically thickened with starches or cereals, can help reduce the number of times those stomach contents get regurgitated back up into the esophagus. Yum.

Special formulas exist for special medical conditions, such as premature babies, or babies with genetic metabolic problems (usually screened at birth). Your pediatrician can guide you here if you need help.

Quick Dr. Diane Formula Tips

- Baby pretty uncomfortable on "regular" infant formula? Try the "gentle" versions.

- Super fussy baby and/or mucus-y stools, or stools with blood in them? Talk to your doctor about possible *milk soy protein intolerance* and if a hypoallergenic or amino acid-based formula would be a better fit.

- Is your baby struggling with reflux? Check out the reflux formulas.

- Constipated baby? Look into formulas that focus on added prebiotics and probiotics to soften the stools, like Enfamil Reguline.

- I usually recommend families *change the formula brand altogether* if a baby is particularly grumpy on one. Similac Infant and Similac Total Comfort both made your baby gassy and pukey? Move over to Gerber or Earth's Best. Different formula brands use different ingredients, and your baby may tolerate one over the other.

- Please know that *generic formulas are just as good as brand-name ones*. It's okay to pick up these cheaper options and know your baby is getting the nutrients he needs.
- Goat's-milk-based formulas can be just as irritating to infant tummies as cow's-milk-based ones, because these proteins are actually pretty similar.
- Give your baby one to two weeks on a new formula to make the call—but of course, if her discomfort is obvious and severe, ignore this tip.
- Changing formulas may change how the poop looks and smells!
- The words "for supplementation" on the formula can mean nothing to me. Any formula can be a supplement to breast milk.

How Do I Mix Formula? What Type of Water Do I Use?

Most folks use powdered formula that comes in cans, so I will focus on how to prepare this type. But please know that there are other versions of formula, including ready-to-feed (pre-mixed and you don't add any water) and concentrated liquid (where you add a little bit of water), and they're all a-ok to use at any age.

To mix powdered formula:

1. Wash your hands.
2. Measure out the water in the bottle first.
3. Add the formula powder to the water in the bottle based on the instructions on the formula can.
4. Try not to "pack" the formula in the scoop—the scoops should be "loose" and leveled.

5. Attach the nipple and cap, and shake well.
6. Throw away the formula within one hour of the baby starting the feed.

As for the type of water to use, don't stress too much about this. If you have a term, healthy baby, I'd just use tap water; however, you may need to *boil* the tap water if:

- Your baby is under eight weeks old.
- Your baby was born prematurely.
- Your baby has a compromised immune system.

The boiling process is not too complicated: boil the water for two minutes, let it cool for five minutes, add the formula powder, then let it cool completely. This kills any bacteria that may be living in the powder (don't worry, infection from this is pretty rare).

Another issue to think about when mixing water with powdered formula is the level of fluoride in city tap water. Sometimes, babies may get too much fluoride this way. Fluoride is safe at low levels—it's actually great for producing strong teeth. Exposure to too much is pretty rare and mainly only causes white streaks on the teeth, but it's not a bad idea to look up the fluoride level on your city's website to assure that it is generally under 0.3 parts per million. Reverse-osmosis filters are great to get rid of fluoride in tap water so you don't have to worry about this. If you live on a well-water system, I'd go with bottled, distilled, or nursery water.

If all of this stresses you the hell out (and I hope it doesn't, but I get it)—just use nursery or distilled water. You can buy it by the gallon, and it's usually pretty affordable. You can even mix it up throughout the first year—boiled nursery water for a few months, then tap water for the fluoride benefits. Or perhaps try the tears of your political enemies. Or fresh water from the springs of Patagonia. You do you, boo. In general, just be safest in the first two months or so, or if your baby is premature or immunocompromised—then mixing it up is totally okay.

An important safety point: Do not "dilute" your formula to make it last longer. Mix it exactly like the container directions state (unless your doc says otherwise). If you can't afford formula, please reach out to your pediatrician or local food bank! We can help!

Cleaning? Sterilizing?

Again, try not to stress too much here. As I tell my patient families—breasts aren't sterile. Bottles don't always need to be.

For healthy term babies, I recommend sterilizing bottles and bottle parts when you first purchase the product. After that first time, I think it's fine to just wash the parts thoroughly with warm water and soap after each use. You can also use your dishwasher if the items are labeled dishwasher-safe. Just use hot settings and heated dry. If your baby was born prematurely or with an immune system dysfunction, talk with your doctor about best practices for sterilizing.

What Temperature Does the Formula Need to Be?

Warm, room temperature, or cold. All are okay. All are safe. It's a myth that cold formula gives babies tummy aches, so feel free to keep it in the fridge for up to twenty-four hours before you start using it.

If you need to warm the formula, try not to use the microwave—it creates hot spots in the liquid that can burn a baby's mouth. You can warm the formula in a bowl of warm water or under running warm water. Just test it on your arm before you feed the baby.

How Do I Transition from Breast Milk to Formula?

There's no protocol here. You can do it overnight, or slowly mix as you change over. Your baby's belly is fully capable of handling a fast or slow change.

How Long Does My Baby Need to Be on Formula?

Most babies need to be on infant formula until they are twelve months old. At that point, the majority of their vitamins and nutrients come from foods, and we transition them to whole milk or another milk alternative.

Should I Order My Formula from Europe?

This is a hot topic lately. Mom groups and message boards really tout the claims that European formula brands, like HIPP and Holle, use better, more "healthy" ingredients than those produced in America. I think for the most part, European formulas are safe and nutritious. But please know there may be some small discrepancies between how formulas are regulated in America and in Europe, and European formulas may not meet all FDA requirements.[2]

Where I tend to get worried is when parents order these formulas online, straight from Europe. When you order from factories overseas, you sometimes lose the ability to know if your formula has been recalled. For example, let's say there is an outbreak of bacteria in Formula Factory #14 in Utah. It makes fifteen or twenty babies very sick. When the FDA realizes this, they force the factory to shut down, do an investigation, and send out a nationwide recall for all the lots of formula that were produced in Formula Factory #14 around that time. When you order from Europe, you lose the ability to know that your cans are safe.

Should I Use Toddler Formula?

Nope. In all my years of practice, I have never once recommended that a child be started on a toddler formula after their first birthday. I think they're unnecessary and nutritionally incomplete, and the American Academy of Pediatrics happens to agree with me. This doesn't mean that certain special conditions like metabolic disorders or severe food allergies might not lead to a child needing extended formula use after age one. Generally, these kids will get guidance about this from their pediatrician or pediatric gastroenterologist.

6

The Period of PURPLE Crying:

Why Weeks 3–12 May Drive You Absolutely Bonkers

When I think about the evenings of those first few weeks (let's face it, months) of my son's life, it's not the sweet snuggles that I remember. It's not the contented sighs of a full belly, or the smiles of a sweet infant falling into slumber. It's the *screaming and grunting*.

    The "fourth trimester" was a hard time for us. Jack was a really fussy baby starting around week three of his life—like many babies are. At the time, I was a brand-new mom and a brand-new pediatrician, so I didn't know this was the status quo for many babies around this age. I mean, I knew it was a grumpy phase, but I didn't realize it was this *miserable*. Every evening, starting around four or five p.m., like clockwork, the grunting and grumpiness would begin. Sometimes it came on suddenly. Sometimes it was a slow workup to the misery. But every night, we experienced a few hours of near-constant tending to him.

Bouncing, rocking, burping, feeding—rinse, repeat. I have so many old videos of me just dancing around the living room, holding him. He seemed so uncomfortable. He grimaced. He arched. He acted like he was starving thirty minutes after his last meal. He spit up a lot more than he used to. This time in his life really made me doubt a lot about myself and what I was doing. Was I making enough breast milk? Was I burping him correctly? Was the formula I was supplementing not good for his tummy? Was he sick? If so, why did he seem to be fine during the day and then do a 180 at night?

Over time, it slowly improved, and eventually, by ten weeks or so, the symptoms disappeared. But not before I tried two new bouncy chairs, two new formula brands, three new pacis, and completely changed my diet. Thus is the plight of the confused parent in the Period of PURPLE Crying. Not all babies go through this phase—but most do experience some version of it.

What is it? Well, PURPLE is an acronym coined by Dr. Ronald G. Barr, a developmental pediatrician at the National Center on Shaken Baby Syndrome. It stands for:

*P*eak of crying. This is the highest phase of crying time for babies.

*U*npredictable. The baby may start and stop crying for no apparent reason.

*R*esistant to soothing.

*P*ained look on the baby's face. Grimacing. Grunting. Bearing down.

*L*ong bouts of crying may last three to five hours per day!

*E*vening crying. Babies tend to love doing this in the late afternoons and evenings (though not always; some poor souls get to experience this nightly at 1:00 a.m.)

The phrase was developed as an educational tool for parents and caregivers so they could understand and anticipate a crying baby, thus hopefully reducing the number of infant injuries and deaths we see from abuse. Because yes—this is a very normal time to feel frustrated and even angry. Almost all babies go through this grumpy phase at some point. For some, it lasts a few days. For others, it lasts months. The most important thing to know is that *it will get better. This is temporary!*

What Causes the Period of PURPLE Crying?

We aren't sure. However, as I mentioned before, I have theories.

- I think babies this age are sort of living in this temporarily dark little confusing world where they are unable to communicate at all, and they pay the most attention to their tummies and their appetites because there isn't much else to focus on.
- I think their brains are starting to sort through a lot of stimulating information as they start to classify day and night into circadian rhythms.
- I think they are in a phase of *rapid growth*, and this growth spurt manifests as a lot of crying in order to ask for more food. More drinking means more gas and more spitting up—two potentially uncomfortable things that are happening a lot more now.
- I do think sometimes their bellies hurt with all the gas bubbles, because they swallow air all day while eating and crying, but I really don't know if it's the main reason they cry each and every night.
- I think they like to "tank up" and eat a lot as their new bedtime develops—thus crying for more frequent food.

- Another theory is "sundowning." This is something we see in older individuals with dementia or Alzheimer's—more agitation, aggression, and anxiety at the end of the day and into the evening hours. Is this a natural time of day for the minds of human beings to feel unrest? *shrug*

What Are Some Typical Things I May See During This Phase?

Well, more crying and fussing. Grunting, grimacing, and arching are more common, too.

Slowly, your sleepy baby will stay awake for longer periods of time and start to have a lot more opinions. And the crying may tend to happen around the *same time each day or night*. This is what makes this phase unique—there can be a pattern to the fussiness. Since they're eating more and more, they'll probably spit up a bit more frequently (more about this in the reflux chapter). They may seem to squirm more and crunch their legs up to their stomach. Their poops may start spacing out a little bit, and they may start to go days in between poops. Pooping may look more dramatic from time to time—with more leg-lifts, crunches, grunting, and crying out.

What Helps?

1. A lot of the stuff discussed in Chapter 2 may help here. Mimicking the womb can be very comforting to babies who are experiencing this new, very stimulating world. I encourage vibrating chairs, swaddling/babywearing, shushing, bouncing, and offering frequent meals. They are hungry.
2. Bicycle legs—bending the legs at the knees and the hips and curling/crunching them up into the stomach in rhythmic

circles. Don't be afraid to really crunch those legs up and circle them around—just wiggling the legs won't do much, but pressing them up into the tummy and curving that pelvic bone under and upward can really help free some farts.

3. Running a bath each night at the same time was very calming for my little screamers and got us into a bedtime routine as well. Soak a washcloth with warm water and rest it on the baby's chest and tummy for a mini spa treatment.

4. Many parents ask if gas drops are okay to use, like simethicone. I think they're fine to try. But—they're not miracle workers. And a few decent data reviews show that they don't really help.[1,2] Same for gripe water.[3]

5. I *do* think a lot of good things can be said about infant probiotics, though! Probiotics are "good bacteria" that aid our own bacterial good guys in helping us digest things. Probiotic drops for babies are easily found on shelves these days, and one systematic review found almost a 50 percent reduction in crying time for breastfed infants if probiotic drops are used for gas pains (formula-fed information pending)![4]

When Should I Worry? When Is It Too Much?

Since it's such a common time for an increase in crying, I do a lot of reassuring of parents at this age. But there are some things that do make me worry:

- Poor weight gain: if a baby is crying a lot during this time and they haven't gained enough weight between their visits with me, I'll often recommend more frequent feeds, or bigger volume of feeds.

- The spit-ups consistently seem really painful: painful reflux is something we can work together to improve (more in the reflux chapter).
- I do worry a bit if the crying is excessive (more than three to four hours a day) and seems to happen all day, not just during a certain time. Sometimes Milk and Soy Protein Intolerance (more on this below) can cause this, or sickness/infection.
- Red blood, thick mucus, or black specks in the poop: again, this makes me think about a medical condition called Milk Soy Protein Intolerance.
- I worry if a baby has a rectal temperature above 100.4 degrees Fahrenheit. A sick baby is often a fussy baby.

Milk and Soy Protein Intolerance (MSPI)

Some babies cry a lot. Like, more than three hours a day, which is our current cutoff as the "normal amount" of total crying for a 24-hour period. Many folks refer to this excessive crying as "colic." Back in the day, we used to just pat parents on the back and say, "this sucks, but you'll pull through."

Nowadays, I tend to look for a reason for the extreme fussiness. And often, that reason is a problem with digesting the proteins in dairy. Cow's milk is for baby cows. It makes sense to me that many human babies (and human adults, for that matter) don't really tolerate cow's milk.

MSPI is a topic that deserves a section all its own. You may also see it called "Cow Milk Protein Intolerance" or "Cow Milk Protein Allergy." This is a temporary condition where a baby cannot digest the proteins found in milk or soy. These proteins are found in many regular formulas and in the foods that breastfeeding moms eat.

MSPI is not lactose intolerance, and it is not a milk allergy. It's a different way to be intolerant of dairy (and soy, and even goat milk proteins, since they are similar). It's a type of inflammation in the gut, which for some babies causes pain. These are the babies that sometimes are fussy *all* day and struggle to sleep unless held. These are the ones that often cannot be put down. And, honestly, some MSPI babies are not fussy at all. Sometimes, the stools are very mucus-y (thick globs of egg whites) or will have spots of blood in them that are red or black. Sometimes they have eczema, a skin rash.

I generally tend to think about MSPI if I come across a very fussy baby. I also think about it if a child struggles to gain weight or has mucus-y or bloody stools. Sometimes, all of the above is happening. Again, I think these babies are often labeled as "colicky" babies. They may have painful reflux—arching, fussiness during and after eating, crying with spit-ups.

Diagnosing it sometimes can be tough. Sometimes I just go with the history of what the patient is experiencing. I will often check the poops for microscopic, hard-to-see blood, sometimes called an *occult blood test*. If the test is positive, it helps support the idea that taking away dairy and soy may help. Sometimes, I ask a pediatric gastroenterologist for help.

To make it better, you just stop giving the baby dairy and soy proteins. So, for breastfeeding babies, I ask mothers to stop eating all dairy and soy. This diet has to be pretty strict. It kinda sucks if you happen to adore the cheese drawer in your fridge, as I do.

Or, I will put the baby on a hypoallergenic formula, like Enfamil Nutramigen or Similac Alimentum. Sometimes we have to go a step further and try amino acid-based formulas, like Neocate or EleCare. It takes time for the inflammation to calm down, so you may not see improvements right away—it can take a few weeks to see a calmer, more comfortable baby. Ask your pediatrician to help you navigate MSPI—it can sometimes be a confusing path.

7

Reflux and Other Problems:

The Reason Your Baby May Sometimes Puke Like That Kid in The Exorcist

My son was a barfer. I smelled like puke for an entire year.

He puked after every meal he ate for eleven months. Eleven. Months.

I had extra outfit changes in my car and in my office. I didn't want to share the smells and stains with families and co-workers. But he was happy. He thrived. He had fat thigh rolls. Sometimes old barf hid in the folds. Mmm.

When I once asked my Facebook readers for any questions they might have about reflux, I received 179 questions within one hour. It's a hot topic in my office and a huge cause of parental stress. Let's cover all the bases here.

What Is Reflux?

Gastroesophageal reflux (GER) is what happens when the contents of the stomach (milk, food, stomach juices) go up into the esophagus. Sometimes, it just stays in the esophagus and goes back down. Not all babies with reflux vomit stuff out. Sometimes it comes all the way up and out the mouth. It can also come out the nose. Don't be alarmed if this happens—the nose is just another hole in the head. We call it Gastroesophageal Reflux Disease (GERD) if the GER is pretty severe, and causing inflammation of the esophagus, a lot of discomfort, and sometimes even wheezing or breathing problems.

How Many Babies Experience Reflux? How Long Does It Last?

The books say "more than half."

I say: All of them. All babies. 100 percent. I watch all babies reflux in my office daily. It's sometimes subtle. A little dribble of milk out the side of the mouth, hiccups, gulping. Healthy infants may experience reflux more than twenty to thirty times a day. It tends to get started around week three to four of life, peaks around two to four months, and in most kids, it resolves by around twelve months.

What Causes Reflux?

Reflux happens in babies because of lower general muscle tone and because of a looser valve between their esophagus and stomach. The sphincter where the esophagus meets the stomach is pretty flimsy in infants. So, stomach contents can easily come up and down. Combine that with the fact that they are laying down most of the time, drinking nothing but fluids, and sometimes swallow a lot of air during nursing or bottle-taking, and it's a perfect recipe for spit-up.

What Are Some Signs of Reflux?

Well, spitting up is the most obvious sign. Some babies spit up once a day. Some babies spit up numerous times after every meal. I had one of each. "Normal" babies can all be very different, and there is a wide range of barfing norms. Sometimes it happens right after eating, and sometimes hours later. Sometimes it's just a dribble out the side of the mouth, and sometimes you're covered in puke. Sometimes it's clear. Sometimes it's chunky. Sometimes it's straight up milk. Sometimes it's just stomach juices. Sometimes it smells acidic. Sometimes not. Other signs of GER:

- Hiccups (so common that a pediatrician made this a book title, ha!);
- An acidic smell here and there;
- Coughing or wheezing, especially when lying down;
- Congestion/snoring, especially after lying down;
- Arching the back;
- Fussing during feeds;
- Gagging/choking out of nowhere;
- Gulping sounds.

What Should I Do About My Baby's Reflux?

This depends on the kiddo. For the vast majority of babies, you don't have to do anything different. We often joke that it's a laundry problem more than a medical problem. Many babies are what we call "happy spitters"—lots of spitting up, lots of mess—but growing well, happy, and thriving. Thankfully, most kids are in this category, and you may just need to try:

- Frequent burping.
- Holding the baby upright for fifteen to twenty minutes after feeds.
- A change of formula (reflux formulas can be helpful here).
- A change of bottle type or nipple flow.
- Thickening of formula or breast milk if other options don't help (let your doctor walk you through this).

Sometimes, it takes more than just these simple methods to help your child with painful reflux. It may require starting a medication or changing a breastfeeding mom's diet to improve symptoms. Which leads us to the next question:

Should We Try a Medication for My Baby's Reflux?

This is sometimes hard for me to talk to parents about because, as a doctor, I really want to "fix" things for you. And it's not that easy. A decade ago, I used to prescribe reflux medications more frequently than I do now. This is because I have read some large studies that make me worry about the future effects of these medications.[1,2] Starting antacid medications for babies poses the question: if we change the pH of the newly developing gut, what will happen to the trillions of bacteria—the natural gut biome—that live inside?

Part of the job of this gut biome is to help our body learn "friend from foe." A large study recently found that children under six months who were put on medications like Prevacid, Nexium, and Pepcid, or any antibiotic, were found to be more prone to food allergies and asthma later in life. Meaning, their body's instinct of knowing "friend from foe" may be off. This doesn't mean your kid *will* have these problems later on, it just means there is a *higher risk* for these problems.

Is it worth the risk? In some cases, *yes*. Some babies are absolutely experiencing painful reflux daily. Some babies even lose weight because they are fighting meals to avoid the pain. They know that eating is going to hurt! Or they will take smaller meals due to the pain. I think these babies deserve a trial of medication to see if it helps.

If a baby is not in daily discomfort, however, I'll often try to talk parents into trying other methods before medicating. And if we do try a medication, we often talk often about weaning it off or stopping it after a few weeks, just to get the baby through the toughest time.

It Seems Like So Much Milk Is Coming Up. When Do I Worry?

Most of the time, it's a smaller volume of milk than you think. I always tell parents, "A stain on your shirt the size of a dinner plate is equal to one ounce." That's pretty impressive, right? Talk to your pediatrician about whether he or she believes your child is gaining weight adequately at checkups to assure your baby is keeping enough in.

I tend to worry if an infant is not gaining weight. I worry if the reflux causes consistent refusal to feed or disruption of feeds. I worry if a baby seems to be in pain most days, knowing all babies have a bad day here and there. I also worry if:

- The vomit looks dark green;
- The child's vomiting is becoming more consistently large and forceful;
- If a baby vomits a large amount after *every time* they eat, seems hungry again afterward, and is not gaining weight well;
- If a baby under three months old has a fever, or seems to be getting lethargic;

- The baby develops breathing problems (rarely, reflux can cause lung issues, such as chronic coughing, wheezing, and pneumonias);
- There's blood in the stools, or very mucus-y stools;
- The child cries or seems fussy for most of the day;
- The baby isn't urinating at least every six to eight hours.

If any of these things are going on, please contact your pediatrician.

There is a condition called *pyloric stenosis* I always keep in the back of my mind, which is what happens when the muscular valve at the end of the stomach get too tight and narrow. This leads to pretty forceful vomiting that gets worse over time (a true "Exorcist" movie moment, over and over), dehydration, constant hunger and fussiness, and weight loss. This problem needs surgery to fix it, and most kids do great.

What Is Milk and Soy Protein Intolerance and How Does It Relate to Reflux?

Milk and Soy Protein Intolerance (a.k.a. MSPI, a.k.a. Cow's Milk Protein Allergy, a.k.a. Cow's Milk Protein Intolerance) happens when a child's digestive system struggles to digest proteins found in cow's milk or soy. They can be exposed through a mother's milk or infant formula. It is *not* the same as lactose intolerance and it's not a food allergy. It can lead to inflammation of the intestines, and I often see these kids really struggle with painful reflux. There's more about MSPI in Chapter 6.

Do I Elevate My Baby at Night So They Won't Spit Up?

I remember many a morning looking into my son's bassinet and seeing him sleeping peacefully in a puddle of dried vomit. The guilt would overwhelm me! And it happened a lot. It was hard not to want to do something different to prevent it from happening. But no, we don't want you to elevate your baby when they sleep. We want you to keep them flat on their backs because this is safest.

While it may seem like elevating the head off the crib makes sense, there really is no evidence that that elevating the head of the baby's bed will significantly help reflux discomfort. Alternatively, there is also no evidence that laying a baby on their back to sleep will cause fatal choking accidents The AAP recommends a flat surface for safest sleep.[3]

Reflux, to some extent, is a part of every baby's life in the first year. And in *most* kids, it totally improves by age four to six months, and almost completely resolves by age twelve months. Talk with your pediatrician about how you can help your baby if some of the options we've talked about here aren't making things better.

8

Solids, Liquids, and Gases

The mother on the phone was adamant: this was *not normal*.

Her sweet two-month-old baby had not had a bowel movement for three days, and it was *stressing everyone the hell out*. Grandma told her to load the baby up with juice. Dad had scoured the internet for hours. Mom had tried bicycling the legs, rubbing the belly, and doing a poop dance. The baby seemed uncomfortable when he stooled earlier from time to time, but his stools had always been soft. She called my office asking for help.

The mysteries of the diaper really plague parents across the globe. And I think it's a lot more stressful than it needs to be in most cases. Let's walk through the normals and not-so-normals of the liquids, solids, and gasses that come out of babies (spoiler: the scenario mentioned above is completely normal for infants this age, and nothing needed to be done. The baby pooped while in my office later that same day because I have magical poop powers).

Why Are My Newborn's Poops So Dark and Sticky?

Newborn poops are literally the weirdest shit. This sticky, tarry stuff is called *meconium*, and it was the "filler" as the tube of the intestines grew in utero. The baby swallowed amniotic fluid, and then the water was absorbed out of it, and the meconium is what was the stuff that was left over. We want them to pass the meconium within twenty-four to forty-eight hours of being born. Then, the poops start transitioning to yellows, browns, and greens as they start to drink more and more breast milk or formula.

How Often Should My Baby Poop and Pee?

In the first day or two of life, we generally want to see two or three pee diapers in a day. Then, as a mother's milk comes in or the baby takes more formula, we want to see urine at least every four to six hours in the first three or so months of life. After that, I want urine to be made at least every six to eight hours. If a child is sick and not making urine this often, I worry about dehydration. Other signs of dehydration in babies might be chapped lips, lethargy, and decreased saliva in the mouth.

We approach poop frequency with a lot less concern than pee frequency. I want a kid to poop at least once in the first 48 hours of life. After that, if a baby has soft poops, is gaining weight well, and seems to be feeling normal, poop frequency honestly doesn't worry me. Most babies poop two to four times a day in the first month. Pooping more than this is normal. Pooping once a week is normal, too.

I like to think of slower poop frequency in terms of growth spurts and eating volumes. When your baby is going through a big growth spurt, it makes sense to me that most of what they eat is being absorbed, right? So, there's not much left over to poop out. Also, some kids just have slower guts. The little food meals may slowly collect in them, and it all comes out together in one big poop. Other baby guts are faster, with more frequent little poops.

What Are Newborn Poops Supposed to Look Like?

Much looser than yours. Some very normal newborn poops soak right into the diaper. Most breast milk poop is yellow, like French's Mustard, with tiny seedy pieces in it. Formula poops are usually yellow, tan, green, or brown.

What Poop Colors Should I Worry About?

Black, white, or red. Those are literally the only poop colors I worry about. And even those colors can often be explained by food dyes, diet, viruses, or supplements. I believe I have seen every poop color that exists in the rainbow.

Why Does My Baby Look Like She's in Pain When She Poops?

This is a very common question I get asked daily. It's certainly understandable that the way babies grunt, grimace, and squirm might make it appear that they're in pain when they're stooling. Even while they grunt, turn red, and look like they're straining, they're usually not hurting a lot. Some folks call this *infant dyschezia*.

You know when you're out and about, and the feeling hits? That tummy feeling that tells you've gotta find a toilet soon? That is a feeling of distension as your poop moves down your poop chute (medical terms only here, people). This particular feeling is new for babies. And while it doesn't hurt, it doesn't feel good, right? It's uncomfortable. As babies start to take larger and larger milk meals, I do think they feel the stretch of those intestines more often, and they cry about it.

Your baby needs to move around and work a lot to poop. They have to learn how to get it out. They're generally horizontal when this is happening. Imagine pooping while lying down. I mean, that doesn't seem easy, right?

You have to engage your pelvic muscles, draw up your legs, twist and turn, and strain to get things movin'. It is completely normal for babies to need to do a lot of work to have a normal, soft bowel movement. If a baby takes a few days to poop, but it comes out pretty soft, that's a-ok.

What Do I Do for Constipation?

So, what if your baby's poops *are* looking pretty large, dry, and/or firm? She might be a little constipated. All children become constipated from time to time.

Constipation is something we define more by texture than how often they poop at this age. So—if it's looking pretty firm, it might be true constipation no matter how often they're pooping.

In the first six months of life, constipation is actually pretty rare. If a breastfed baby is constipated, I usually recommend starting an infant probiotic drop. If a formula-fed baby is constipated, I again recommend a probiotic, but a formula brand change may also help. Some formulas are specially made for constipation, like Enfamil Reguline.

For babies over six months, you can offer a bit more water each day, along with pureed or table fiber-rich foods like raisins, figs, lentils, berries, prunes, and pears. If you feel your baby's constipation is super painful for them, or she's dealing with chronic constipation, it's worth a visit with your pediatrician or a pediatric gastroenterologist. There are absolutely safe medications we can use to help your little one feel better.

What Do I Do for Diarrhea?

Diarrhea is sometimes hard to define in the first six months of life. Baby stools are generally much looser than ours, especially if breastfed. That being said, if your baby's poop suddenly changes, and it has quickly become watery and smells or looks different, you can assume your kid probably has diarrhea.

All children get diarrhea at some point in their lives. Most of the time, it's a new tummy germ, or *acute gastroenteritis*. Many babies catch this from their parents, their siblings, or daycare. They may spit up more with these viruses, too. Usually, babies will poop more frequently and more loosely, and it may last for one to two weeks. Medications can also cause diarrhea, like antibiotics. The most important thing to do is to make sure the baby isn't getting dehydrated during diarrheal illnesses. You want to assure they're drinking frequently, watch for urine every six to eight hours, and make sure they have moist eyes and a moist mouth.

I tend to worry if a baby is super lethargic with their diarrhea—so tired they can't drink enough to keep up with the water they're losing. I worry a bit if there is blood in the stool, or their urine production has slowed down to less than every six to eight hours, or if they seem to be in a lot of pain. I'd call your doctor if any of this is happening.

We generally don't really use medications to stop diarrhea in babies unless it's severe or they're in the hospital. I sort of want the body to "flush it all out." And since antibiotics kill the *good* germs as well as the bad germs, sometimes they don't help diarrhea at all, and things stay loose.

Some babies under six months get chronically looser, greener, more mucus-y stools when they experience a digestion problem called Milk Soy Protein Intolerance (MSPI). Dietary changes in breastfeeding moms, or changing to hypoallergenic formula, can help. I talk more about this in Chapter 6.

What Are These Orange or Pink Spots in My Newborn's Diaper?

Pink or orange spots in a newborn's diaper, also known as "brick dust," are urate crystals and are completely normal. They are peed out due to the urine being concentrated, and are related to the dehydration most babies experience in the first few days of life. They should go away on their own. If you see pink dots in the diaper after the first few weeks of life, best to bring it up with your doctor.

What Is the Best Way to Burp a Baby? How Often Do I Need to Burp Her?

Babies swallow a lot of air. They do this when they eat and when they cry. You have to jiggle the gas bubbles in the stomach and line up the exit ramp perfectly to get those burps out. And babies are pretty floppy for the first few months of their life, so lining their chest up perfectly—and getting their esophagus nice and straight—can be hard.

There are many methods for burping, and none of them are the perfect solution for each kid. Some babies burp better when laid prone on their stomachs. Some over your shoulder. Some while suspended in the air. Try hand pats, stretching/straightening the chest, and circular wiggles of the butt and tummy.

I recommend spending a *few minutes* burping your child every 2 ounces or so in these early few months to help get out any air bubbles. But guess what? *Burping isn't medically necessary.* You don't *have* to do it. If it doesn't come out the top, that air is gonna continue on through the intestines and pop out as a fart later. Give it the old college try for a few minutes, then move on with your life.

Once babies are able to hold their bodies upright more easily, you don't have to burp them anymore. They can adjust, shift, line up that esophagus (like we do), and get the burps out themselves. This happens around months four to six. It's awesome!

My Baby Farts a Lot. Is This Normal?

Abso-freakin-lutely. I almost titled this book *Trucker Farts*. But my sweet literary agent gently said "um, no." (hi, Carolyn!)

9

Four to Seven Months: The Happy Potato Stage

I lurched over to the exam table to keep the (very active) four-month-old from rolling off the edge. She then sneeze-farted and giggled.

"Things are just . . . so much better than they were," his parents breathed out, smiling.

Amen. This age is one of my favorites. And it kind of sucks that most parents who are on maternity/paternity leave have to go back to work when things are just getting so damned *fun*.

Those first four months are about survival. The next few months? This is when the fun begins (at least, in my humble opinion—many people love the newborn stage, and I get it, but I'll take these squealing rolly pollies over other ages any day)!

What Is a Happy Potato?

Over the years, I have lovingly referred to age four to seven months as the "Happy Potato Stage." This is an age group where I see babies generally become more happy, more interactive, and more content with routine. Thus leading to parents who are . . . more happy, more interactive, and relieved by a routine.

When I think about it a bit, it makes sense: in the first three months, babies find themselves in a dark, mostly internal-focused world where they are dealing with their essential needs. Blind to their surroundings. Crying from hunger. Grunting with stomach bubbles. Fussing when fatigue creeps up. Unable to move their bodies the way they want. Angry about the barf coming out the nose. Wary of a place that feels nothing like the womb they were used to.

Compared to the first three months of life, Happy Potatoes are more aware of their surroundings. They're less focused on internal needs and become more interested in the goings-on of the world around them. To be fair, the grumpies and fussies will still show up once in a while at this stage. But perhaps the internal battles won't be as loud and interesting as talking to the dog or the new fun skill of chewing on a toy.

Babies this age can see better and can watch you across the room. They may sometimes get a little mad if they aren't propped up all the time—because seeing all the goings-on is fun! You'll see lots of planking and straining to try to sit up and take it all in.

Happy potatoes are learning how to self-entertain by grasping and studying objects and their hands. They're learning how to move their bodies independently—the sudden ability to roll over to that out-of-reach toy is pretty cool! They're watching you and mimicking you from time to time. They're finding easy delight in learning about the world around them.

But they're not yet old enough to move too far away or defy you. And many of them are just mostly immobile, fat, and delicious. Those rolls. Sigh. I love the wrist-hand junction. But this quiet before the storm—the storm that is having a fully mobile child—is a time I hope you really cherish and enjoy with your baby.

What Are Some Changes I May See at This Age?

There are some classic changes I see in this age group that often come up in check-ups. Drooling really revs up, for example. For some babies, it's mild, and for others it's Niagara Face Falls. Babies also start putting everything in their mouth. Before you go running for the meds, read the teething chapter—this actually has little to do with teething and more to do with exploration of objects and building a great immune system. It's called *infant mouthing*.

Babies this age are so much more aware of their environment—their vision and hearing are getting a lot better. So, it's harder to sneak around them, ha! And they're better able to wiggle, and in some cases roll or slowly scoot over to whatever attracts their attention—so no more throwing them in the middle of your bed or on the changing table while you grab something across the room. Take it from this pediatrician (whose four-month-old rolled riiiight off her bed)—it ain't safe anymore.

Many of the "tummy issues" you struggled with in the first few months of life may improve at this age. Muscle tone is building, and babies are better able to burp out their gas and wiggle out their toots. Pooping starts to get a little easier when they're spending a good portion of the day upright and are more in tune with which body movements are needed to get it out. Reflux may improve or may worsen; this changes from kid to kid and mostly involves more puking due to pressure on the belly when they're on the floor playing.

Their wake times are getting longer and longer, and their three or four daily naps may, sometimes barely reach thirty minutes. These little "refresher naps" are pretty normal since the nighttime sleep stage is now a significant part of their day. Most babies sleep about ten to twelve hours at night (some babies still need one to two feeds during the night sleep). Don't worry—the naps will get longer again later on.

And oh yes—I can't move on without mentioning the famous Four Month Sleep Regression. I've capitalized it as it deserves all the notoriety it gets. I'll touch on it more in the sleep chapter, but at four months, even the best sleepers may suddenly start to wake more often at night. This is due to a real biological change in the growing brain's sleep cycles. They have more "shallow" portions of sleep in their night, thus arousing more often. And when they wake—well, sometimes they demand you come over and put them back to sleep. Over and over and over. It's exhausting, and I'll walk through some ways you both can get better sleep later on.

What Do I Do with My Baby at This Age? How Do I Entertain Them?

One of the most common things I wondered to myself as I raised my own Happy Potatoes was, okay, what do I *do* with them all day? They seemed to be awake a lot more than in the first few months of their lives, and I needed ideas for how to fill up that free time.

The answer is: it's totally okay to do a little bit of everything and a little bit of nothing.

I love just *talking* to babies at this age. They enjoy it so much! It doesn't matter what you talk about: I educated my infants with vivid discussions of what the Kardashians had been wearing recently. Talking to your baby will encourage their own speech development and help them learn their own means of communication through facial expressions and sounds. They'll mimic changes in volume and pitch, too, and it's pretty damn cute. It also helps bonding with your baby.

Put your baby on the floor. Please. Some Happy Potatoes certainly are potato-like. They need a lot of floor time at this age because we want them to start building the strength to lift their heads, roll their bodies, and coordinate their hands and arms when reaching for objects. And guess what? They may get a little pissed off when you put them on the floor because they want to be upright! And maybe be held! 'Cause they have to see everything going on in the room! But you are going to give them a little tough love and plenty of floor time because *frustration is motivation* and if they're mad, it'll entice them to start strengthening and coordinating those new movements. Trust me as a mom whose baby had motor developmental delays due to how ridiculously stubborn and lazy she was: it's okay to give a little "tough love" sometimes in order to help them. Put them on the floor.

Run errands together. Do not be afraid to take this baby out and about! With a nice robust immune system, a schedule that is less demanding, no ability to crawl away yet, and the skills to take in the sights and sounds with ease, your Happy Potato is a great candidate for patio lunches, grocery hauls, book clubs, and checking out the new restaurant. A trip to the farmers market is a nice reprieve from the monotony for you—and a really fun smorgasbord of new things to see and hear and experience for your baby.

What About Going Outside? Can I Use Sunscreen? DEET?

Take your baby outside. Hell, let them even get in the dirt. Being outside is so beneficial to kids this age. First off—it's calming. Any parent of an infant can tell you they almost always calm down and stop crying when taken out. Seeing the trees sway, hearing the branches scrape and the birds sing, and feeling the wind blow through the fourteen hairs on the top of their head can be an amazing sensory experience for an infant. Digging in the dirt and grasping some crunchy leaves is a brand-new feeling, too. Being outside and *in* nature often can also benefit their immune system, which is being exposed to all sorts of new things.

Baby skin burns more easily than adult skin, so I'd keep him completely shaded from the sun until six months. If full shade can't happen, consider some sunscreen if the baby is over two months old and if you plan to be outside in direct sunlight for more than fifteen minutes. There is no magical brand that is best. I prefer thick creams over sprays. I prefer the *physical* or *mineral* sunscreens over the chemical sunscreens. Look for words like *zinc oxide* and *titanium dioxide*. These ingredients literally physically block the harmful rays from reaching the skin. Apply fifteen to thirty minutes before going outside, and then every one to two hours while you're out there.

If it is warm and the mosquitos are rampant, consider DEET. DEET gets a bad rap, and I think it's confused by many folks with the old banned pesticide *DDT*. It is not harmful to babies or kids and is the best way to prevent insect bites when outside. DEET can be used on kids as young as two months. I know, I know—the thought of putting a synthetic compound on a sweet baby makes me cringe, too. But honestly—it's okay for a few hours at a time. Scary things like neurotoxicity have actually only occurred in massive doses after prolonged exposure, and even then, it's super rare.

If you have aerosolized spray, do what I do—spray it on your hands, then rub it on their arms, legs, neck, ankles, and torso. Don't spray it on them directly and try to avoid inhalation. Don't put it on their hands. Avoid the eyes. Give them a bath when you're done with outside time. DEET comes in different percentages—10–70 percent. I'd stick with the 10–20 percent range. Ten percent will get you about two hours. Twenty-four percent gets you about five hours of protection. If your children are older, you can use higher concentrations if you'll be outside longer than five hours. The higher the concentration, the longer the effect will last.

Which Toys Are Worth the Money?

Toys make up a big part of the Happy Potato's world. There is no need to buy every high-tech baby toy that Amazon has to offer. Babies this age love to engage with any object, as they are naturally curious creatures.

Car keys hold the same intrigue as a musical toy. An empty water bottle is totally thrilling! And even more exciting with some water or a few beans in it. Let your baby hold all kinds of objects. First, they'll study with their eyes. Then, their mouths. And then, as they gain more arm and hand control, they'll start twisting and turning the object, and even shaking it to see if it makes noise.

I do think some toys *are* worth the purchase. I love baby rattles and any other grippable things that make noise. When babies hold these objects and shake them, they start to associate the noise with the movement. Love those crunchy books they can grasp and wiggle. Objects that dangle in front of them are great, too. These types of toys help a great brain-to-arm connection to start forming as they try reaching for them.

Same for things they can kick and then hear a noise—I love those little keyboards made for floor time! Rubber teethers with grippy parts are great for hand-eye coordination. Musical instruments are great for when babies are sitting upright and can whack at them.

As they start to hone their fine motor skills more, look for things that encourage more complex use of their hands. Baby socks with grippable animals are fun. Wheels they can spin will encourage new arm movements. I also love things like stacking cups, wooden blocks, or the pole you can stack rings on.

The point here is that you certainly don't need a smorgasbord of electronic or expensive toys. Some of the simplest and oldest ones can be super stimulating for the developing Happy Potato.

Life with your Happy Potato will hopefully be filled with giggles, learning, and enjoying their new experiences. Soak it all in—this fun phase is tragically and beautifully temporary.

10

"Sleep Is for the Weak."—Most Babies

I've struggled with the introduction of this chapter for days. Which one of my (sort of nightmarish) infant sleep stories will I tell you? My sweet friend's story? The one where she didn't sleep a full night for the entire first two years of her son's life? My neighbor's story? The one where he and his baby stared at each other for four hours in a row one night? A patient family's story—of which I have hundreds—with visions of their bleary, tearful eyes swimming in my mind?

I'll just tell you my own. My first infant, Jack, was the most excellent sleeper. The kid was two months old and sleeping ten to twelve hours a night. It was amazing. I was the envy of all the parents in my universe. I was the Sleep Queen. Diane Arnaout, Patron Saint of Sleep. All hail and bow down to my knowledge and expertise.

Then, the Four-Month Sleep Regression hit, and the little turd woke up every one to two hours. Every night. For weeks. And my crown was flung off my head, and my body was flung off my high horse. And I cried. A lot. And he cried a lot. And I was thrust into the wild world of chronic exhaustion and maternal stress. I learned a lot about infant sleep at this time (more than the general science of sleep that med school had taught me) and about the vast array of different methods and ideas about sleep training.

A good number of studies have shown that when babies don't sleep well, it takes a pretty big toll on not only their health, but their *parents'* health as well. Poor infant sleep has been linked to parental sleep deprivation and parental depression,[1-4] unsurprisingly. It even can affect how a mother bonds with her infant.[5] A few decent studies out there have linked poor infant sleep to significant attention deficit, anxiety, and other behavioral problems later in life,[6,7] but a few other systematic reviews deny this relationship (because perhaps there are too many other confounding factors, and this is generally a hard thing to study?)

I'll be honest—I haven't written much about sleep online over the years because I find the topic to be a bit controversial (hell, it's hard to find anything that *isn't* controversial on social media these days). And I get it. Not everyone feels the same way about it.

There are attachment parenting advocates who believe that babies cry to express their needs, and any night crying needs to be attended to. Many believe babies should be touching their parents all night long. Other parenting styles may deduce that the only way to get a kid to sleep all night without needing constant help is by allowing him to "cry it out" early. I think most parents probably fall somewhere in the middle.

So, who's right? Well—honestly, I think there are a lot of different ways to raise a child, and different sleep training methods work for different families. Oh, and *please feel free to ignore every damned word I say in this chapter if it doesn't apply to your parenting style or your kid.* You know your baby best. No matter which pathways you take to get better sleep, the two things I think are most important for you are to (1) be consistent and (2) be safe. Please refer back to the first chapter of this book to learn about how to keep your and your baby's sleep adventures as *safe* as possible.

Writing a single chapter about sleep is a challenge because, as I'm sure you know, there are entire books out there dedicated to it. Hell, there are also websites, podcasts, social media accounts, and entire businesses capitalizing on the struggle of the exhausted parent. There's *so* much volume and variety of information about infant sleep at your fingertips, including sample schedules by age, charts galore, general tips and tricks, and different methods for sleep training. And although I generally tell you to avoid internet searches when it comes to your kid, if you need help with sleep, have a look online. You're bound to find something that may help. Hopefully, I can give you a backbone of knowledge here as you move forward with becoming sleep-savvy.

Why Is Sleep Important for Babies?

Sleep is so important. You need it, and your baby needs it. Sleep is when your body grows, repairs, rests, and heals. For babies, there are huge amounts of body and brain growth and development that happen in sleep.

The results of a bad night's sleep are similar for you both—a next day of irritability, emotionality, and frustration. Chronically bad sleep? Then you're both set up for cognitive brain dysfunction, attention span issues, behavioral issues, increased chances of illness, and even growth problems over time.

Is It Normal for My Baby to Make Noises While She Sleeps?

Oh yes yes yes. Some babies make *so much noise* when they sleep. I can't tell you how many videos I get sent on our office portal system with videos attached of beautifully resting babies who just happen to have fart noises coming out of their faces. Wheezes, sighs, hums, grunts—all normal. Parents really worry about the grunting noises and the grunty faces. Please know that if she hasn't been acting sick recently and has been breathing and eating comfortably with good energy during the day, your baby is most likely fine and not in any pain. Also—they're probably sleeping while they do all the movements and noises. This is called "active sleep" and some babies are a lot more active than others.

What Are Wake Times?

I know the pictures and videos are so dang cute, but when I see a baby falling asleep with his face in his food in the high chair, or tipping over passed out on the play mat toys, I get a little sad. This is because his parents probably don't understand the importance of being aware of wake times and sleepy signs, and the kid is probably exhausted.

Wake times are the amount of time that passes from the first wakeup to the beginning of the next sleep. The smaller and younger the baby, the shorter the wake time. Wake times throughout the first year generally look like this:

Newborns to Two-Month Olds: 45 to 90 minutes;

Two- to Four-Month Olds: 60 to 100 minutes;

Four- to Six-Month Olds: 1.5 to 2.5 hours;

Six- to Nine-Month Olds: 2.5 to 3.5 hours;

Ten- to Twelve Month Olds: 2.5 to 4 hours.

(*Morning wake times tend to be shorter than afternoon and evening wake times.*)

Keeping your baby's wake times in the back of your head is a great way to plan your day and also ensure your baby gets the best sleep possible. So, for example, if your four-month-old baby wakes at 9:30 from his nap, chances are good that he will start to get tired for his next nap around 11:00–11:30. Around this time, start looking for sleepy signs. These are things like yawning, glazed-over-looking eyes, getting grumpy, and/or rubbing their eyes or ears. Once you see these signs—*that* is the time to head into nap mode.

What Does It Look Like When My Baby Is Overtired?

If you miss the sleepy signs, or your baby is hell-bent on not sleeping and stays awake longer than he should, he may eventually head into "overtired mode." Any seasoned parent will warn you to avoid letting your kid get overtired. The misery of it actually makes scientific sense: when an infant is overtired, the body has to somehow get some extra energy to maintain alertness. So, stress hormones are released—cortisol and adrenaline, to be specific—and the child goes into overdrive. In infants, this looks like a pissed off, fussy, even jittery baby. They're angry, cry a lot, and move a lot. And these hormones, which help us in "fight or flight" mode, make it *harder* for your baby to fall asleep. You can understand why we're trying to avoid it.

If your baby is overtired, and you get them ready for their nap, they're likely going to cry more than usual and may need some help falling asleep. The room needs to be dark, quiet, and cool. Calm your own breathing down and rock your baby. He may fight and cry, but eventually, his little body will shut things down.

How Soon Can I Start a Schedule?

You can start a schedule or routine as soon as you get home from the hospital. Start your day around the same time, and feed at least every three hours during the day. As your baby grows, the schedule will change. There are lots of sample schedules for all ages online if you like something concrete to follow. *It's important to be flexible here, especially in the first three months.* Babies do not follow the rules some days. There are growth spurts and sleepy days and sick days to be accounted for. So please know that some days your kid is gonna rock that routine. And other days are gonna be a total shitshow, and that's okay. Tomorrow is a fresh start.

How Many Naps Should My Kid Be Taking?

In the first month of life, your kiddo is going to be sleeping a lot. In fact, the majority of the day, when not occupied with eating and pooping, will consist of sleep. But then . . . they start waking up! And you can loosely expect the following nap routines (It is completely normal for some kids to have different nap schedules, but this is the general trend I see in my office):

- 0–2 months: 5–6+ naps per day;
- 2–4 months: 4 naps;
- 4–7 months: 3 naps;
- 7–12 months: 2 naps.

Again—this is a very loose observation. All babies are different, and nap frequencies often depend on how much nighttime sleep they're getting.

So, How Do I Set My Baby Up for Nighttime Sleep Success?

I think there are a few things you need to know before you can expect your kid to sleep through the night (defined here as eight hours in a row).

First off, most babies need to build fat on their bodies and gain enough weight before they can sleep for longer periods of time. For example, I wouldn't expect an eight-pounds baby to be able to go more than four hours in a row at night without eating. A ten-pounds baby? five hours. A twelve-pounds baby? About six hours, max. And this is just a general trend I see in my office—there are definitely exceptions.

Second, it's important to know that all babies are different. You are going to hear stories from friend A and friend B about how their little darlings slept through the night at six weeks old. And I want you to take that information and throw it in the diaper pail along with any other comparisons you're making to other babies. Your kid is unique, and what works for one may not work for another. Some babies crave constant touch at night. These infants may need different forms of sleep training compared to the baby who prefers independence while sleeping.

My next piece of advice—infants need to eat enough volume during the day to be able to sleep longer stretches at night. And *"snacking" during the day will lead to snacking at night.* Meaning, if your baby takes frequent small meals throughout the day, you can expect the same thing to probably happen at night. So, the goal is to get your baby to eventually take bigger meals more time apart.

That being said—little tiny newborns are not capable of huge meals! And some days babies go through growth spurts and need to eat more frequently! So please don't stress about this a ton. Just keep this idea tucked away somewhere in your mind, as a general rule. And if you can convince your infant to start taking larger volumes by maybe making them wait a teensy bit longer to get the meal, or by increasing the flow of the bottle, perhaps this will set the tone for bigger meals throughout the day (e.g., a two-month-old will go longer until the next meal after finishing a four-ounce bottle compared to a two-ounce bottle).

Another tip: after one month of age, it's best to make all sleep "look and feel" the same. This means fewer naps in the living room during the daytimes and more naps in the crib or bassinet they sleep in at night. Let all sleep happen in the same place and consider using blackout curtains and a sound machine. Babies will soon get used to the same air conditioner sounds, the same feeling of the mattress, the same smells, and the same levels of darkness. This is how the baby's body, which is becoming more aware of the environment, will start to know "oh, I'm here again. This must mean it's time for sleep."

I've mentioned it before, but a swaddle is safe and effective for babies under four months. Swaddles help suppress the startle reflex, which babies gradually lose at four months. They also start rolling around this age—so it is best to take them out of the swaddle at four months and move into a sleep sack.

A sound machine is also super effective at helping babies sleep longer stretches. Consistent sound mimics the womb and helps blur out all the noises of the house. Just make sure to keep the volume no louder than 50–60 decibels (think electric toothbrush volume) and at least seven or eight feet away from the baby's head to protect his little ears.

Consider starting a nighttime routine around four to six weeks old. Bath, massage, feed, read a book. Or whatever you want it to be. Bedtime routines are great at helping a baby know that nighttime sleep is coming, and their body soon starts to anticipate that sleep.

What Is the Eat-Play-Sleep Routine?

The Eat-Play-Sleep routine is a general pattern to follow during the day with your baby from maybe ages six weeks until around maybe six months. It's definitely not a routine you *have* to do by any means, and plenty of babies are great sleepers without it. But I like some of the general principles it encourages.

The gist: when your baby first wakes in the morning, feed her. When the meal is done, it's time to play. This means talking, floor time, going for a walk, running an errand together, toy time, whatever you want. This may be for twenty to thirty minutes or two-plus hours long, depending on the baby's age. Then, it's time for a nap.

The goal of Eat-Play-Sleep is to put your baby down to sleep for a nap *without feeding them again*. This encourages the child to (1) spread a little more time between the last meal and the next meal (see the section above—we want to *avoid snacking*) and (2) fall asleep without always needing to eat. When your baby wakes from her nap, she will be vigorous and hungry and it's time to start the cycle again with a nice big meal. Flexibility is always allowed, of course. If baby is just not feeling it today, and wants to eat more often than this—just go with it.

It's a great routine to follow during the day that helps reduce "snacking" and gently teaches your baby to fall asleep without always needing to eat. In the late evenings, I say ditch the routine, though. Many kids in the first six months will "tank up" and cluster feed at this time of day, just before bed, so the pattern tends to flop during this time of day.

Again—some days are gonna go so great with Eat-Play-Sleep! And some days are going to be total failures. Some days, your baby is just *not* going to go down for that nap without eating again. And it's okay to scrap things midday and start fresh tomorrow.

What Is Sleep Training?

"Sleep training" is what I'll define as any modification you make in your habits to help your infant learn to go to sleep on his own. The end goal is to teach your baby not to depend on lots of help and work from you (rocking, shushing, feedings) to fall asleep. You are essentially teaching them how to soothe themselves back to sleep without your help.

There are different forms of sleep training. The most commonly discussed (and probably most controversial) is the *Cry It Out* or *Extinction* method. This is when you walk away and pledge not togo to the baby until a certain time of night or morning. Extinction method generally takes three or four nights, and then the baby has learned how to self-soothe and can sleep through the night.

Another type is the *Ferber Method*, a.k.a. the *Gradual Extinction* method. The Ferber Method was made popular by Dr. Richard Ferber in his 1985 self-help book, *Solve Your Child's Sleep Problems*. This method is more gradual. You initially only leave the room for only a few minutes at a time, slowly growing longer and longer stretches to gently and gradually teach the baby how to self-soothe.

Yet another method includes staying in the room while your baby fusses, but not picking them up or tending to them. Essentially this method teaches the baby—"I'm here, you're not alone! But I'm not going to do all the "fixing" so you can try to go back to sleep on your own."

I typically don't believe all children are ready for all these methods at the same time. Premature babies, babies with growth issues, or those with underlying medical problems are the first that come to mind as examples of this. But in general, I do believe most developmentally normal babies who meet two criteria—six months old and at least fifteen pounds of weight—are ready for one of the methods above if their parents want to try it.

Does Sleep Training Even Work?

Short answer: yes.

Long answer: yes, in most cases. Several studies have found that the varying methods of sleep training and sleep behavioral modification really do help babies learn to sleep for longer periods of time more consistently.

And in my practice, I find that families who are motivated to self-educate and learn more about sleep training (and then implement some of the ideas at home) are generally experiencing better quality and longer amounts of sleep as a family than those who don't.

It's So Hard for Me to Hear My Baby Fuss! Is Sleep Training Safe for Babies?

I sometimes remind parents that sleep training can actually *reduce* long-term crying over time.

Think about how often an eight-month-old who wakes up two or three times a night needs to cry to be attended to. Multiply those minutes by seven days in the week. Then four weeks a month. Now think about sleep training: if your baby learns to put himself back to sleep on his own after a three- to seven-night training period, total crying minutes, over time, is pretty reduced.

Randomized control studies have shown me that sleep training does not harm the attachment between parent and child[8,9] and longitudinal data shows me sleep training does not create adverse behavioral problems or parental attachment disorders when studied in toddlers years later (one study even followed kids for five years).[10-13]

Learning and studying all the options along with the data as a young pediatrician is why I eventually did a combination of the types of sleep training for my own kids. After months of exhaustion, my son responded quickly and beautifully to the Extinction method—and after three nights he was a champion sleeper again (and still is to this day). My daughter responded better to a more gradual process. All babies are different in how they will respond. I would never have done any sleep training if I felt it would harm them in any way in the short or long term, or threaten our attachment to each other. The data showed me that just wasn't the case.

Quick Tips by Age

Six Weeks to Three Months

A big step you can take at around six to eight weeks old is to start putting your baby down to sleep when *drowsy*. By waiting until your baby is super tired, and almost but not quite asleep, you are helping her understand where she is going to be sleeping (and waking later on). Imagine falling asleep in your mom's arms. Then, a few hours later, waking up in your crib. It seems like it might feel a little scary, right? By letting her see her surroundings while falling asleep, you help her avoid this scenario.

If she absolutely needs to be rocked to sleep? No biggie—just do it! But after you lay her in the crib, jiggle, or tickle her little foot a bit, to *almost* arouse her, but let her fall back asleep on her own.

If you start putting your baby down for sleep drowsy but awake around six weeks of age, I think it is *completely safe* to let them fuss for five to ten minutes to see if they can do it on their own. You can do this with naps and/or bedtime sleep. I used to try it a few times daily with my own kids—when I noticed their wake time was coming up, and they started to yawn and show other sleepy signs, I'd swaddle them and put them in their crib. Sound machine on, dark window curtains drawn, snuggle quickly, walk out. After waiting those few minutes, if they hadn't started calming and getting sleepy on their own, I'd go in and help. Many children this age still need tons of help with soothing—this is developmentally normal. We're just testing the waters and learning some new things!

Dream feeds are a great tool at this stage. A dream feed is when you gently partially wake your baby in a dark room, and give them a sleepy feed around the time you're going to bed. Typically, parents do this around 10:30 p.m.–12:00 a.m. The goal is to push the next feed to a more palatable time later in the morning.

Four Months: The Dreaded Four-Month Sleep Regression

The infamous Four-Month Sleep Regression is actually the only consistent, honest-to-goodness developmental and biological sleep regression nearly all babies experience. At this age, even some of the best sleepers may start waking every few hours all night long.

This happens because in their brain, sleep cycles change from that deep newborn sleep (you know—the sleep where you can vacuum next to their head and they don't wake up) to a different type of cyclical sleep pattern.

They now have many deep dips in sleep followed by shallow, lighter sleep periods. Our human brains do this to "check our surroundings" throughout the night to make sure we are safe. Babies can go through these cycles three to five times a night.

If they arouse themselves, sometimes they can sink right back into sleep, and sometimes they don't. Sometimes they arouse completely and then cry. They're like, "Hey, uh, I'm awake. I need you to come over here and do that thing you do so I can fall back asleep again." Sometimes they realize that a whimper or a bit of fussing doesn't get you over there ASAP, so they'll really scream like they're dying because it gets you up faster. The fact that this is the age where they're learning to move around more and roll over in the crib isn't helping anything, either.

If your baby starts waking a lot at night, and this is a new development, the first piece of advice I have for you is to *not jump up and tend to them right away*. Give it a little time. I'd wait it out for ten or fifteen minutes at this age to see if they can fall back asleep on their own.

If you do need to tend to them, try to do as little "fixing" as possible. I rubbed my son's tummy while he lay in the crib, tried a paci, or picked him up in his sleep sack and shushed him quietly. Keep the room dark and try to be as quiet as you can. Feeding was my last resort, especially because he had been sleeping through the night with no need for food prior to the regression, but if I did feed, I tried to give as little volume as possible.

Some babies get through this regression really quickly, while it may go on for months for others. I don't think babies are really ready for Cry It Out methods until both the six-month and fifteen-pound milestones are reached, but it's okay to do extended lengths of time before you soothe your kiddo back to sleep. As I said before, I'd probably limit it to ten or fifteen minutes at four months, or whatever feels right to you.

Six Months and Older

Remember that weight plays a role in whether or not your baby can sleep through the night, so if your baby is under fifteen pounds at this age and is still waking to eat at night—this is completely normal and necessary.

However, if she is heavier and was sleeping through the night when she hit that regression, it's okay to get a little more hesitant to get up and "fix" the situation. There are a lot of ways that people deal with sleep training at this age.

Some exhausted families dig in their heels and do the Extinction method. Again, this is safe for most babies over six months and fifteen pounds. I find that the first night is definitely the hardest with this method, with the longest amount of crying. Some kids cry for ten minutes, and some for thirty-five. Subsequent second and third nights get better, and most families tell me the whole process takes three to four nights total. Their child eventually sleeps really well through each night and wakes up happy and rested in the morning.

If this option is not for you—and it's absolutely not for some folks, and that's totally okay—you can try the more gradual methods, like Ferber. If neither method sounds okay to you, that's fine! Just keep trying to "fix" with the least amount of fixing you can do when your baby wakes. The less picking up, rocking, and holding you do, the easier it will be for your baby to get used to going to sleep without these things. Try standing next to the crib and rubbing her back or tummy, making soothing quiet sounds, giving some bottom pops and pats, and offering a pacifier. At six months of age, most babies are fine to drink water from a sippy cup—another thing you can offer at night instead of a milk meal.

What About "Sleep Hiccups"?

Sometimes, parents with babies who sleep really well may experience a hiccup or regression here and there. This is what happens when your good sleeper goes through an illness or maybe a family vacation. Suddenly, she needs you more at night because things are scary, or new. Totally expect this—it's normal! And temporary. Your sick baby may need frequent snacks at night if she hasn't been able to keep much down during the day. Please don't hesitate to help her through the tough nights when change like this happens. When the trip is over, or the sickness resolves, pick yourself up by the bootstraps and start over fresh if you need to—generally babies pick it up again on their own much faster when they've learned how to self-soothe before.

When Can My Baby Sleep in Her Own Room?

I think this really depends on the family, the situation, and the home structure. In general, the AAP recommends parents keep their babies in their own sleep space, in the parents' room, for at least six months. Then, the baby can be moved to their own room between six and twelve months. This is the timeline generally considered safest to avoid SIDS death.

But many families choose to move the baby sooner, especially if things like a parent's snoring or job requirements wake the child. One study[14] showed that room-sharing between four and nine months led to less nighttime sleep for babies and parents, and more unsafe sleep practices.

My own baby was such a noisy, grunty, and farty sleeper, sleep was impossible for me most nights. I moved him to his own room around four months and bought a good baby monitor. To this day there's no place Jack wants to sleep more than his own bed!

11

Sight, Hearing, and Baby Squeaks

The Covid pandemic sucked.

I know, understatement of the decade. But one thing I really hated was that I had to wear a mask for every single patient encounter for years, including my visits with young babies. I really enjoy interacting and encouraging engagement from babies—mostly because: omigah! Cute baby smiles! But also, I like to assess how they're doing developmentally—specifically noting their vision and social cues.

Interestingly, the masks didn't change a thing. Babies of all ages knew to look right into my eyes. And when my eyes crinkled up? That meant I was smiling—and they smiled right back, astonishingly. It was such a cool thing to see them pick up on those subtle biological signs with their vision at such a young age. If you can believe it, even newborns are pre-programmed to start picking up on light and dark visual patterns that represent human faces![1]

How Much Can My Baby See?

As I mentioned, newborns mostly see things in light and dark shapes. They are programmed right away to recognize light arrangements that represent faces. Newborns cannot focus on anything more than a few inches from their face. Their visual acuity at birth is about 20/400, which is about 12 inches.[2] You might often see their eyes wobble and move differently than ours do.

Around six weeks of age, I want to see an infant start to study her parent's face. Before two months of age, I want her to give her parents social smiles (not the gassy or sleepy smiles; a social smile is when you smile and she smiles back). A three-month-old should be able to follow an object from side to side and move her head to do this. By four to six months, depth perception improves, and babies should be able to follow their parent's movements across the room. Six-month-olds should easily recognize familiar people who walk in the room, and should be able to reach out and grab a nearby toy. We generally assume a baby has developed their full adult visual capabilities by around twelve months.

What Are Red Flags for Vision Problems?

I worry if a two-month-old doesn't fixate on and study a parent's face or hasn't smiled at her parents yet. I worry if a four-month-old can't follow a parent's movement across a room, or if they don't seem to be able to reach out and "bat" at a toy.

If one of your baby's upper eyelids hangs lower than the other, let your pediatrician know. You also need to let us know if one pupil (black dot in the middle) seems to always be bigger than the other, or if one eye seems to focus on you, but the other eye wanders.

Is It Normal for My Baby to Be Cross-Eyed?

Yep, we will see babies go cross-eyed quite a bit when they are newborns. We want this to improve by three or four months of age.

At that point, I'd only expect a tiny bit of crossing if they're trying hard to focus on something really close to their face. If a baby's eyes cross often after four months of age, I send them to see a pediatric ophthalmologist.

What Is a "Lazy Eye"?

Sometimes, a baby is born with or develops eye muscles that don't coordinate properly, or has one eye be weaker than the other. This may look like one eye that turns in, out, up, or down, while the other one appears focused. Or it may look like the baby goes cross-eyed more often than other babies her age. Sometimes it's more noticeable when the baby is tired. This should be evaluated and treated by a pediatric ophthalmologist. Eye patching, eye glasses, and surgery are different approaches to treatment.

It's worth mentioning that some babies *look* like they have in-turned or crossed eyes, but it may be an optical illusion. *Pseudostrabismus* is when eyes appear to be misaligned but are actually visually straight—they look crossed because of a baby's facial features—like a wide nasal bridge, or folds of skin over the inner eyelids. Nothing needs to be done for this—the baby's eyes are just fine! Your doctor will be able to walk you through this if they notice it.

When Will I Know My Baby's Eye Color?

I get this question daily. Babies can be born with eyes of any color. They mostly look gray/blue to me initially. They can quickly change over the first month of life. Generally, you will know your baby's true eye color by age six to twelve months. One study even shows that you can't determine your child's stable adult eye color by age six years! And that 10–15 percent of the Caucasian population may have eye color changes into adolescence and adulthood.[3]

How Do I Know If My Baby Can Hear?

In the United States, newborn hearing is tested in one of two ways—Otoacoustic Emissions (OAE) testing or Auditory Brainstem Response (ABR) testing. OAE testing involves playing a soft noise in the baby's ear and measuring the "echo" response that happens with normal hearing. ABR testing involves small electrodes on the baby's scalp testing the brainstem response to sound played in the ears.

Try not to panic if your baby fails their newborn hearing screen—one of my kids did. This is usually due to fluids in the ear canal, leftover from birth, that can skew the results. Hospitals generally repeat the hearing screen in a few weeks if this happens. If a baby is born at home or at a birthing center, I generally refer them to see an audiologist to screen their hearing in the first month of life.

Most parents can see signs of good hearing from day one of a baby's life. Newborns may turn their heads toward sounds in the room. By three months, a baby should be turning toward or calming to their parent's voice pretty regularly. Sometimes you will see the Moro, or "startle" reflex. This is when the arms suddenly punch out, and can be triggered with a sudden noise as well.

When and How Do I Protect My Baby's Hearing?

Generally, sounds below 75 decibels (dB) are considered safe for human hearing. This might be something as loud as a vacuum cleaner, for example. Eighty-five decibels seems to be where our ear hair cells start to develop damage. Think of a food blender or a lawn mower. Short exposures to something this loud are okay, but prolonged exposures can cause pretty significant hearing damage.[4]

If you are going to be somewhere where loud noise is prolonged, like a concert, fireworks show, or air show, consider putting noise-muffling or noise-canceling ear muffs on your baby to prevent hearing damage.

Infant sound machines (white noise machines) can also be too loud for comfort in some cases.[5] Try to keep your baby's sound machine at least six or seven feet away from them in the room, and keep it under 50 decibels (like a quiet conversation or the shower or dishwasher running).

What Sounds Should My Baby Be Making During Their First Year?

- First three months—cooing sounds like "uh," "ooh," and "aah."
- Four months—giggles! laughs, blowing "raspberries."
- Six months to nine months—squeals, pterodactyl screeches, and some consonant babbling like "dadada" and "bababa."
- Nine to twelve months—lots of consonant babbling, experimenting with new letters like *p* and *g*, and may even start to say a word or two appropriately ("dada" when daddy walks in the room).

How Do I Promote Language Development in the First Year?

The best thing you can do with your baby to encourage language growth is to *talk to him*. Even if you feel ridiculous, chat with your newborn. Hell, I spent a good portion of my maternity leave chatting with baby Jack about celebrity gossip. Prop him up on your legs on the couch or chair, and spend some time talking at least two or three times a day. Over time, you will see him start to study your face and facial expressions. Then, you will start to hear coos as a response to your speech. Next, he will start to mimic your facial expressions and respond (a smile for a smile! A giggle for a giggle). With time, he'll engage in back-and-forth conversation-like babbles with you.

Repetition works well here. Just think about how the famous Miss Rachel opens her show with the same recognizable words! Saying similar words when you first glimpse your baby in the morning, like "Hi, Baby! It's Mama!" starts to set a pattern to speech inflection, word choices, and cues. Speaking slowly at times and saying a word repetitively can be helpful if you observe your baby studying your face and mouth intently.

Reading books is also great for encouraging language development[6] if coming up with your own topics of conversation is difficult. I also think just narrating what you're doing is a great way to expose your baby to language. "I am going to make you some delicious food! Let's get out the steamed carrots. Okay, now I am going to cut them into pieces for you. Let's find a bowl to put them in."

Should I Expose My Baby to More Than One Language?

Absolutely. Early exposure to more than one language is guaranteed to help a child become fluent in the future! I say the more languages, the merrier. Speaking more than one language around a baby does *not* confuse them and may even lead to some later cognitive advantages over kids who are only exposed to one language![7]

12

Teething Is Horrific (and Other Myths)

"No one got an hour of sleep for an entire month in our house," texts a friend who is telling me the horror stories about her daughter's teething issues during her sixth month. "I laugh now like it's funny, but honestly, we were all miserable."

"She screamed like a banshee on crack," to quote another.

"I even bought the damned brown rock necklace just to get a little peace."

These are common tales I hear in my office every day. The teething period is no joke for many families. Why is it that such a common and universally human event is blamed for so many bad days? Let's bite into the truths and myths about teething and all things related.

What Is Teething? When Does It Happen?

Teething is the process of a baby's tooth moving from its little pocket deep in the gums to the outside world.

I'd say that on average, babies get their first tooth around age six months. But many babies don't get a first tooth until after a year. I've seen babies *born* with teeth, and I've seen some kids not get their first tooth until seventeen months. It's considered "delayed teething" if a child has no teeth by eighteen months. I usually look into evaluating for possible medical problems if this happens.

The first teeth that usually come in are the bottom central incisors. These are the little tiny bunny teeth in the middle. That's where you'll want to look first if you think your baby is teething. The last teeth I see are the second set of molars, or the "two-year molars," typically in toddlers aged two- to three-year old. You get more teeth later, but this is a discussion of the baby, or "primary" teeth only.

Babies Can Be Born with Teeth?!

Yes! They're called *natal teeth*. They're not common, but when they happen, they often have to be pulled out by a dentist. Their roots may be poorly developed, so they can be wiggly and unstable, and we don't want a baby to choke on it if it falls out.

Why Are My Baby's Hands in His Mouth, and Why Is He Constantly Drooling?

At every four-month-old well check, I ask parents if their baby has started grasping things and putting objects and their hands in their mouth. Spoiler: it's usually not due to a new tooth.

We've dubbed this cute behavior *infant mouthing*. The mouthing usually comes with a lot of drooling. Everyone assumes the reason for this is that a new tooth is coming in. And sure, babies can get a first tooth at four months (a bit on the early side, but it happens). But your baby puts everything in her mouth for other reasons.

Her mouth, at that time, is likely her most finely tuned and sensitive body part. It is the best thing she has for exploring their environment. Eyes? Still focusing and developing. Hands and fingers? Still learning how to use and perfect the movements of those guys. But the mouth? It's super-packed with concentrated nerve cells that are excellent for feeling out textures and objects.

Another reason for mouthing? Well, I (and others) strongly believe it strengthens their immune system. Sorry to gross you out, but that toy she's cramming in her mouth? It's covered in trillions of tiny microbes. That teething ring? Bathing in harmless germs. Small children put things in their mouths until they are two to three-years old, no matter what their teething status, and I think this is a beautiful way to expose their body to germs and build a nice memory of them. Our mouth immune system and gut biome play a huge role in the growing immune system memory of early life. These cells are constantly learning and building antibodies against the "bad guys" and getting exposed to a few bad guys every day (not enough to actually make you sick) is actually a pretty great thing.

I think it's kinda crucial for small kids to put things in their mouths to expose their bodies to the outside world. This way, the inside body knows what's going on all around them. Not doing so might stimulate things like asthma and allergies later in life, because these biomes help us understand "friend from foe." So . . . let your baby put stuff in her mouth. Maybe avoid choke-able stuff, hot sauce, medications, and, you know . . . live bugs.

What Symptoms Does Teething Actually Cause?

Despite what grandma says, teething is associated with irritability, discomfort, and poor sleep in babies.

That's about it.

There are a *lot* of misconceptions out there about what symptoms are caused by teething.[1]

Fever is a symptom that is a bit debatable. See next section.

What Symptoms Does Teething Not Cause?

Based on my practice experiences and the data I've read, I do not believe teething causes a lot of the symptoms that parents and grandparents tend to rely on as a teething guide.

I don't think teething causes significant fevers. I don't believe it causes rashes or diarrhea. And since all babies are putting their hands in their mouths (sometimes aggressively) as they're evolving through the normal stages of infant mouthing, I don't know if I can reliably tell if any of this behavior is absolutely indicative of teething pain.

I'm also not sure teething pain lasts weeks and weeks. It may only last about one week. One study of 125 children claimed that the timeline for when a baby's tooth really hurts may be shorter than you think—symptoms were only obviously more frequent in the four days before a tooth emerged, the day it cut through, and three days after. The study also claimed that congestion, sleep problems, loose stools, increased stool number, decreased appetite, cough, rashes (other than facial rashes), fever over 102 degrees Fahrenheit, and vomiting were not significantly associated with a tooth coming in. Other smaller studies confirm similar results.[2]

Fever is a particular symptom that a lot of parents brush off as being due to a new tooth. You can understand why this is of interest to me—if I have a baby sitting in front of me with a new 102 degrees Fahrenheit fever which a parent claims is due to teething, do I just assume that's all it is? Or do I need to go hunting for a different cause, like a new ear infection or UTI?

In general, I tend not to blame higher fevers on teeth. With a 102 degrees Fahrenheit fever, I'm gonna start looking for a different cause. However, studies are mixed on whether teething causes increased temperature. A few show that yes—teething can raise core temperature, but it's usually very mild and may not even be high enough to call a "fever" (100.4 degrees Fahrenheit). One study did show a temperature difference only if the temperature was taken rectally, and this difference was small.[3]

What Should I Do for My Child's Teething Symptoms?

As with most of the universal baby stages and experiences, I tend to recommend "less is more."

It's not that I want your child to suffer! I just think there are a lot of "snake oil" products out there (particularly the homeopathic varieties) that haven't been studied well enough to make sure they work and that they're *safe* in these age groups. One product, Hyland's baby teething tablets, was even recalled by the FDA a few years ago because of the potentially toxic levels of belladonna in them. What sparse studies do exist about homeopathy options basically state their ineffectiveness and lack of safety trials.[4] One retrospective study[5] did show improvements in symptoms with hyaluronic acid gel but the study was small (about fifty babies) and didn't have a "placebo" gel to compare/control the results.

If it's been a particularly bad week, and a parent can see obvious inflammation of the gums and a new tooth cutting through, by all means—use as many comfort measures as you can! Extra snuggle time is super effective. I liked to constantly offer my babies things for them to soothe their gums on. I put teething rings and toys in the fridge (not the freezer—the rubbers can get pretty hard) so the coolness can calm the inflamed gums. I also put cold berries or other soft foods in the teethers with the food nets. Rubbing the gums with your own clean fingers, and offering those fingers for chewing, can also be helpful. I think pain-relieving medications like acetaminophen (and ibuprofen over six months) are completely fine to use as needed if sleep is being affected.

Are Those Amber Teething Necklaces Helpful?

They're a huge waste of money, and they're potentially dangerous.

When you look at the websites selling the Baltic amber teething necklaces, you're going to find a lot of pretty extraordinary claims. Claims that the amber reduces inflammation, lessens pain, calms babies, and creates happy feelings. It's hard to even comment on the claims made by the websites selling these things because, honestly, they're kind of an insult to the biochemical and physiological sciences:

- It radiates soothing energy and absorbs negative energy.
- Aligns ethereal and physical energies, cleanses the environment of the mind.
- Promotes positive thinking and attitude.
- Breaks the cycle of chronic inflammation by changing the body's magnetic fields.

Any product that makes corny magical claims like this should make you go running for the hills. Just sayin'.

The more plausible (and I use this term lightly) explanation for why amber teething necklaces are theorized to work is that amber has small amounts of something called succinic acid in it. This succinic acid is supposed to absorb into the warm skin of the baby and help with all the things. Amber requires extreme heat and pressure to form from tree resin. And most biochemical sites and studies tell me that the amber must be heated to somewhere around 390–400 degrees Fahrenheit to release the succinic acid. If your kid is this temperature, we need to talk.

I can literally find zero evidence that succinic acid, when placed on the body in amber as its vessel, can be absorbed and reduce pain and inflammation. One website exclaimed that 8 percent of the surface of amber is succinic acid, but it lists no source for that number. And if that were true... how do we know this is even okay for kids? Is it safe for a child's body? What's the right dosing for succinic acid delivered in this manner? Frustratingly, I've got nothin' for you here.

There is literally not one study about the effectiveness of amber teething necklaces on any of the major search engines. I did find studies that disprove the link.[5,6,7] There are plenty of commentaries you can find on these databases discussing how dangerous these damned things are.

There have been cases of children being strangled and killed by the necklaces. There are also instances of children who have choked on the beads of these necklaces. I don't know a single physician parent who has used one of these on their own child, and I wouldn't put one on my own kid. My conclusion for you, friends, is that not only do I have no evidence that amber teething necklaces work, but I think they have proven themselves to be too dangerous to even attempt to seek any benefit from them.

13

FOOD!

Ten years ago, I remember my husband walking in the door after a long day of work and then stopping dead in his tracks when he saw the absolute chaos happening in the kitchen.

I had just received a very high-tech homemade food pouching "system." And my ass was sweating over boiling chicken and steaming carrots while squishing all of it into tubes to create pouched chicken-and-carrots. More of the gray slop ended up on the counter, on the floor, and in my hair than in the damned pouches—all for the sake of making my baby healthy homemade first foods.

It was a valiant effort that exhausted this working mom within a few weeks. Eventually, I was pretty grateful I had the opportunity to make food at home—and lots of great baby food options for purchase at the grocery store. Moral of the story: making homemade baby food is a great idea and excellent nutrition for your child unless you are prone to mild-to-moderate meltdowns, at which point store-bought food is also a great idea and excellent nutrition for your child.

Feeding your baby can be a super joyful time. It's so thrilling to see them try out this new and exciting activity, and it's fun to experiment with new recipes and flavors. And let's be honest—it's hilarious and messy and a great reason to bust out the camera. For a new parent feeding their baby for the first time, though, the rules can be a little daunting—and they really don't need to be. Let's break it down into super simple steps.

When Do I Start Introducing Foods to My Baby?

I invite parents to start solid foods when their baby can hold his head up well and sit up easily with minimal support. I would also like the child to seem interested in eating, usually by watching you closely when you eat and maybe even leaning forward toward you. Notice how I didn't give you an age—I tend to go more by ability than by a number. For most kids, this happens around five or six months old. Some babies, especially those born premature, may need to start later than this. I don't recommend any solids before four months of age.

Remember that solid foods aren't the priority under age one—we really want babies to get the majority of their nutrition from formula or breast milk until their first birthday. I recommend parents try to give at least 20–24 ounces of milk each day, with food as an accessory. If your baby can't seem to get at least 20 ounces of milk a day, you may want to back off on the volume of foods you're feeding her.

Recommendations for Starting New Foods (By Age)

Four to Five Months: Zero to One Meal a Day

Some babies are ready for solids at four to five months of age, and some are not. I always recommend discussing this with your pediatrician. We consider things like motor development and family history of food allergies when it comes to starting foods.

We generally want you to start something super simple when your baby first starts eating solids. I recommend a simple grain like oatmeal or barley cereal (I'm not a fan of rice cereal—I worry about daily exposure to the amount of arsenic in it). Make sure to get the containers that say "fortified cereal" so that your baby will get the extra iron. These cereals are easy to digest. You can offer anywhere from one teaspoon to three tablespoons of it at a time, and you can loosen the texture with breast milk or water until it's pretty runny.

I'd offer it once a day with a spoon while your baby sits upright in a high chair. It's gonna be a hot mess at first, and he may take a week or so to get the hang of it. Part of the purpose of this whole spoon-feeding process is to teach babies how to open their mouth in time, eat off a utensil, and coordinate the mouth muscles to swallow the solid food appropriately. There is a tongue-thrust reflex you may see for a bit as he's learning how to do this.

Just an FYI: we generally don't put cereals in bottles unless a child is dealing with some pretty severe reflux.

Six to Seven Months: One to Two Meals a Day

Now it's time to start a variety of more flavorful foods! Fun times!

Interesting fact—your baby likely starts to understand flavor preference *in utero*![1,2] So, the best way to start them on the right track is to eat a variety of different foods during pregnancy, if you can believe it. I didn't know this fact when I made my first child entirely out of sour candy. But offering lots of different foods starting at six months can also get kids on the right track to lots of food acceptance.

Most families start vegetable, fruit, and meat purees around this age (I'll discuss another option called *Baby-Led Weaning* later in the chapter). Give maybe two to three tablespoons of food at a meal. Some kids may want less volume, some more, and it's okay to follow their hunger cues.

There's no specific way that you have to introduce foods. It's a myth that you have to do veggies first and then fruits—there's no data that shows that sweeter foods will inhibit acceptance of other foods. I generally notice that parents often forget meats while thinking about first food choices. It's totally fine to offer chicken, beef, and fish in those first few weeks!

The AAP recommends that parents introduce a new food every three to five days. I disagree with this. I think it's okay to try a new food every twenty-four to forty-eight hours. Look at me, bein' all controversial. Hear me out.

If we waited three to five days to offer new foods to babies, this means they'd only be exposed to seven to ten new foods a month. And I want them to be exposed to more than that as early as possible in their lives. This will hopefully reduce the chances for food allergies later on. I also want babies to get *early* and *repeated* exposure to the same foods as much as possible, and as I mentioned earlier, this increases food acceptance over time.[3,4]

But, don't we want to spread out new foods by a few days to see if they have a reaction? As the person who is typically called first when a baby has an allergic reaction, I can tell you that most typical allergic reactions (hives, for example) happen within a few hours after eating the offending food. Another, different kind of reaction called food protein-induced enterocolitis syndrome (FPIES) shows itself within two to six hours, typically. I'll teach you more about these problems in the next chapter. So, I argue, why wait three to five days between foods? I like the idea of introducing new single ingredients one day at a time.

Speaking of allergies, this is the age when I want most kids to start to be exposed to the allergenic foods—especially peanuts and eggs. Methods to introduce peanut early include adding warm water to creamy (*not* crunchy) peanut butter to thin its consistency, or to try powdered peanut butter in something like oatmeal cereal. I like parents to offer peanuts at least two or three times a week. See more about peanut introduction later in this chapter. As for eggs, introduce baked egg around six to eight months—like in a soft banana bread or pancake. If he eats it with no issues or reactions, start offering scrambled eggs each week!

Eight to Twelve Months: Three Meals a Day

At this age, most babies are eating three meals a day: breakfast, lunch, and dinner. Many families are progressing into different sizes of bites and textures. I encourage parents to offer the baby some of the same foods the adults are eating, straight from the table. I also think it's great for them to start feeding themselves at this age if they haven't already, by picking up small pieces of food on their tray (this is the age where a finger movement called the "Pincer grasp" is practiced and perfected). And it's always a great idea to sit your baby at the table with you and eat as a family.

It's okay if the foods have a little spice or salt on them. However, we generally ask you to avoid lots of strongly flavored foods because there's thought that babies may reject more bland and natural foods after having a majority of strong flavored offerings. I try to avoid added sugars in general until age two (although that first birthday cake is a notable exception).

Babies this age do great with bites of soft veggies, fruits, scrambled eggs, soft fish, cottage cheese, unsweetened yogurts, beans, lentils, nut butters, small bites of meats, pastas, potatoes, tofu, and more. The only thing I ask parents to avoid is honey. Honey should be offered only after the first birthday because it can be contaminated by bacteria that causes infant botulism.[5,6] This is a rare but nasty disease, and by waiting until the immune system is ready before offering honey, the risk for it goes down.

Should I Make My Baby's Food or Buy It?

I think parents put a lot of pressure on themselves to take the time and effort to make their baby's food at home. Knowing exactly what is going into your kid's mouth comes with a sense of security. I understand it—and I did it myself! But I do think that store-bought pureed foods, especially the simple one-ingredient varieties, are generally safe and very healthy. For busy working families, they can certainly be more convenient.

Reading labels and understanding what the ingredients mean, is important when you shop for baby food. For example, it can be scary to see something called *ascorbic acid* on a pouch ingredient list which is supposed to contain only pureed carrots. But ascorbic acid is merely Vitamin C—a really important nutrient for our bodies. And a natural preservative that many companies use in baby foods. It's also important to make sure the food doesn't contain any added salts or sugars. Ultra-processed foods can contain a lot of stuff in them (and words on those ingredient lists) that you just wouldn't find in a home kitchen.

Your baby is only eating pureed foods for a short period of time, and if you want to make these foods at home, go for it! Roasting, boiling, and steaming fruits, veggies, and meats are easy to do and are much less costly than store-bought. After introducing one ingredient and then another with no reactions, feel free to combine foods into tasty combos. After my pouch-food-system nightmare, I actually became a fan of just throwing the slop into ice cube trays and popping out and defrosting a cube or two when it was time to eat.

Gagging and Barfing and Coughing: Oh My!

I hear concerns daily in my office about the confusing way your baby may handle first foods. In particular, they do a lot of—sometimes very aggressive—gagging. It's actually completely normal for your baby to gag once in a while when experimenting with solid foods.

Your baby's body is actually pretty good at protecting his airway. This means if any texture makes it to the back part of the mouth that he may not be ready for—boom. Gagville. Gagging does improve with time, as he gets used to the thicker and changing textures.

Other troubling actions I hear about are coughing—which is a reflex that clears our airway—and even vomiting while learning to eat solids. These are all reflexes that are, to a certain extent, very normal. Sometimes the barfing even happens a few moments after the food has happily made it down to the stomach. Again—the body has super protective reflexes and sensitive pathways! And if it was a particularly chunky meal, his body may think he's choking (when he's not) and since throwing up is a natural reflex we all experience when choking—ta-da. Avocado all over your floor.

There are limits to what is normal, of course. If your child vomits *numerous times* after eating a food, or seems to puke every time he eats that particular food, you may want to pause and talk to your pediatrician about this possibly being a symptom of a food allergy or something called FPIES. And if you feel like your baby coughs and gags excessively, without improvement over a few weeks, talk to your doctor about possibly speaking with a speech or feeding therapist to assure nothing is wrong with how he's swallowing. More discussion about choking and swallowing problems comes in the next chapter.

What's the Deal with Peanuts?

Peanut allergy is one of the most common and severe food allergies that humans experience. Thanks to a pretty cool study called the Learning Early about Peanut Allergy or *LEAP trials*[7] published in 2015, we learned that introducing peanuts *early* to high-risk children actually reduced the number of kids who would later on become allergic!

"High risk" babies are considered babies who have severe eczema or who also have another known food allergy, like egg allergy (I also sometimes include families with a strong history of food allergies in this group, but this isn't data-based). This study changed our general outlook on food introduction in babies and led the way for other studies to repeat similar findings.[8]

The AAP's general consensus about peanuts is as follows:[9]

- High-risk infants (presence of *severe eczema and/or egg allergy*) should be introduced to peanut as early as *four to six months of age*, following successful feeding of other foods to make sure the infant is developmentally ready. Allergy testing is actually advised prior to peanut introduction for some in this group.

- Infants with *mild-to-moderate eczema should be introduced to peanut around six months of age* to reduce the risk of peanut allergy.

- Infants with no eczema or history of food allergy who are not at increased risk should be given peanuts freely in the diet together with other solid foods according to how their family prefers.

Given this guidance, you can understand why I believe early introduction of peanut is so important. If your baby deals with severe eczema (think eczema covering large portions of his body, or eczema so bad you've needed to visit with a dermatologist) or egg allergy, I think you should introduce peanut around four or five months—and maybe even under the guidance of a pediatric allergist.

Is Baby-Led Weaning Really Better?

This is a common question in my office. And it's a hot topic on social media, too.

Baby-Led Weaning (BLW) is the term we use when a family allows their baby to essentially feed himself. This means no spoon-feeding purees (typically no purees at all), offering small or large pieces of table foods from day one, and letting the baby decide what and how much goes in his mouth at mealtime. Advocates for it claim that babies who do BLW are better able to gauge when they feel full and are less prone to being overweight. It's also thought that the brain more quickly and easily learns how to chew and swallow foods safely. BLW is also a great way to have your baby sit at the table with you and enjoy a lot of the same things you're eating, while watching you bite and chew and learning more about the eating process.

Some critics are concerned that babies who feed this way may not get enough calories, iron, or other nutrients. Some feel babies may get too much fat, sugar, or salt in their diet, because they're eating foods with adults—whose foods may contain more of these things in general. Others feel six-month-old babies may be more prone to choking when they are handed a large steamed carrot, or pieces of carrot, to feed themselves rather than a bowl of pureed carrot.

So, what does the data show? Well, a lot of these risks and benefits haven't actually been proven or disproven with good studies yet.[10-13] Nor are the existing studies very good, or very big (remember that sample size plays a big role—looking at trends among fourteen babies versus *four thousand* babies makes a huge difference in our trust of an outcome). In literally almost every systematic review of BLW that I can find, the results are essentially, "we don't know if this risk (or benefit) is real, because current studies aren't good enough to prove it."

My thoughts? I think BLW is great if done correctly and safely. I think babies aren't ready for it before six months old (six months corrected age if born premature) and need to be really good at sitting up in a high chair and have good head control. They should be interested in eating and be able to reach out, pick up foods, and put them in their mouth. I'd avoid harder or very firm foods in general, like nuts, whole grapes, raw vegetables, hot dogs, and steak. I think if you're really worried about choking, move slowly at a pace that you're both comfortable with. And try to set aside foods for the baby while you're cooking, before adding lots of salt or sugar.

Overall, I don't think feeding your baby needs to be so black-and-white. If you want to give your baby purees first, go for it. If you want to do BLW, go for it. Most families I see do a combination of both, as did I with my own kids. They're all successfully eating McDonald's french fries off the floor of your car in five years, either way.

What About Water? Juice?

No water until age six months. At that point—have at it! We generally recommend starting with mealtimes only and then, in the next few months, throughout the day as needed. It's okay to offer for night wake-ups, too, before you offer breast milk or formula.

Juice has always been a big no for me before age one (and after it, frankly). Juice is essentially sugar water. I'd much rather your kid eat the meat of the fruit—where most of the nutrients live—rather than drink the juice of the fruit.

When Do I Start Sippy Cups?

Go ahead and start sippy cups (or open cups) around age six months. Speech therapists tend to recommend straw or open-rim cups over the traditional spout cups as they promote better oral motor skills.

You can offer water in them throughout the day or during meals. There is no maximum or minimum amount of water we want you to offer. Try to wean off bottles completely and just use cups around the first birthday.

Are There Gonna Be Poop Changes?

There are absolutely going to be changes in your baby's stool when you start introducing more foods into their diet.

Some kids start experiencing firmer stools, or even hard stools when they start to eat solids. It's a pretty common stage for constipation to make an appearance. Consider offering more fiber-rich foods, fruits, and veggies, and remember that water is allowed after age six months, so a few ounces a day can help here too.

You're also gonna start to see different colors in your baby's stool. Berries, tomatoes, beets, greens, food dyes—all have made it into my inbox poop color pictures. Some foods come out digested a bit acidic, and may cause diaper rashes that resemble burns. Using barrier diaper creams can help here as prevention when you identify the offending food.

And don't forget about the smell—poop smells change a lot once you start introducing foods. Gut bacteria are what create our poop smells and gasses, and feeding them different things leads to different odiferous productions. Ah—the glamorous nasal adventures of being a parent. No one tells you these things at the baby showers.

14

When Food Goes Wrong

I'll never forget the day my eighteen-month-old experienced his first food allergy. We were sitting in a deli finishing up a meal when he tackled his fruit bowl. Filling it to the brim was cantaloupe (why do American fruit bowls universally consist of like 90 percent cantaloupe?) and he grabbed a hunk with his fat hand and devoured it. Fifteen minutes later, I noticed his left ear was suddenly red and flushed. Huh. That's weird. Maybe he's a bit warm? Then a few minutes later, I noticed pink welts raised on his cheek. A few moments after that, there was a bit of lip swelling. Some hives popped up on the arm.

It scared me. We drove home and I quickly gave him a dose of an antihistamine, cetirizine, also known as Zyrtec. I watched his breathing closely and monitored his activity level—all seemed okay except for some scratching of the face here and there. After about an hour, his symptoms were completely gone. After that experience, I was so nervous about Jack experiencing new foods. A few months later, I actually pulled him out of a school we loved after cantaloupe accidentally made it to his plate during a holiday meal.

Food sometimes goes wrong. And there are a lot of ways babies can struggle with the process of learning to eat new things. Let's dive in and learn when to worry and when to take a deep breath.

Food Allergies

It's estimated that at least one in nine adults[1] in the world deals with a food allergy, and it is definitely becoming increasingly more common over time. I have personal theories it may be related to our judicious use of antibiotics in pregnancy and infancy, along with hygiene and sanitation practices across the globe—but that's a different discussion for a different day. With how common it is, it's no wonder that we get called at the office at least once a week to help parents navigate what to do when their child has an allergic reaction.

Food allergy occurs when a baby's immune system mistakenly labels a food protein as a bad guy. This can happen when the baby eats, touches, or inhales the food's particles. There is an antibody present in the blood called IgE, and it freaks out when it sees the food, and makes other cells release a lot of chemicals.

The most common reactions I see happen within a few minutes to a couple of hours of eating the food, and the most common symptom is *hives*. These look like raised pink welts on the skin, almost like weirdly shaped bug bites. They can be anywhere on the skin and can cause swelling of the face and ears. Hives may itch. I also often see *flushing* of the skin.

Another symptom of an allergy is vomiting pretty soon after eating the food. Sometimes puking happens when a baby eats a food with more texture than she's used to, so it can be hard to realize what it is at first. But if your kid pukes soon after (and each time) she eats a certain food, it could be an allergy.

Other signs of food allergy in babies may be shortness of breath, flushing of the skin, extreme fussiness, drooling, hoarseness, wheezing, coughing, scratching at the mouth, sudden unusual lethargy, swollen lips, or diarrhea.

Rarely, a baby may experience *anaphylaxis*. Anaphylaxis is a severe and potentially life-threatening allergic reaction involving *more than one body system* (this is a very simple definition for a pretty rapid and complicated process, but I say it this way so parents know what to look for). For example, hives and vomiting. Vomiting and wheezing. Severe fatigue and hives. *Any* combination of the signs I listed in the paragraph above, or of breathing difficulty, dizziness, confusion, or sudden severe fatigue/sleepiness during an allergic reaction should be taken *very seriously*.

The treatment for anaphylaxis is epinephrine (a.k.a. "an EpiPen"). If you are worried your baby is possibly experiencing anaphylaxis, the first thing to do is make sure she's comfortable and can breathe. Next—use your epinephrine pen or nasal device, if you have one. This is usually injected in the muscle on the side of the thigh or sprayed in the nose. I will often call in a prescription for epinephrine for any child who has had an obvious food allergy. I tell parents: if you are thinking about or wondering if you should be using the Epi, *just use the Epi*. It can absolutely save your child's life. Next—call an ambulance. You can give an antihistamine like cetirizine (Zyrtec) or diphenhydramine (Benadryl) if you aren't sure what to do and your baby can safely swallow, but these have been proven not to be effective in a real anaphylactic reaction—only epinephrine helps here.

Babies with food allergies may need to be followed by a pediatric allergist, especially if their reaction was severe. I like an allergy to be confirmed (sometimes skin testing done by the allergist can help here), and I want families to be as educated as possible about their child's allergy. Most kids outgrow their food allergies with time. Over the years, allergists can do something called an oral food challenge to see if a child is able to eat the food again. About 45 percent of infants with food allergy still deal with it around age ten.[2]

What Are the Most Common Foods That Kids Are Allergic to?

The nine most common food allergens are:

- Eggs
- Milk
- Peanuts
- Tree nuts (almonds, hazelnuts, walnuts, brazil nuts, cashews, pecans, pistachios, and macadamia nuts)
- Soy
- Sesame
- Wheat
- Crustacean shellfish (shrimp, crab, lobster)
- Fish

Other common foods kids can be allergic to are fruits, such as apples, peaches, melons, and cantaloupe, and mollusks like mussels and oysters.

FPIES

Food protein-induced enterocolitis syndrome (FPIES) is a rare type of delayed allergic reaction to a certain food. It's what happens when a food triggers the immune system to freak out in the digestive tract (instead of the blood). At least, that's how I simplify it in my brain. I usually suspect FPIES if a family calls me and says something like, "Johnny ate oatmeal cereal last night with dinner, and then vomited for six hours straight overnight!" It can be caused by literally any food, but oats, cow's milk, rice, and soy are the most common triggers.

The vomiting (and diarrhea) often starts one to four hours after eating the offending food, and it can happen over and over and *over*. I don't see hives with FPIES. It's honestly sometimes hard to diagnose. We can only go by the story, and there are no labs that help us confirm it. Sometimes it can be severe, and the kids often get super fatigued and stressed. Sometimes when parents or doctors don't realize FPIES is happening, the baby may not gain weight appropriately.

Often, we treat FPIES with vomiting medications like ondansetron (Zofran). Some kids get so sick they need rehydration with IV fluids in the ER. Most babies eventually outgrow it by ages three to five and do just fine with the offending foods.

Lactose Intolerance

Depending on your source, it has been determined that something like 65–68 percent of the world's population is intolerant of lactose. If you think about it, we're the only species that drinks *another species'* milk. So, it makes sense to me that a large portion of us doesn't feel so well when we drink it.

There are actually a lot of ways a little human can be intolerant of dairy. Some have Milk and Soy Protein Intolerance (MSPI, discussed in Chapter 6), which is a temporary condition that shows up as reflux, fussiness, and mucus or blood in stools early in life. Another way to be intolerant is to have a true milk allergy—to have antibodies in the blood that give you hives or vomiting when you drink milk.

The most common way for humans to be intolerant of dairy is *lactose intolerance*, which means the child's body doesn't know how to digest the sugar, or lactose, in cow's milk. They don't have enough of the enzyme *lactase* to help break it down. So, the lactose sugars get digested by gut bacteria, which produce gas. Yum. Many lactose intolerant people can have *some* dairy, or even some types of dairies, with no issues. And whether or not you feel bad may depend on the amount consumed.

The most common symptoms of lactose intolerance are bloating, diarrhea, and gas. Most cases of lactose intolerance show up after infancy. I just wanted to include it here so you understand all the different ways our body can, um, hate dairy.

Troubles with Swallowing

All babies must take on the task of learning how to swallow and breathe at the same time. The lesson begins at birth, and I often hear of newborns coughing here and there while nursing as they start to coordinate this—let's face it, kinda difficult—task of drinking and breathing simultaneously.

If a baby struggles with swallowing milk from a breast or bottle, or even food, and it doesn't seem to be improving over time, I will often have them evaluated for swallowing difficulty, or *dysphagia*. The baby may have lots of coughing and gagging and might need many breaks while taking a bottle or breast. They may drool or leak milk from the mouth, or arch and be irritable.

When babies learn to eat solid foods, there again lies the challenge. How do the tongue and throat need to move to push a soft clump of mashed potato from the tongue to the back of the mouth, down the throat, and into the esophagus? There are actually a whole lot of muscles and nerves involved in this process. They may need repeat attempts at swallowing, pocket food in their cheeks, have lots of gagging, or frequent vomiting if they're struggling.

Rarely, a baby will only present with lots of respiratory problems— like one child I saw for a year who had "asthma symptoms," coughing and wheezing, which never improved on asthma meds. It wasn't until we eventually realized he was aspirating (some of the liquids he swallowed went down the lung pipe instead of the stomach pipe, which led to lung inflammation) that things got a lot better.

Sometimes dysphagia comes along with other medical problems, like cerebral palsy, cleft lip or palate, nervous system disorders, or prematurity. If I'm worried about swallowing problems, I may order something called a *modified barium swallow study* to see the details of how a baby swallows or ask a specialist for an evaluation. Sometimes thickening the consistency of liquids really helps. Speech Language Pathologists, speech therapists, and occupational therapists are the experts in all things swallowing, and are the main folks I call to help with a baby who is struggling.

Choking

Let me start out this section by saying, in fifteen years of practice, I've never lost a baby to a choking episode. Babies generally have really good protective reflexes and mechanisms in place (like coughing, gagging, and vomiting) to prevent choking as they learn to eat foods.

There are two pipes in the throat and neck—one for air and one for food (trachea and esophagus, respectfully). Choking is what happens when a piece of food gets lodged in the air pipe. Sometimes it completely blocks it, and sometimes it just partially blocks it.

If your baby is crying or coughing during a choking event, air is still able to move down the windpipe, and this is good. Sometimes they wheeze and drool if this happens. If your baby suddenly looks alarmed and becomes silent, air is unable to get into the lungs. And this is every parent's worst nightmare (or at least, my nightmare).

Toys, balloons, and coins are other common things babies put in their mouths that lead to choking—a reminder to be vigilant once your baby starts to reach for and grasp objects.

If you believe your baby is choking, you should perform alternating five back blows followed by five chest thrusts, while someone is calling 9-1-1 and getting them on the speaker phone. I recommend sitting down and holding your baby face-down. Lay the infant's torso on your nondominant arm. After five blows delivered between the shoulder blades, turn the baby over and perform five chest compressions.[3] I recommend using the meaty bottom part of your palm to deliver these thrusts—and don't be gentle. We're trying to use pressure, vibration, and air in the lungs to *pop* the blockage upward. We do not recommend a "finger sweep" in the mouth to find the food at this age—this may push it back down again.

The Heimlich Maneuver can be used on kids over the age of one. You can get down on your knees behind them and place a clenched fist just above the belly button. Thrust upward, aiming up and back. *I highly recommend every parent sit down at some point before their baby reaches grasping age and get online to watch detailed videos of how these maneuvers are done.*

A lot of families ask me about the anti-choking suction devices. These are devices you can slip onto the baby's face or into the mouth that have suction levers on them that can be pumped up and down. The goal is to use this suction to un-wedge the food from the trachea. When you look at the data, there's not much to go by. Most of the studies are done on mannequins or cadavers (dead bodies). One recent systematic review didn't find any encouraging or discouraging evidence for or against them.[4]

My take on these devices? Get one if available and affordable to you. It's something to try if the back and chest thrusts don't work and you're waiting on the ambulance.

Whew. This was stressful to read, huh? My blood pressure is up. Thank goodness the next section has very little to do with your kid potentially dying.

Why Is My Kid's Skin Turning Yellow?

If your baby has started enjoying foods, and you start to notice a yellow or orange tinge to his skin, please do not run immediately to Google and look up "my baby is jaundiced oh Mylanta what do I do??"

Chances are excellent that he's just experiencing a completely harmless condition called *carotenemia*. This is something you may see from time to time if your baby really enjoys orange foods like carrots, sweet potatoes, and squash. There is an increase of something called *beta carotene* in the blood, which is a version of vitamin A, and is safe! It should go away on its own. If your baby's eyes are also yellow—this is different, and you should bring it up with your doctor. This actually could be jaundice, and we take it pretty seriously after the first few months of life.

15

Scroll, Cry, Repeat:

How to Spot Online Garbage and Save Your Sanity

Can I take a few minutes to talk with you about our lord and savior, Google?

And, social media in general? And Instagram? TikTok? Facebook?

Parents are online now more than ever.[1] And in the middle of the night, when you're wondering what to do about your little one's weird diaper rash, it can certainly be a godsend to have all that information easily in your hands. Not to mention the fifty hash-tagged Instagram posts and twenty TikTok videos about how that diaper brand you just bought is totally the cause of it. Or no, wait, it's that cream you use. That specific cream that will obviously cause your kid to have butt cancer in a few decades. You need to put some turmeric on it.

I think parenting in this age of technology and global communications is hard as hell. It sort of simultaneously rocks that we have this infinite bucket of information available at our fingertips—

and yet it sucks, as the weight of it all can stress us out and suffocate us with guilt.

Let's not forget the Covid-19 years (as much as we want to). The pandemic kept us all cooped up in our houses. We all spent a lot more time online, sending social media traffic numbers soaring. We were seeing posts about just about everything, now at an accelerated rate—posts about silly stuff, crafting, cooking, oh my God, the bread baking—and about medicine, vaccines, and science. And the seismic increase in the amount of absolute *garbage* information out there, often pushed with biased and political undertones, has really made it hard to understand online fact from fiction in the last few years.

Not all is bad. Studies have shown that parents being on the internet more has improved their relationship with their doctors in many ways. One study[2] showed that patients used the information found online to help them prepare for their visit, ask better questions, and understand what their physicians told them. This was shown to empower patients to play a more active role in their disease management, to be more effective in talking with their docs, and helped them understand what was going on with their bodies.

And, to be fair, *I* write a lot and post on social media. And I have gained a following over the past ten years just by sharing what I know. And because of social media, I get to write this book to help you out. I think now more than ever, there are a ton of credentialed medical folks online, trying to fight the good fight against medical misinformation.

But I can't *tell* you how many times I've been on my phone late at night and have come across a video on TikTok that has something like 1.2 million views which is dispelling misinformation declaring *These Ten* (completely normal) *Newborn Behaviors Absolutely Mean Your Kid Has Severe Autism!!!*, and this shit makes me want to punch myself in my own face. There is so much out there that is *literally not true*.

So: arm yourself, soldier. I am coming in hot.

Here is a comprehensive list, by me, a doctor with a medical degree, to help you understand how *doctors* use online information—and how to decipher fact from fiction.

1. *Don't just read the headline.* Companies want clicks. Influencers want engagement. It drives their numbers up. An eye-catching headline may totally be bogus or completely unrelated to what the actual article says.
2. If someone makes a video claiming some medical fact, and you can find no other videos repeating that fact, and you can find no reputable sources online repeating said fact, said "fact" is most likely bullshit.
3. I tend to find more reputable sources at websites that end in "edu" or "org."
4. If you see a post that has questionable spelling errors, CAPS LOCK, or excessive use of exclamation points!!! . . . ignore it (unless it's mine, of course).
5. Just because someone uses an app to put words on a picture doesn't make it true. And there are some very *believable*-looking pictures with overlying text out there that are completely made up.
6. If someone online is telling you that a certain medication or supplement is the *best thing they've ever tried*, and you can click on a link to buy said item, chances are excellent that the person is not to be trusted in that assessment. This includes some online doctors.
7. If you follow a doctor online, or someone who claims to be a doctor, look up their credentials. Are they board-certified in their field? Do they have MD or DO behind their name? Did they lose their medical license a few years ago? There are *many* online nurse practitioners, nurses, physician assistants,

chiropractors, alternative medicine gurus, and naturopathic practitioners who use the title *doctor*. Are they giving you information based on their training—or their opinions? This is not to say that their ideas and viewpoints aren't valid—but if a chiropractor is *going outside the scope of practice* to lecture you about vaccines, move on. This isn't his ballpark. Same for the podiatrist teaching you about your cholesterol meds.

8. Along those same lines—if one doctor says one thing, and *literally thousands* of doctors say something else? You really have to stop for a second and think—is this special doctor stating legitimate and little-known information? Or is this guy just trying to sell something? (Guess which is more common?)

9. If someone cites studies, look at them. For example, if a lady on TikTok exclaims: "sleep training will harm your baby beyond repair! Studies prove this!"—don't be afraid to look at those medical studies. And then look up studies that say the opposite, and compare the information.

10. *You can find a medical study to support almost any viewpoint.* That's why I think the general public needs to know how to understand what a good study is.

11. When you look at medical studies, here are some tips on how to know if it's legit or not:

    - *How many* test subjects were in the study? I'm more likely to believe the outcome of a 4,000-kid study over a 14-kid study.
    - *Are there any biases*? (i.e., did the author of a butt cream study get paid by said butt cream company to run the study?)
    - *Who published it?* Look for a peer-reviewed journal with a good reputation. Good journals take the time to weed out the crap. I'm going to believe the New England Journal

of Medicine over the Small Town Kansas Library of Cook Books Publishing Company.
- *Can the information be replicated?* Meaning, did other studies show similar findings? We love a reassuring repeat.
- The most informative studies, in my opinion, are things called *randomized control trials* (RCTs). If you want to know how effective a treatment is for a medical problem, RCTs are the way to go. This is because the treatment is compared to a "no treatment" group, to keep the outcomes fair. "Randomized" means the test subjects are randomly put into groups. One group gets the treatment, and the other group gets a placebo (fake treatment). It's even better if the study is *"double blind"*—meaning both the participants and the doctors have no idea who got which.
- It also helps to look up things called *systematic reviews*. This is when someone takes a look at *a large group of studies* that they have deemed good, and makes an overall assessment about a topic based on this collection.
- Look for studies that are *peer-reviewed*. This is basically quality control—people in the same field, like other doctors in the same specialty, who review the information and consider it good and valid.
- If you have no idea whether a study is valid, *ask someone who knows*. People send me studies all the time that I'm happy to interpret for them.

12. *Again: ask a medical professional you trust if you see something worrisome online.* If all of it seems to be too confusing, or you can't understand if a post is to be believed or not, talk with your doctor. Chances are excellent that we've heard the concern before, and we can walk you through what is fact and what is fiction.

16

The Absolute Brilliance of Your Kid's Immune System

My toddler son once woke up with a fever of 105.7 degrees Fahrenheit. I remember the day clearly. It was a workday for me, and I had my first patient scheduled to see me in twenty minutes, and boom—he spiked the highest temp he'd ever had. I totally freaked out, just like all parents do. And I cried a little, because I had to go take care of other people's kids, but couldn't take care of my own baby that morning. After some deep breathing, the wave of emotions subsided, and I asked myself: what do I tell my patient families to do in this scenario?

Once I tried a few different thermometers and they all read the same number, I gave him a dose of ibuprofen, and put him in a warm bath (not cold—warm) and let him play. I watched him closely and gave instructions to my husband. I made sure he was breathing okay and able to drink. He seemed fine, just super grumpy.

After about 45 minutes, his dad rechecked his temp. It was 102 degrees Fahrenheit. He was sitting on the couch, drinking water and talking comfortably. And I was okay with this. And throughout the day, he did fine. He had a fever for three days, and a runny nose and a little cough, and it went away. He had a virus, and his body took care of it.

I tell you this story to illustrate some points:

1. Pediatricians freak out about their own kids, too.
2. Fever is a natural and normal part of being a kid, and it *helps* the body fight off infection. Even the high ones can often be a-okay, and
3. The immune system is an amazing and complicated beast, of which I am in constant awe.

Does My Baby Have a Strong Immune System When She's Born?

Yes and no. Your baby is born with her own collection of immune system cells. I've always thought it was pretty cool that newborns actually *borrow* antibodies from their mother in utero (antibodies are the ones that recognize bad guys and bind to them, so the rest of the immune system can beat them up and kill it). The antibodies pass from mom to baby through the placenta. When baby is born, these antibodies float around to help protect her until around six months of age. It's not perfect protection, but it's something!

As soon as she comes out into the world, her body immediately starts to be covered with microbes.[1,2] Your baby's immune system starts "learning" about these bacteria, viruses, yeasts, and fungus ASAP, and the immune system cells provide some protection to the kiddo right away.

That being said, your baby has never been out in the world. She has hung out in the mostly sterile uterus for nine months, and now, she may be more susceptible to things that *you and I's* immune system has already learned about in the past. We already have that army assembled. Babies do not.

This is why, when a baby under the age of three months has a fever or is acting odd, we tend to take it a lot more seriously than in older babies. That new immune system is decent, but fresh and new. And it may not yet know how to fight off the germs that my body or your body's immune system could take care of easily. Babies this age are more susceptible to germs getting into places where they don't belong, like the bloodstream or the nervous system fluid.

Is My Baby's Immune System Able to Handle More Than One Germ at a Time?

Hell yes! And it's *awesome*.

Your baby's body is covered with somewhere between *thirty trillion and one hundred trillion microbes*.[3,4] Take a minute to let that sink in. This means your kid is absolutely saturated, inside and outside, with viruses, fungi, yeasts, bacteria, and protozoa. In eyeballs. In nostrils. In the gut. Most of these germs are completely harmless. Sometimes even dangerous germs live on our bodies, and for some unknown reason, most of the time they cause no issues.

At any given moment, your baby's immune system is interacting with trillions of foreign microbes. And it's learning about them, sorting them, avoiding them, labeling them, attacking them, neutralizing them, and absorbing them in *millions of interactions per minute*, constantly.

When the baby's body meets an organism it has never seen before (an antigen), it takes notes about the new invader and creates memory cells (antibodies) so that if it comes across that germ again, it will remember it quicker and attack faster. Isn't that cool? This is also how vaccination works. More on that later.

So yes—chances are excellent that your baby can handle more than one germ at a time. They can have a rash and a tummy bug, deal with pink eyes and a cold. Or even more than one cold virus at a time. And babies can handle vaccines on the same day as a cold! And the cold won't make the vaccines less effective. And the vaccines won't make the cold worse. Isn't the immune system freakin' amazing?

What Are Lymph Nodes and What Do They Do?

Your baby has hundreds of lymph nodes in her body. Some people call them "glands." The most common lymph nodes parents notice are typically on the back lower head, or in the neck. Baby necks are lean and so sometimes it's easy to see and feel them. They feel like tiny rubbery balls or lima beans under the skin.

Lymph nodes are awesome. They do a lot of things, like filter some of the fluids in our body. They're also "hotels," or temporary houses, for some of our white blood cells. If we have inflammation or an infection somewhere, the lymph nodes nearby might get bigger for a few days or weeks.

They're all over because they help and drain different areas of the body. Ear infection? Sometimes the lymph node behind the ear gets big. Zit on your chin? You'll suddenly feel a little bump underneath your chin. Bug bite on the thigh? The lymph node in your groin gets bigger.

If your child has a new cold, you may suddenly feel the lymph nodes in the head and neck, and that's okay. They're just doing their job and draining the area while temporarily housing the white blood cells. Sometimes I can feel a lymph node all the time—and as long as it stays small, doesn't grow rapidly, and no more lymph nodes appear to grow around it, I don't worry.

What Happens When My Kid Spikes a Fever?

Every time your baby gets a fever, I want you to read this process to remind yourself about *why* we have fevers and take a deep breath.

1. A germ (virus or bacteria) enters your body. One of your immune cells floating around notices it. It freaks out. It makes a whole bunch of chemicals to freak everybody else out. HIGH ALERT, EVERYONE!

2. The chemicals reach your brain (the hypothalamus, in particular). The hypothalamus says OK GUYS, GET THE ARMY OUT THERE, STAT. DO YOUR THANG. I'LL MAKE THIS PLACE REAL HOT TO HELP OUT!
3. The brain thermostat is set at a new number. Instead of 98 degrees Fahrenheit, he is now going to reset at 102 degrees Fahrenheit.
4. Heart rate speeds up. Breathing speeds up. Blood vessels open and flush. The body is physically pushing the blood around faster, to get the white blood cells there quicker.
5. Muscles shiver, generating heat. You start making more immune cells. They travel around faster. They talk to each other more effectively. They "stick" to the bad guys better.
6. You feel cold because your new "set" thermostat wants you to be 102 degrees Fahrenheit. You're not there yet, so your body is trying to get you there. You shiver. Your muscles ache.
7. Soon, the germ can't replicate as much as it wants to. It can't divide and conquer. Maybe even its protective coating starts to break down a little bit. The hot environment makes the germ weaker, and it dies faster.
8. After a few days of fever, you beat the germ! Thank you, glorious fever and fabulous immune system!

History and literature generally tell us that trying to constantly *suppress* a fever may not always be a good thing and may actually make it *harder* for people to get over an illness.[5] There is also some data that shows that suppressing fever may make it easier to give the germ to others, if you can believe it![6]

When it comes to fever, I generally tell parents to *treat the kid, not the number*. If your baby has a fever under three months of age, call your doctor or go to the ER. However, if he's over three months of age, and despite the fever, seems comfortable, is resting well, drinking well, and breathing well, it's okay to wait a bit. Call the doc in the morning. If the baby is over six months, it's even okay to wait and watch for two or three days before giving us a call.

If he's feeling and drinking well, it's okay to just let the fever do its thing. If he seems to be in pain or uncomfortable, then it's okay to treat it with medication! Acetaminophen is used under age six months, and after six months, either ibuprofen or acetaminophen can be used.

Are There Any Vitamins or Supplements That Can "Boost" My Baby's Immune System?

Short answer? No. Only vaccination can "boost" the immune system to make it work better than it already does.

Long answer: No, but there are vitamins that *support* a healthy immune system. Almost all of those vitamins (Vitamin A, Vitamin C, Vitamin E, Folate, zinc, and selenium) come from a healthy diet. Vitamin D comes from sunlight and fortified foods or supplements. If you're deficient in these vitamins, you may experience more infections overall.[7,8] So, I generally have no worries about how a kid's immune system is gonna fare in daycare if the baby is eating a well-rounded diet and of course, getting adequate breast milk or formula (supplementing Vitamin D if breastfed).

How Much Sickness Is Too Sick? How Do I Know If My Baby Has an Immune System Problem?

On almost a daily basis, I talk with worried parents about how often their baby is getting sick. And, nearly 99 percent of the time, the frequency at which their child is getting sick is completely normal.

This is because if your child is in a situation where they are around even one or two other children, *they are absolutely going to get sick, and often*. And this is a good thing, remember? We are teaching and building that fresh immune system!

Babies in daycare almost immediately develop a runny nose (and even fever sometimes) within three to four days of starting. There is this whole smorgasbord of community germs swimming around daycare rooms, and lots of little potatoes who aren't able to cover the coughs and sneezes coming out of their faces. Until your baby has been exposed to just about everything, she is likely going to experience things like snot, fever, coughing, vomiting, diarrhea, pink eye, and rashes on and off throughout the first year of daycare. We lovingly refer to this process as the "daycare drip"—the seemingly never-ending river of nasal drainage that comes and goes from that nose. I also see a pattern of "ocean waves" of the cold symptoms—some days it's pouring, some days it's drying and yellowing and thickening. Then it's clear again and back with a vengeance. This is the nature of recurring colds—an ebb and flow.

So, when do I worry? I worry that a child may have an immune system deficiency if they seem to have infections that *require hospitalization to get better*. I worry if they deal with frequent skin infections called *abscesses*, frequent lung infections called *pneumonias*, or deal with a blood infection called *sepsis*. I also sometimes worry if a baby takes a *long time to clear up* most infections (most cold symptoms last ten to fourteen days from beginning to end in infants), or has *more severe versions* of illnesses, like UTIs that turn into kidney infection or blood infections quickly. *Poor growth* and *severe eczema*, teamed up with some of these other symptoms, also makes me wonder about an immune system deficiency.

Honestly, it can sometimes be hard to know if a kid is experiencing just super crappy and frequent daycare illnesses, or if there is an underlying problem. Our friends the pediatric immunologists can help. These are doctors whose literal job is to help identity and treat immune system issues, and I often will send a baby over to see them if I am worried about how often or how severely they're getting sick.

17

Vaccines. Vaccines!

When I was training as a pediatric resident in the Texas Medical Center, I spent three years immersed in rapid-fire and comprehensive learning at a world-renowned, internationally recognized medical city. Translation: I went to a good medical school and I saw some shit. I cared for thousands of patients. Could tell you hundreds of stories. Of heartache. Triumph. Disease. Death. I own a collection of experiences that make me smile, and others I sometimes wish I could forget. One I will never forget, however, is the Grunty Baby.

The Grunty Baby was a sweet six-week-old infant whom I saw in a clinic for a regularly scheduled checkup. The baby and parents were there for routine care and the first set of vaccinations. Baby was just starting to smile and coo. The family was enjoying these fun changes. But the attending doctor and I noticed the baby was doing some abnormal breathing that day in the clinic—a special sound called *grunting*. This is a rhythmic, unique kind of exhalation sound that babies make when their body is in distress. Doctors are trained to identify it—and act quickly if they hear it.

The parents reported that the baby had been tired lately. Not eating well. Less alert. Red flag. Red flag. Red flag.

So, the baby was admitted to the hospital.

And, twenty-four hours later, that beautiful baby was dead.

Devastating isn't even the word for it. Heartbreaking. Shocking. This poor family. That sweet baby. We residents were *stunned*, and we had just been given our first encounter with a very mean, often deadly bacteria called *Haemophilus influenzae*. The baby died of meningitis, an infection of the membranes around the brain and spinal cord, caused by *Haemophilus*—which is a germ we have a vaccine for. The Intensive Care Unit doctor told us the baby's cerebrospinal fluid (CSF), or fluid around the brain and spine, came out "looking like pus"—a pretty gruesome description, given that CSF usually looks like water. The *Haemophilus influenzae type b* (Hib) vaccine was one that the baby was supposed to get that day in the clinic, had they not been so sick. I think about that baby and that family all the time.

The story goes that in 1796, a fellow named Edward Jenner noticed that dairymaids, the local women who milked the cows, were often exposed to a mild virus called cowpox, which gave them pox sores on their hands. These women, after dealing with cowpox, never got the disease that was killing hundreds of thousands of *humans* at the time—smallpox. Somehow, the cowpox was protective to these dairymaids. Farmers in the area had actually known this fact for years.

When Jenner extracted the pus out of cowpox lesions and inoculated a little boy with it, the boy got a mild illness and was fine after about a day. Then—Jenner took the pus out of smallpox lesions and injected the boy with it—and the boy never got ill with smallpox. He then exposed him to smallpox many more times over the next few months—and the boy never got sick. This was some of the first proof that exposing humans to a *milder* or *dead* version of a germ could help protect them from a deadlier version of the disease.

I pretty strongly believe that vaccination is the most freakin' brilliant and life-saving scientific advancement of the twenty-first century. We have *rocked* this vaccine thing. We eradicated smallpox, which killed *hundreds of millions of people* over the past century. That's it—poof—gone. Polio is essentially nonexistent (though it creeps back sometimes in underdeveloped communities). We have rapidly improved infant mortality death rates by nearly eradicating certain types of infections. Infectious deaths all over the world have declined steadily over time as we find ways to get more communities vaccinated.

And yet so many families in our country doubt their safety, their efficacy, and their worth. So many people fear vaccines. If you find yourself in this group, I actually understand how you feel.

When your child is sick, maybe even in the hospital, invasive or painful treatments like IV medicines, shots, IV fluids, surgeries, and medical procedures feel like the right thing to do to save your baby from pain, trauma, or even death. These things may hurt—but in the end, if they save your kid's life, it feels so worth it, right?

It can feel very wrong, however, to inject your *well* baby with painful and unnatural-feeling things in vials. The baby feels good—and then you make them feel not good. And they're so small. And social media posts are screaming at you about *toxins*! Chemicals! Aborted fetal cells!

I know it may feel like a conundrum.

And as parents, we all just want to do what we feel is best to keep our kids healthy and happy.

I'm hopeful the information I give you here gives you a better sense of why I did not hesitate to vaccinate my own babies on time and on schedule, and why *I fear the diseases more than the risks.*

What Are Vaccines and How Do They Work?

I'm going to try my best to make a lot of complicated (but cool) science super simple.

You know that scene in the movie *The Matrix*, when Neo is strapped in that chair and they're giving him a crash course on combat and self-defense, and they upload things really quickly into his brain? And then he was all like, "I know Kung Fu?" Spectacular scene. I wish I could have uploaded medical school and saved four years of my life. Anyways. Vaccines are those uploaded programs.

Vaccination basically works by giving your body the blueprint to make an army. When we inject a dead or weakened germ into your baby's muscle, it tricks your body into thinking an infection is happening. Certain white blood cells float by, and suddenly they see—Oh, crap! What's that thing? Do we know that thing? No! It's a foreign invader! Quick! Time to put together an army, pronto!

After a shot, your body starts to create something called antibodies. This way, if the real disease shows up a little while later, the body can *easily and quickly* identify it and subdue it right away. The germ has no chance to even start replicating itself before it's destroyed. It's so cool.

Are There Any Harmful Ingredients in Vaccines?

Not that I know of. And the reason I know this is because all vaccines undergo pretty rigorous testing to assure *all the components* are safe. And, most vaccines are made in pretty similar fashion. And most vaccines at this point have been given *hundreds of millions of times* across the world—so we have a pretty good understanding of their human safety record.

First, you need the germ. Or, rather, a dead or weakened germ. Or, sometimes a piece of a germ. We call this the *antigen*. The antigen is the part that's going to get our kid's body to make *antibodies*, or—the army.

Next, you add a preservative. This is super important, otherwise everything in the vaccine would turn into a dud during transport from lab to distribution center to clinic. Before we put preservatives in vaccines, the shots could also get infested with bacteria and cause scary fatal infections in kids. Some vaccines may even have a microscopic amount of antibiotic in the vaccine to keep it from getting contaminated. This is the teensiest amount, and usually in the group of antibiotics that create the least allergic reactions in humans—streptomycin and neomycin, for example.

Also, most vaccines need an *adjuvant*.[1,2] An adjuvant is something that

- Encourages the body to make a big fat immune response;
- Helps scientists use *less* of the weakened or dead germ to make the vaccine;
- Makes it so that fewer shots are needed to fully vaccinate a patient; and
- Can help the vaccine last longer before they expire.

We *want* the immune system to get revved up so it will make a big army. If we throw a tiny bit of an adjuvant like aluminum salts in with the vaccine, it helps a tiny response turn into a big one. Don't worry about the aluminum salts—it's found in breast milk and drinking water, too. Aluminum is one of the most abundant elements on Earth, and is in our water, food, and air.

Last up—*stabilizers*. These are things that are added to the vaccine to protect the contents of the vial and keep the germ parts from adhering to the sides of the vial. These are things like amino acids, proteins such as gelatin or albumin, or sugars like sucrose or lactose.

What Are the Diseases We Vaccinate Against?

I think one of the blessings of living in a developed country is the ignorant bliss we enjoy on a day-to-day basis. Vaccination is a privilege that most of us don't think twice about.

In many underdeveloped countries, people will desperately wait in lines to hopefully have the chance to be vaccinated. And if I talk with a family who is hesitant about vaccination, I almost always bring up true stories about the diseases themselves. This makes the ghost of an illness feel a lot more real and reminds folks why we pediatricians believe so strongly in vaccination.

"But Dr. Diane, why are there *so many* vaccines? It seems like too many these days?!" Well friend, because there are so many germs that are potentially deadly in the world, especially to babies, and science has adapted and evolved its best weapons. I say, the more vaccines, the merrier. And because of vaccines, childhood survival rates have increased across the world. Walk through any older cemetery and have a look at the dates of birth and death on the smaller tombstones. We have come a long way.

Here's a super-quick breakdown of the diseases we vaccinate against in babies (these are not *all* the vaccines we give, just those in the infant period):

Hepatitis B (HBV): A virus that can infect the liver. It can cause chronic liver failure, and liver cancer. Children can get HBV by being born to a mother who has HBV, or contact with an infected person's blood or bodily fluids, such as sharing toothbrushes or bath towels, or by being bitten by an infected kiddo (think daycare and playgrounds). Hepatitis B causes 800,000–1 million deaths per year[3] (mostly from the liver cancer it causes in the chronically infected). One of the only vaccines that prevents *cancer*.

Diphtheria: A super-serious bacterial throat infection that can cause a thick film-like lining of the nose and throat. It can also cause large, slow-healing ulcers on the skin. 5–10 percent of those infected (in children under five years old, 20 percent) die, *even if you've had antibiotics*, mostly due to the toxin spreading in the blood and causing organ damage—like the heart, kidneys, and neurological systems.

Tetanus: The classic "step on a nail" scenario. It's a bacterium that lives in soil, dust, and surfaces of metals. If you step on that nail, and the bacteria get into your bloodstream, expect some interesting symptoms to show up in a few weeks. This includes trouble swallowing, seizures, sudden painful muscle spasms, lockjaw, and trouble breathing. You will be in the hospital for a few months if you catch it, and you'll probably need to be on a breathing machine for a while. Fatality rates between 6 and 72 percent based on how good the hospitals are around you.[4]

Pertussis (Whooping Cough): Babies with whooping cough start out with a runny nose, fever, and a slight cough. Typical cold stuff. Then, the coughing gets worse and worse. And the coughing comes in fits. And sometimes the baby starts to vomit with the cough. And the baby starts to turn blue with the fits of coughing, and struggles to get a breath in again (and when they finally do, they make that characteristic "whoop" sound). The bacterium that causes pertussis is relentless and does not improve with antibiotics (we give it anyway to keep it from spreading). Many babies with pertussis need ICU care and 3–4 percent die. The younger the baby, the higher the chance for severe disease. This is why we recommend pregnant women get the pertussis vaccine, along with any other person who plans to be around the newborn in the early months of life. Maternal vaccination in the third trimester is a fantastic way to assure your baby is protected.[5] Get on YouTube and look up "baby with pertussis" and try to watch the videos without tearing up. These babies truly do suffer.

Haemophilus influenzae type B (Hib): Remember Grunty Baby? That's what *H. influenzae* bacteria can do to an unvaccinated child. It was the leading cause of meningitis before the vaccine came out. It can also cause ear infections, blood infections (sepsis), pneumonias, and skin infections. Oh, and something horrific called *epiglottitis*. There's a flap behind the back of your tongue called the epiglottis. It helps with swallowing and protecting the breathing tube, or trachea. *H. influenzae* loves to make this guy get suddenly infected, huge, and swollen. You rapidly develop high fever, drooling, trouble swallowing, and trouble breathing. It is considered a medical emergency, because your breathing can get cut off from all the swelling. It's terrifying.

Polio: A very contagious virus that makes you feel tired, achy, and feverish, kinda like you have the flu. Some people have a bad headache and stiffness in the arms and legs. Then, in an unfortunate few (about one person in 200), it can lead to paralysis of the legs and arms. Five to ten percent of people with paralysis die because it affects the breathing muscles, too. It's a devastating disease. There is no cure. Look up "iron lung," the old breathing machines that used to help people breathe through polio.

Pneumococcal disease (Streptococcus pneumoniae): A real jerk of a bacterium that causes ear infections, bronchitis, sinusitis. Sometimes it gets invasive and can get into the blood, cause pneumonias, cause bacterial meningitis, and can burrow itself deeply to infect bones and joints. The pneumococcal vaccines are fantastic at helping kids not get ear infections, but also the nasty invasive stuff.[6]

Rotavirus: A virus that causes severe diarrhea and vomiting in babies. I know a child who experienced diarrhea over forty times in one day due to rotavirus. It can cause severe dehydration, and many children require IV fluids and hospital support. It used to be the number one disease that put kids in the hospital for diarrhea before the vaccine was developed.

Measles: One of the most contagious viruses on the planet. It causes high fever, coughing, red eyes, runny nose, and a rash. No big deal, right? Except that the measles virus loves to suppress a child's immune system for weeks to even years after infection. This means children suffering from measles may develop bacterial pneumonia, or the virus may attack the nervous system and cause something called *encephalitis*, or brain inflammation. Or, it may even make the immune system forget everything it has learned up to that point! This is called *immune amnesia*. Measles makes children more susceptible to *other* deadly germs while infected. *SSPE*, or *subacute sclerosing panencephalitis*, is what we fear the most. It is a brain disorder following measles that occurs several years later, where the patient slowly starts to experience seizures, cognitive decline, blindness, and progressive loss of normal body functions, followed by death. There is no cure.

Mumps: A viral illness that, you guessed it, starts out mild with fatigue, fever, and a headache. It progresses to cause *parotitis*, or inflammation of the parotid glands in the head, leading to the characteristic swollen mumps face we see in pictures. It also causes inflammation in other parts of the body, like the ovaries, testicles, and brain and spinal cord. It can cause people to become sterile (not able to have a baby). There is no cure.

Hepatitis A: A virus that can cause big lymph nodes, fever, fatigue, loss of appetite, dark urine, and jaundice—and occasionally a severe liver infection. You can catch it from drinking contaminated water or eating contaminated foods (think frozen foods, restaurant food) or being in close contact with infected people. Most of the time, the infection is mild, but some people experience full liver failure. There is no cure.

Varicella-Zoster (Chicken Pox, Shingles): The varicella virus causes fever, aches, and sore throat. It also causes the famous chicken pox rash—itchy and sometimes painful bumps all over the body. Many of us had it as kids, and for most of us, it was mild. It's the secondary infections that prompted the development of the vaccine in the 1990s—especially the skin infections from the sores, where extensive scarring can happen. Some people get something called "disseminated primary varicella" where the virus takes over the whole body, which has a high death rate. There are some rare neurological complications too, called encephalitis or Guillain Barre Syndrome. Varicella also can cause some horrible pneumonias, which also carry a high death rate.

Flu (Influenza): We've all had the flu. It's a virus that may knock us out for a week with fever, chills, a hacking cough, and a sore throat. But for some reason, in some kids, the flu causes a huge flare of inflammation in the lungs, making it hard for the lungs to process oxygen for the body. The flu can also make you more susceptible to secondary infections with bacteria—I have seen many children with double pneumonia while battling the flu. And I will never forget the healthy child I saw in my training who caught the flu and within a few weeks needed a heart transplant. The flu inflamed and weakened the heart so much (myocarditis) that it stopped being able to pump blood effectively. Children who are under five years old, and children who may have an underlying health condition like diabetes or asthma, are more prone to severe flu disease. The reason there is a yearly, changing vaccine for it is because it mutates yearly. Getting a flu vaccine can prevent children from catching the illness[7] and can reduce hospitalization and death[8-10] overall.

Covid-19: Covid in most infants is a mild illness; however, I am sure you're seeing a trend here: *sometimes it isn't mild.* The nasal congestion, sore throat, and coughing that infants experience can start to become severe in some, requiring oxygen and hospital support. Covid has caused plenty of childhood deaths in the past few years.[11] The Covid vaccine seems to be pretty good at preventing severe illness[12] *and* preventing the complications of long Covid.[13,14]

Should I "Spread Out" Vaccines?

I completely understand why people want to vaccinate, but don't want to get "too many at once." Your baby feels so small, and getting two, three, or even four shots at a time feels like it could be too overwhelming for their little bodies to handle, right?

The way I reason through it: our body deals with *millions* of interactions with bacteria, viruses, protozoa, yeast, and fungi daily, both on the surface and deep inside the body (more about this in the immune system chapter). Eating a bite of food? Introduces *millions* of microbes to your gut. Picking your nose shoves a few mil up the nostril. The nipple of a bottle? More and more millions. And the immune system in the mouth and gut is primed and ready and very, very capable of dealing with lots of new germs at once.

Getting vaccines, which are introducing anywhere from three to twenty new antigens to the body at one time, is not something that is going to overwhelm this well-oiled ship. I know this all seems super-simplified, but I have never worried about "overwhelming" my kid's immune system with several shots after learning about how strong and complex the immune system actually is.

I also find that babies who are on an "alternative" vaccine schedule may be at risk *of catching* the disease if not vaccinated on time. The CDC vaccine schedule was designed meticulously and *purposefully* to get kids vaccinated at the times when they are the most vulnerable—early childhood. Its intent is not to "load up" babies with tons of shots—the vaccines are given when they're given *so that the baby is the most protected he can be in the shortest amount of time.*

Why are the same shots given over and over? Well, we "boost" some vaccines a few times because when they're studied, it may have been found that they work better this way—and the protection lasts a lot longer when you "remind" the immune system about that bad guy a few times.

Also, this may seem less important, but I feel a need to say it—spreading out the shots means that your baby is going to feel pain more often. If the whole point is to not overwhelm them, it feels right to just get all the pokes at the same time to minimize crying time.

Do Vaccines Cause Autism?

This myth keeps coming back around, no doubt fueled by the loudest on social media, and it hurts my heart to see parents worry about this. Not only because it's false, but because it minimizes the experience of parents of autistic children, and flimsily blames routine shots as the cause of a very complex condition that is slowly becoming more understood over time—thus diagnosed more readily and easily.

The rumor was propagated by an individual in the UK (Andrew Wakefield) who eventually lost his medical license for publishing falsified information in 1998 about twelve kids in a lousy study he performed. He essentially blamed the measles-mumps-rubella vaccine (MMR) for their autism diagnoses. Several people and organizations attempted to reproduce his findings, and surprise surprise—no one could. Wakefield's study included twelve kids; other studies included *over half a million children*. And, shocker, it was also discovered that he was going to potentially make over 40 million dollars in a deal for "testing kits" for the disease.

All that nonsense to say—the public was duped, the study was retracted, and Wakefield lost his license, but the harm was already done. I think the belief keeps being revisited because at age twelve to eighteen months, around the time a child gets their first MMR vaccine, happens to be the same age we start to suspect autism in many children. This is the age where they often start to show us speech regressions and speech delays, and changes in interpersonal interactions.

So, I can say with confidence that *vaccines do not cause autism*, and I have listed a *lot* of data sources for you in the "Further Reading" section at the end of the book to further reassure you (nine studies involving huge and very reassuring amounts of data and test subjects).

What Are Some Side Effects of Vaccines I May See in My Baby? Are There Any Serious Adverse Effects?

Since the whole job of vaccines is to "rev up" the immune system, it is super normal to see symptoms afterward that mean the immune system is working hard.

The area where the baby got the shot may become warm and red—this means the immune system rushed to the area and infiltrated it quickly. Your baby may sleep a lot on the day he got his vaccines, he may have a low-grade temperature, and he may be pretty grumpy. This is great—it just means the vaccines *worked*, and important things are happening. An army is being made! Some kids may hold their breath when they get vaccines, or have an emotional response to the anticipation of the shot—and may faint. This is not super common, but it happens sometimes.

But What About "Vaccine Injuries"?

In my fifteen years of practicing pediatrics, along with several years of hospital training, I have never seen a child suffer a severe reaction to a vaccine. This is not to say it doesn't happen—it does. The job of the vaccine is to "rev up" the immune system, and sometimes it does *too good* of a job. If the immune system gets too worked up, inflammatory or allergic reactions may happen. Things like anaphylaxis occur very rarely, at a rate of 1 in 100,000–1,000,000 doses.[15,16]

This incidence is so low that I very strongly feel the benefits of vaccination far outweigh the risks.

What you'll read on social media is about the vaguely described problem of "vaccine injuries." Do I believe there are some children out there who have been harmed by vaccines, like an allergic reaction for example? Absolutely. Do I believe it happens at the substantial rate that many anti-vaxxers online claim it does? Not at all. I think a lot of things are blamed on vaccination without substantial medical proof.

I can't tell you how many stories I have heard along the lines of, "my neighbor's niece had a seizure six weeks after her flu shot!" It's really hard to assume causation in many of these cases. But I understand how invasive vaccines feel, and how easy it is to connect them to a new problem in the next few months. I think you should hear these stories, but understand and remember the old adage: *correlation doesn't necessarily mean causation.*

Dr. Diane, Do You Vaccinate Your Kids?

For those of you who feel inclined to take a more natural route to parenting, I hear you. Treating kids naturally and letting their immune systems work hard to beat infections, certainly sounds like a good way to go. I hold myself in your ranks. I try to avoid medications for my kids in general, when I can. I let fevers burn if my child otherwise seems okay. I wait out the fluid in my kid's ears before starting the Amoxicillin. I try dietary changes before starting the constipation meds.

But if you're thinking you want to go all-natural and skip vaccines, please know *there is nothing more natural than disease and death*. And the more we choose to opt out of vaccination, the more these diseases are going to creep back into our lives and communities. And since I have had very personal and up-close experience with how these diseases can ravage a child's body, I choose to vaccinate my kids on schedule, *without an ounce of hesitation*.

18

What Could Go Wrong?

Common Medical Ailments That May Come Up

The first year of life just feels so . . . delicate.

Baby giraffes can walk within a few hours of being born. Our offspring? Well, they're helpless little vulnerable blobs for a while, aren't they? Illnesses and ailments can feel really scary at this age. Allow me to walk you through some of the most common stuff I see in the first year of life. You may have seen some of these topics in prior pages—but let's solidity that info here as a quick reference.

Eye Goo/Pink Eye

Yellow and green eye drainage is something I hear a lot about in the first year of life. And believe it or not, it can have a couple of different causes. Sometimes, it's due to a tear duct blockage. Sometimes, it's due to a germ getting into the eye.

If you see goo in your baby's eyes in the first few weeks of life, chances are great that it is a blocked tear duct. Pull down your bottom eyelid and look in a mirror. See that little dot on your lower eyelid, toward your nose? That's part of the tear drainage system. Our tears wash over our eyes throughout the day then drain down that teeny tube, the lacrimal duct, into and down our nose. Sometimes, these tear ducts don't work very well in the first few months of life. They can get sticky, stuck, and blocked, or may not be fully formed yet. This is called *lacrimal duct stenosis,* and parents typically complain that one or both of their baby's eyes seem to always be teary, or have yellow goo or crusts.

Just a heads up—tears may be clear, but they almost always *dry* to a yellowish goo.

Lacrimal duct stenosis is usually nothing to worry about. You often just have to wipe the tears and goop away, and with time, it will go away on its own.

Sometimes we recommend a *nasolacrimal massage* to help. It's also called the "Crigler massage"—there are some great YouTube videos about it. Take a warm washcloth and wrap it around your finger. Point your finger at the inner corner of the eye, near the nose bridge. Massage the area and then push downward, down the area where the cheek meets the nose. The hope is to help the tear ducts drain downward on the inside. Do this maybe two or three times a day. The eye drainage may come and go a few times in a child's first few months. And, rarely, if the tear duct blockage continues after nine months of life, I'll send kiddos to a pediatric ophthalmologist. There are procedures they can do that'll fix the problem for good.

Sometimes, eye goop is caused by an infection.

You know how when you have a cold, you wake up in the morning feeling gross, and you have to walk over to the mirror to rub away all the crusties from your eyes? That's the cold making you tear up more. Those tears dried overnight and now they are eye boogers. This is the most common thing I see that causes pink crusty eyes in babies.

Yep—most pink eyes in babies are viral. And viral means there is no cure. It just needs a little time to go away on its own.

You should suspect your baby's pink eyes are viral if she also happens to have new snot dripping out from her nose, or a new cough or fever. Remember this fact—the clear stuff that comes out of our face, whether it's tears or snot, turns yellow or even green when it dries up. So, since viral conjunctivitis makes babies tear up more, you will often see more yellow crusties in those eyes.

The classic pink eye we all think about can absolutely be caused by bacteria. The white of the eye turns pretty red, and thick green goo will seem to never stop coming out. I tend to suspect it is bacterial (and will need an antibiotic drop) if only one eye is suddenly red, if it doesn't show up with new viral symptoms like a runny nose, or if the stuff coming out of the eyeball is super thick and constant. Go to your doctor anytime you're worried about pink eye. We can have a look and get the story and make an educated guess on whether the wait-and-see approach or eye drops are needed.

Flat Head (Plagiocephaly)

At some point, you may notice that your little one has a flat area on his head, or that the whole back of the skull seems to be changing shape over time. *Deformational plagiocephaly* is what we call it when a baby has a flat side, or flat back, of the head. This can lead to asymmetry of the face, ears, and skull, and it's actually pretty common, because baby heads are soft and take new shapes easily.

Sometimes it's caused in utero, from the pressure of mom's pelvic bones, for example. Rarely, it's caused by a tight neck muscle that causes a head tilt or head stiffness, called *torticollis*. Really rarely, it's caused by the bones of the skull fusing too early (*craniosynostosis*). Most commonly, it's caused by the positions we lay them in for hours each day (like how we recommend they are always on their back to sleep).

If it's mild, it's almost always gonna improve with lots of tummy time, or time spent propped up. Basically, if he's awake, try to keep him off the back/side of their heads. Once they start rolling over around four months of age, he'll flip to his belly to sleep, and the head will usually round itself out over time. The vast majority of babies I see with flat spots do absolutely fine without needing any other therapies.

If it's moderate to severe, some babies need more than positioning to help. We can enlist the help of a physical therapist to assist with neck movement and strength. Osteopathic Manipulative Treatment (OMT) done by a trained DO physician has also been proven to be effective in studies.[1,2] If severe enough—and by severe, I mean causing noticeable asymmetry of the forehead, cheeks, eye sockets, face shape, and/or ears—I may send a baby to be evaluated for a cranial helmet. The helmet "hugs" the skull bones and only allows for growth in certain directions. Over time, this leads to gradual re-shaping of the skull. Helmets work best if used as early as possible, and sometimes can be a little costly.

Baby Acne

Almost every baby I see experiences a little baby acne starting between weeks two and four. These are little red bumps on the face and neck that appear around this age. Sometimes the little red bumps even have white spots on them, just like a teenager's acne. It has a little bit to do with hormone fluctuations and a lot to do with more oil production in the skin. It's temporary and almost always goes away on its own. I know it looks pretty bad sometimes—but it doesn't hurt or bother them! If you want to try to do something about it, we usually just recommend a soft scrub with a gentle baby body cleanser daily. Some moms swear that putting breast milk on it helps. It always improves with time, so it's hard to know if it's the breast milk or the tincture of time that makes it go away.

Cradle Cap

Cradle cap, or *seborrheic dermatitis*, is super common starting at age three weeks and sometimes continuing for months (or years). Cradle cap looks like yellowish scales on the scalp. I often see it in the eyebrows and behind the ears, too. It is not painful or dangerous, just annoying. Again, we think it's due to mom's hormones circulating, along with increased oil production in the skin at this age. When the excess oil meets up with dead, sloughing skin cells, little scales form. There are a few ways to treat it, though your doc may tell you to just leave it alone—cradle cap almost always improves with time (though it can be a bit of a wait). Applying an oil to it, like baby oil, and letting that sit on the skin for a bit can soften the scales and loosen things up. Then, you can gently scrub the scales off with a toothbrush or cradle cap brush. Sometimes, if it's really bad, we might recommend an antifungal or steroid shampoo or cream to help things along.

Diaper Rashes

Diaper rashes are probably the most common rashes I see in young babies. And it's understandable—imagine wearing a diaper yourself! Think about how warm and sticky things get in there. A diaper is a contraption that holds in a lot of moisture and heat. Combine that with body parts that are almost always covered in sweat, urine, poo, bacteria, and yeast, and you have the perfect environment for skin breakdown.

Diaper dermatitis is what happens when your baby squirts out so many poops and pees, and you're wiping so much that the skin starts to get red and irritated and even ulcers appear. It's painful and common. And it takes a long time to heal—the skin has to repair itself layer by layer.

The way you make it better is by doing the opposite of what has been going on in that diaper—make it dry, and wipe it less. You can dry things out by having some diaper-free time throughout the day. Think tummy time on towels. You can also change diapers more frequently. You can wipe less by gently patting instead of sweeping the area, or running that booty under warm tap water. Barrier the heck out of that skin by thickly coating it with diaper creams that contain petroleum or zinc oxide. I always tell parents, "Frost that butt like a cake!" This isn't going to fix it, but is going to help all the poop, pee, and sweat to not touch the skin constantly.

Parents of babies who have started to eat may deal with some pretty gnarly diaper rashes related to the new foods he's eating. Some foods, especially those with natural acids in them like lemons, oranges, strawberries, raspberries, tomato sauces, and tomatoes (among others) can make the stools come out acidic. All it needs is a minute or two in the diaper to create an almost burn-like rash on their poor bottom.

Diarrhea from a tummy bug can also cause this acidity. This type of rash looks like a large area of reddened skin, sometimes with sores and ulcers. It's painful and I feel so bad for these poor baby booties!

Like a burn, this type of rash is going to take time to heal. I usually see maybe 5 percent improvement each day, and it may take weeks for the skin to look normal again. You have to apply *thick* barrier creams to the area with each diaper change, so that future pee and poop don't touch and irritate the angry skin. Calmoseptine is a great option if you can find it online. Sometimes there are some stronger medicated creams we pediatricians can call in for you—but most of these poor booties do just fine with love, attention, and time.

Some diaper rashes aren't caused by all the poop and wiping. Some are caused by infection. The most common infection in this area is with yeast. Yeast loves to create a rash that looks like red dots and loves to be in the folds in the groin area. Or—super red skin in the diaper with a border of red dots. Your doctor can prescribe a cream or oral medicine to make this rash go away.

Rarely, some severe diaper rashes are caused by bacteria. It may even come with a fever. Similar treatment here—this may need medicine from a doctor to get better.

Fever

I dive deep into *why* babies have fever in the immune system chapter (Chapter 16!), but felt it was important to discuss fever here, too. Please note: we manage fever differently in the first three months of life compared to older ages.

Under Three Months Old

The definition of fever in a baby is a rectal temperature of 100.4 degrees Fahrenheit (38 degrees Celsius) or higher.

So, no, 99.5 or 100.1 degrees Fahrenheit is *not* considered a true fever. We want you to take the temperature rectally—as opposed to an ear thermometer or forehead scanner—with a digital or old-school mercury thermometer because it is the most accurate reading of the real body temperature. And—accuracy is important at this age.

Interestingly, in the first few weeks of life, the *opposite* may happen, and a newborn's temperature may go *lower* than normal when they are dealing with an infection (under 97 degrees Fahrenheit, for example). We take cold babies just as seriously as hot babies in those first few weeks!

If your baby has a fever, they may act more tired or fussy. They may or may not feel warmer, and often look flushed in the cheeks. There are lots of causes of fever, but infection is what we worry about the most in this age group. You can help them feel better by offering a dose of infant acetaminophen (a.k.a. Tylenol©).

If your under-three-month-old baby has a fever, you need to, at the very least, call your doctor immediately for guidance. Most babies in this age group need to head to the emergency room at the hospital, because there are specific blood, urine, and sometimes spinal fluid tests we have to do to make sure they aren't super sick. We also sometimes have to put them on IV antibiotics as soon as possible. Babies this age tend to take a small infection and turn it into a big infection (like sepsis or meningitis) really easily. And while these big bad infections are rare, it's important that we rule them out.

Three Months and Older

If your baby is now over three months old and spikes a fever, there is no need to panic. Now that she's a bit older, her immune system is rockin' and rollin'. It spiked that fever to help fight the germ. And we aren't *as* worried about a severe infection taking over if they do have a temp above 100.4 degrees Fahrenheit. It doesn't mean they don't rarely get severe infections—it's just less common.

You don't necessarily have to run her to the emergency room if your baby has a fever over three months of age. Take a minute to look at your baby as a whole. Is she breathing comfortably? Is she drinking enough to make urine every six to eight hours? Is she able to sleep comfortably? She might be a little fussy, and want to take some longer naps, but in this age group it's okay to put a call in to your doctor and talk through a plan.

Make her comfortable with acetaminophen if she seems fussy. Offer lots of fluids, because fever can be dehydrating. You can give babies this age infant electrolyte-replenishing drinks (like Pedialyte©, for example) in small amounts to keep them hydrated. Watch her closely, and hopefully within a few days she will be feeling much better.

I worry about a fever in a baby over three months old if it lasts longer than four days, or the numbers seem to be trending up instead of down over time. I always worry if they can't seem to drink enough to pee every six to eight hours, or if they seem extremely fussy to the point where it is hard to calm them down. Again—call your doctor if you're worried at all. It's our job to help you through this.

Belly Button Stuff

I have to give mad love to all the new parents dealing with their newborn's weird belly button. The *umbilicus* is truly a foreign body part. It's kinda gross. It's hard to know how to deal with it, how to keep it clean, and how to know what's normal and what's not and . . . you're doing great, sweetie.

The umbilical cord typically falls off before week three. If it stays on longer than four weeks, talk with your doctor.

After it falls off, it's totally normal for you to see old blood crusties, sometimes even a bit of fresh blood, and yellow gunk from time to time. There are little blood vessels starting to dry up even after the cord falls off, so you'll see some dots of red and yellow on the clothes or diaper here and there. This should improve with time, as things continue to shrink and dry.

Sometimes, the belly button may look like it sticks outwards. This is normal and it may be something called an *umbilical hernia*. Umbilical hernias are what happen when a little bit of intestine pokes through a hole or weak spot in the abdominal muscle. It may stick out more when the baby is straining or crying. It's not painful or dangerous at all. I actually see these almost every day in my office. With time, the muscle will slowly close and the hernia will go away. This can take anywhere from a few weeks to five years! So, we usually just recommend you watch it and as long as the bulge can be easily pushed back into the belly, you're good. After age five, if a child still has a hernia, we ask a surgeon to help close the hole. If the belly button sticks out a lot suddenly, seems to be changing colors, won't easily go back in, or seems to be causing inconsolable pain to the baby—see a doc ASAP. There is a super rare complication called an *incarcerated umbilical hernia* that can happen if the intestine gets "stuck" in that weak spot. I've only seen this once in my career.

Another issue you might see with the belly button is something called an *umbilical granuloma*. A granuloma is a little bit of tissue that forms on the belly button after everything heals up. Sometimes it's moist and can be yellow, pink, or red. It's not dangerous, just kinda like a skin tag. It may go away on its own, or your doctor can apply something called silver nitrate on it that can help it go away. Call your doc if you notice spreading redness around the belly button, red streaks, fever, or a whole lot of yellow drainage coming out of it, just to be on the safe side.

Eczema

Eczema is what we call it when a baby has spots or body areas that look like inflamed, reddened, dry skin. It can be itchy, but not always. I see eczema every single day in my office. I see it in children of all genders, ages, and races, and during all seasons of the year.

Eczema's nature is to flare up, calm down, and flare up again. It comes and goes. It can be affected by the things you put on the skin, weather and temperature changes, foods, clothing, detergents, or it may appear *for no reason at all*. Because genetics.

There are many kinds of eczema. And eczema looks different in babies than in older kids and adults. It is located on different parts of the body at different ages. Sometimes it looks like just dry skin. In babies, it often looks like a ringworm patch—a circle of different skin that suddenly appears and may even have some clearing in the center of it. Sometimes eczema looks like inflamed skin in the folds of the elbows and knees. Babies tend to get it on the shoulders and the face and scalp a lot, too.

Some children with eczema are sensitive to certain foods. Meaning, their eczema gets worse if they eat certain things. However, most kids with eczema have zero problems with food. Why do some kids get eczema and some don't? The answer is usually genetics. Atopic families are more prone to have kids with eczema. This is an important word: *atopic* means your family is prone to eczema, allergies, and asthma—your body is sensitive in general. I kinda think of atopy as an "overactive" immune system. But many kids with eczema don't necessarily have families who struggle with this. I also tend to see more eczema in kids who have Milk Soy Protein Intolerance.

If your baby has eczema, don't be afraid to bathe them often. It doesn't make it worse—it actually can make it better. Try to give them lukewarm baths that aren't too hot and use a cleanser that doesn't have fragrances and says things like "gentle" or "hypoallergenic" on the bottle. When you take them out of the bathtub, just pat them dry gently. Then, immediately apply a moisturizer—the main treatment for eczema. We want the skin to hold on to the moisture as much as possible. This means lathering on petroleum jelly, Aquaphor, Vanicream, Eucerin, Cerave, Aveeno—you name it, you use it—a lot. Avoid lotions. I happen to like the thick clear stuff the best, like petroleum jelly or Aquaphor or Cerave Healing Ointment. Some kids may be so sensitive they're allergic to the components in some of these products, so just good old petroleum jelly (Vaseline) is the best thing if other products aren't helping. If you're moisturizing daily, and your baby seems content, the eczema isn't worsening, and it doesn't seem itchy, you're good to just do this every day.

If a child has severe eczema and really struggles with itching, we think more about treatments with medications. Steroid creams work well for spot-treating the super itchy spots. I don't like to use these long-term, but they can help a baby feel more comfortable for a little while. There are also nonsteroidal medications we can use for the more miserable cases. We also use things like antihistamines to help with the itch, and rarely antibiotics if the broken skin has got infected (bacteria love eczema). Sometimes I have my patients see a dermatologist to help with the more severe cases. Most eczema improves with time, and over half of kids have their eczema go completely away between ages five and fifteen.

Drool Rashes

Babies get a lot of rashes because of drooling. When they start the mouthing behaviors—putting everything in their mouth to explore and build an immune system—more drool tends to come out. And all this moisture can absolutely lead to some bumpy rashes. I see this a lot on the chin, cheeks, and neck. Sometimes it looks like little pink dots and sometimes it's patches of dry and inflamed skin. Try your best to keep the areas as dry as possible if you think drool is the culprit.

The neck rolls and other skin rolls may get red from time to time when they're sweaty and moist. We love our rolly polly babies, but this is a common problem with those delicious fat rolls. The redness can get really impressive. Sweat and old skin cells can collect in there and make things raw. The main treatment is just drying the heck out of the rolls throughout the day with towels. If it seems to be pretty bad and bothers your baby, you may want to talk with your doc about whether an anti-yeast cream or antibiotic is needed. This is rare, though.

Common Colds

Colds are the number one infectious illness your baby is going to deal with in the first year of their life if they are around other children in any capacity. And I know how completely helpless it feels when your baby is dealing with one. So, let's march through all the things that happen with a cold virus. And remember—colds are viral infections, which means there is no cure for them.

Say the baby on the floor next to your baby sneezes in the daycare classroom. From that sneeze, literally millions of viral particles will be launched into the air, desperately seeking a living organism. Let's say some of those droplets land on your baby's teething toy, which then, of course goes right into your baby's mouth. Ta-da! A new cold will be coming home with her for you to enjoy. This happens sometimes a couple times each week—which means your baby may harbor more than one virus at a time. And is also why it seems like the snot is never-ending when they're in childcare. And don't stress about this—we *want* them to get sick from time to time. This builds army after army of antibodies that are ready and waiting for any future bad guys.

That cold virus—adenovirus, rhinovirus, enterovirus, or one of many others—makes its way to the nose and the throat, and within a few days, symptoms start. A runny nose, a sore throat (maybe manifesting as some grumpiness or poor eating), and even a fever may appear. The stuffy and drippy nose is so frustrating to babies, who really want to breathe through their little nostrils. The fever may last three to five days. The drainage will get worse for the first couple of days, then start to dry. At this point, it usually goes from clear to colored yellow or green. *It's a myth that kids get green boogers only with bacterial infections*—most viral colds involve yellow or green snot. That snot has white blood cells, nostril skin cells, and old dead viruses in it. You just see "the junk" more easily as it dries out.

The cold then "moves to the chest," which generally freaks everyone out but is actually normal. It's okay to feel vibrations in the chest while your kiddo coughs. The cough is the *cleanup process* in most cases. Coughing pulls the old mucus up out of the pipes of the lungs, and then the baby swallows it down the other pipe—down to the stomach! Yum. Then, we digest all that mucus and poop it out. This is why babies often get loose weird stools with colds, too. The cough starts and may last for seven to ten days and is natural and important!

Colds are viral, and there is no cure for them. Most colds clear up on their own in about a week or a week and a half. The best ways to comfort your baby when they have a cold are:

- Suction the nose a lot. There are all kinds of bulbs, suction hoses, and even electronic options here.
- Use nasal saline sprays and rinses.
- Give pain meds as needed. Under six months, use Acetaminophen. After six months, you can try Ibuprofen. This is for the headaches, body aches, and sore throat your baby can't tell you about.
- Use a humidifier in the room (to be clear, this cures nothing, but does moisten the mucus membranes). Having a dry, painful nose and throat sucks in the mornings when you have a cold, right?
- Keep your baby hydrated. She may not want to drink the same volumes as before she got sick, but you want her to pee at least every six to eight hours and small frequent meals can help.
- If the nose is super stuffed, it's hard to breathe when taking the breast or bottle. So suction beforehand and give her lots of breathing breaks while eating!

Overall, babies get several colds per year (and if in daycare—I'm talking *several*). Like eight to twelve a year. And each one can have symptoms that last seven to ten days total. When you do the math, it makes sense as to why we call the continual nasal drainage the "daycare drip."

When Do I Worry?

- If a baby has a fever for more than three to four days with the new cold.

- Fever under three months old? See a doctor or ER, as soon as possible.
- If fevers are going up over time, instead of trending down.
- If the coughing is growing more severe over time, maybe even making her gag or vomit.
- If the baby seems to be breathing faster than usual or have a hard time catching her breath.
- If the baby is using extra chest, rib, or collarbone muscles to breathe.
- Any baby who is hard to arouse/wake up needs to be seen in the ER as soon as possible.
- Any baby who cannot drink enough to pee every eight hours needs to be seen as soon as possible.

Ear Infections

There are two kinds of ear infections we see in kids. Otitis *media* and otitis *externa*. Otitis media is an inner-ear infection, and the one we see most commonly in babies. This is the type I'm gonna focus on here.

Ear infections are caused by colds. Because colds cause snot.

Baby head and inner-ear drainage systems sometimes don't work well. The *eustachian tubes* are the culprit. They're narrow and slant more horizontal than vertical in babies compared to adults, and when a cold hits, these tubes often swell up and don't work well.

If the drainage system swells up, the snot and mucus deep in the ear have nowhere to go. So, it just sits there. Often, when the cold gets better, it drains out on its own. I'll often tell parents to "wait it out" when I see clear, nonconcerning fluid behind the eardrum on my exam.

But sometimes, before it can drain out, bacteria find the mucus party. And then things get painful, pressure in the ear builds, and a child may have a fever. Some kids even get a bit dizzy/clumsy since this is near the equilibrium center, and many babies can't hear well when they have an ear infection. This is when we use oral antibiotics to help out.

Sometimes, the pus builds up and the eardrum pops. This is called a *ruptured tympanic membrane* and don't panic—it's okay—we just use antibiotic drops in the ear to help out here. You may see a lot of drainage come out of the ear. It's honestly like a zit popping—the kid usually feels better and the eardrum will heal up on its own with time. This is how our ears used to "cure" the infection before antibiotics came around.

Viral Rashes

Babies are unique when it comes to rashes. They get a *lot* more rashes than we adults do. And anytime they get a virus, like a cold or a tummy bug, it is very common for babies to suddenly have a new rash appear.

Viral rashes are something I see in the office daily. They don't worry me much, but I know they can be so stressful for parents. Out of nowhere, your kid, who is getting over a cold, suddenly has red dots all over her little body. Usually, these rashes look like someone took a pink marker and put dots everywhere, especially on the chest, stomach, and back skin. Some viruses, like Fifths Disease, give babies rashy red cheeks, too.

These rashes are harmless, and I kind of view them as the virus waving at me: "Hello! I'm in here."

I always look at the *overall picture* when it comes to rashes—how is the baby acting? Does she seem to be feeling okay? Does the rash bother her? Is she drinking and breathing okay? If this is the case, it's usually fine to watch a rash like this for a few days. If you feel the rash is worsening or changing over time—like becoming painful, itchy, weepy, or the baby is acting sick—head into your doctor's office.

Hives

I parked this section right after *viral rashes* for a reason. Sometimes, viruses (like colds and tummy bugs) cause hives. Yes—hives. Viruses are probably the most common cause of hives that I see in babies, believe it or not. I think most parents see hives and worry about new exposure to things like new soaps, lotions, medications, or foods. All of these can cause hives as well.

Rather than little dots, hives are welts of varying shapes and sizes that are raised and can be felt with your hand. They may be in different shapes, may move around and grow and shrink quickly. They are sometimes itchy. Sometimes babies are a little fussy with them.

If you can't think of anything new your baby might be exposed to, it's probably okay to chalk it up to a new germ, especially if they've recently had a runny nose, cough, or some diarrhea. The most common causes of hives that I see caused by foods are probably peanut, dairy, and egg, but any food can cause allergy. Stop the offending food and give your doctor a call if you notice any hives after a new food.

Scary as I know hives can be, they're usually pretty harmless, other than causing itchiness. We usually use antihistamines like cetirizine (Zyrtec) to help them go away, but they may come and go for a few days.

I do worry if a child shows signs of *anaphylaxis*. Anaphylaxis is a severe allergic reaction that involves more than one body system. For example, if a child eats something and then develops hives *and* vomiting. Or new hives and drooling. Or vomiting and loud breathing. If you're worried about anaphylaxis, call 9-1-1 and give your child and use injectable *epinephrine* or nasal spray as soon as possible if you have one. If hives appear with a new food, your doctor may prescribe epinephrine for you to carry. More on this in Chapter 13.

RSV

Respiratory Syncytial Virus (RSV) is a phrase that, when spoken, may make any pediatric medical professional within a half mile shudder. This is a virus that puts thousands of kids and older adults in the hospital yearly. Did you know that 90 percent of kids have had RSV by age two? And chances are excellent that a recent cold you had may have been RSV. It is one of the most common viruses that circulates in schools and daycares each and every year, and usually it's a late fall and winter virus.

RSV starts out with typical cold symptoms: runny nose, sneezing, congestion, fussiness, and sometimes fever. The whole illness from start to finish may last two to three weeks.

Days three to five are usually the worst days, and the time when the "lung stuff" may start to appear. We call this *bronchiolitis*. Babies may start to have coughing fits, breathe faster here and there, and struggle with being able to handle all the gagging, mucus and secretions.

The tiniest little branches in the lungs are called the *bronchioles*. And RSV loves to get things super inflamed and super mucus-y here. Because of this, some kids with RSV may start *wheezing*. This is a whistling sound you may start to hear from the throat and chest. I describe it as a "pack-a-day-smoker" sound. It's not coming from the stuffy nose, but instead the whistles are coming from the tighter narrower airways in the lungs.

In most kids, RSV is usually just a very snotty cold. Not all babies get the lung issues, but if they do, we watch them pretty closely for *fast breathing* and *retractions* (using the chest wall and collarbone muscles to breathe). If your kiddo is difficult to arouse, won't drink, has a blue tinge to the lips, tongue or gums, isn't peeing every six to eight hours, or is breathing so hard they cannot seem to catch their breath, you need to get to the closest ER (or call 9-1-1) so they can be monitored and given oxygen and support if needed.

Those most at risk for severe RSV are babies under twelve months old, kids born with lung, heart, or neuromuscular problems (who may have a hard time coughing or swallowing), and patients of any age with asthma or immune system problems.

Treatment for RSV? Suction. Suction. Suction. The snot is intense. You may even want to invest in one of those good electric suction devices. Nasal saline helps, too. The salt in it helps draw out mucus deep in the nostrils. If your baby is struggling to drink normal meals, offer small amounts of breast milk, formula, infant electrolyte drinks, and water (if over six months), every fifteen to thirty minutes—they may struggle to drink big meals when they're all stuffed up. It's okay to use pain and fever meds—RSV makes them feel miserable with the sore throat, body aches, and headaches.

For the kids with wheezing, there is a medication called albuterol, given aerosolized as a "breathing treatment," that may help—or may not.[3] Sometimes it helps to open up the tiny airways, and sometimes it doesn't. It can be given at home or in the hospital.

The truth is, not much really helps RSV as much as the tincture of time. If your baby is hospitalized, he may need help with keeping his oxygen levels up and may require large amounts of suctioning. He is supported and helped through the worst of it.

And again, thankfully, most babies do just fine at home.

Want to hear something that really sucks? When babies get a pretty bad RSV infection and then get over it, they now have an increased risk to *wheeze with future illness*. Even if that future illness is not RSV, a child may start to wheeze more often, for a few months to years, because of the past RSV infection. Stupid virus.

To *prevent* RSV, consider one of two shots given in the fall and winter. The RSV vaccine given to pregnant women during the third trimester of pregnancy is a great way to protect babies before they even come out of the womb. Mom gets the vaccine and then develops the antibodies that cross the placenta and go into the infant's bloodstream. It should protect the baby through their first RSV season.

The other shot to consider, if the maternal vaccine isn't given, is *Nirsevimab*. Nirsevimab is not a vaccine shot. It is an antibody shot. This means, instead of *asking the infant's body to make an army* against RSV, which is what vaccines are designed to do, this shot *is* the standing army. It's given to babies under eight months old who are going into their first RSV season, and to some older kids who have underlying health conditions. It works really well to keep babies from developing severe RSV! Data shows fantastically reduced rates[4] of hospitalization in babies who get this shot, and I've seen how well it works in my own practice these past few years. Side effects are minimal (some leg tenderness at the injection site) and I highly recommend it!

Tummy Bugs (Throwing Up and Diarrhea)

At some point in your child's life, he is going to get a tummy bug. "Tummy bugs" are the endearing term parents have given to the misery that is *acute gastroenteritis*. Tummy bugs are usually caused by a virus (no cure), though less often can be due to bacteria. When babies get a tummy bug, liquids may start coming out of both orifices. I sort of like to think of the body panicking and "flushing out" the bad guy, from the top and the bottom. It usually comes on quick with some exorcist-style pukes, and then the watery poops may follow. Sometimes it's just throwing up, and sometimes it's just diarrhea. It can last from one day to several weeks.

Many babies are fussy because, well, think about the last time you had a stomach bug. It sucks, right? Many babies experience the same nausea and tummy cramps. Some have fever. Some babies throw up for a day, then it gets better, then they throw up again (this often throws parents for a loop because they assume it's a "24-hour thing" when really the stomach remains pretty irritable for a few days). Diarrhea causes cramping and gas and butt pain and diaper rashes. Babies may not eat or drink nearly as much as they usually do—and that's what you'll need to keep an eye on. Hydration is key to getting your kid through the illness, and dehydration is what usually (and rarely) puts kids in the hospital.

Formula or breast milk is totally fine to offer if your kid is sick—don't believe the old wives' tales about "no milk." Babies over six months can be offered water, too. Electrolyte drinks like Pedialyte are great to start offering if a baby refuses to take milk for a few hours. It has things like sodium and sugar in it to keep the electrolytes in the blood normal. Small amounts of the beverage at a time—even a teaspoon or two every ten to fifteen minutes—can keep a baby out of the hospital. The goal is for them to pee every six to eight hours.

When do I worry? I always want to see a kiddo if parents feel they're struggling to keep him hydrated. We tend to watch babies under three months old really closely—if not peeing every six hours, acting much more tired than usual, and not able to drink small amounts of formula or breast milk throughout the day—to the ER you go. Kids older than three months can often do well at home if they take small amounts of electrolyte drink (like two to three teaspoons at a time) throughout the day and keep peeing, but if they seem to vomit it all up no matter how small the sips, get seen by a doctor soon. If your baby has been sick and is acting so tired that it's hard to wake them, go to the ER.

The Flu

Influenza, a.k.a. "The Flu," is one of the most common winter viruses in the entire world. It is a *respiratory* virus. We medical people cringe a little bit when we hear folk say terms like "stomach flu." The flu certainly can make kids barf and have stomach pains. But the essence of the flu—the true misery of it—lies within its respiratory problems.

Rivers of snot. A horrible headache. A cough that rattles the bones. A very sore throat. A fever so high it makes you shake and quiver. All of this is classic flu—and the body aches are some of the worst I think humans can experience. Babies can't tell you they're feeling all of this, so they're just going to cry, and sleep, and whimper, and cry some more. I tend to think of the flu in bigger kiddos when I walk into my exam room and the poor kid is lying face-down on my exam table, miserable and wrapped in three blankets.

The main treatment we have for flu is to support babies through it, with lots of nose suctioning, fever reducers, snuggles, and hydration with formula, breast milk, or electrolyte beverages. The flu is a virus, and viruses have no cure. They usually just have to run their course. We do, however, have some medications that can slow it down and punch it in the face if we catch it early enough. Oseltamivir (Tamiflu) and Baloxavir marboxil (Xofluza) are examples, and your doctor may prescribe one if we can determine it's the flu early in the first few days.

Most babies do fine and can get over the flu on their own. It's at least a week of sickness, sometimes more. The cough can linger for one or two weeks afterward. I tend to worry a bit if a baby experiences more than four or five days of fever. I worry if the fevers are trending upward instead of down over time. I worry if a baby seems to be struggling to breathe, and their breathing seems fast or labored—get to the ER as soon as possible if this happens. I also want babies to go to the hospital if they can't seem to drink enough to pee every six to eight hours, if they seem to be acting abnormally confused, or if are hard to wake up.

Sometimes, rarely, influenza can get severe. Babies with underlying medical problems, like prematurity, lung disease, heart disease, diabetes, and asthma are more prone to this. And the flu can make your body more prone to get opportunistic bacterial infections while you're fighting it off, like pneumonia. The flu can also cause severe lung inflammation and heart inflammation. Around the world, it's estimated that 28,000 children under eighteen die from influenza-related lower respiratory tract infections each year (and the majority of these deaths occur in children under four years old).[5]

The flu is constantly moving and changing, and every year as different strains circle the globe. Each year we try our best to match the yearly flu vaccine to the strains that are circulating—and sometimes it works well, while other times it unfortunately doesn't. But the flu vaccine is the biggest preventative weapon we have against severe flu, and I (and every doctor I know) get it for my kids yearly . . . because I never want to sit in a hospital room with regrets. There's a lot of myth and lore out there about the flu shot. The truth is, it's safe and usually pretty helpful to prevent hospitalization and death. Starting at six months, I highly recommend getting your baby a flu vaccine each year. If your baby is under six months old, ask that anyone who is around her often be vaccinated.

COVID-19

SARS-CoV-2, a.k.a. COVID-19, a.k.a. the 2020 Pandemic Scourge of the Earth, was a virus that entered our stratosphere in 2019 and made a whole lotta people *super sick* for a while. Thankfully, while it still causes tremendous trouble for some folks, it has generally mutated to be less deadly over time (and the vaccines helped, too). For most babies, Covid is a mild illness (there are exceptions here, of course). We actually noticed this somewhat early on in the pandemic—a respiratory virus that was generally less severe in infants? A rarity, indeed.

Covid tends to cause a runny nose, congestion, fever, sore throat, and often stomach problems like diarrhea and vomiting in babies. It is viral, which means there is no cure. While there are some medications and infusions used in older populations, we tend to not use them in kids unless they're being hospitalized or have underlying health conditions that make them prone to severe illness. We just try to support babies through Covid, like we would treat a cold: making sure they're not struggling to breathe, assuring they stay hydrated, suctioning all the snot, and keeping them elevated, hydrated, and comfortable.

The Covid vaccines are safe and have been effective most seasons they've been used. Studies in older kids show very decent protection from severe disease and "long Covid."[6,7] I'd consider getting them for your baby, especially if she has an underlying health condition like asthma, diabetes, prematurity, or any lung or heart disease.

Roseola

Allow me to introduce you to a total turd of a virus. It's called roseola and I hate it.

Many years ago, my nine-month-old daughter suddenly spiked a high fever for many days. Five days, to be exact. Her temp was as high as 104–105 degrees Fahrenheit.

As I have trained you to do when it comes to fever, I didn't freak out—but I did watch her really closely. And I took her to her pediatrician and they tested her for things like the flu and a urinary tract infection—all negative. Her fever was super high, but she had no other symptoms. Just fever, fussiness, and tiredness. I was clueless as to what was going on, and I was worried.

Then, the fever suddenly stopped on day five. Woohoo! But then, a rash appeared immediately all over her body. The rash didn't itch or hurt. It was then I knew. Ahhh. This is *roseola*.

Roseola is a real stinker because it can trick us medical folks and parents into thinking a kid is super sick with that high temperature. And while babies do feel completely lousy, this virus goes away on its own, and they do totally fine afterward. Roseola loves to pop up in small kids (six months to two years) in the spring and fall months.

It's important to remember the story: fevers for three to five days, then it stops, and BOOM the rash shows up. This is how roseola behaves, and it's pretty unique to this virus.

Always check in with your doctor if your baby is younger than six months and having fevers this high, if you're worried they're not drinking enough, if they have other new symptoms showing up, if they seem to be breathing harder, or if you're just not sure what the heck to do.

Hand, Foot, and Mouth Disease

I always hear the *Jaws* music playing in my head when I see these little ones toddle into my office. New rash . . . fever . . . won't eat much. "Please doc, don't say it's Hand, Foot, and Mouth—I'm terrified about it!"

- No, it's not that cattle disease with a similar name. Heehee.
- Yes, it's super contagious.
- Nope—no reason to freak out. We see it all the time. You probably had it when you were a kid.
- Go get some popsicles. I'm gonna prescribe them.

Hand, Foot, and Mouth Disease (HFMD) is caused by a virus and typically happens in kids under age five. It loves to spread in the spring and summer months. Big kids and adults can get it too, and it tends to be more miserable the older you get. HFMD loves to spread in daycare classrooms like fire. Usually, kids catch it by getting oral secretions or fecal secretions in their mouth or airway from a buddy. I'll let your imagination run wild on the methods kids go through to experience this fun transfer of germs.

Soon after catching it (like three to five days), kids start with a fever and a new rash. Sometimes they have a runny nose or other cold symptoms. I think the rash is pretty unique. They're usually pink or red spots with/without thick bubbles of fluid. Typical HFMD appears on and inside the mouth, the palms of the hands and soles of the feet. Hence the name. I joke with parents that it should be called "Hand-Foot-Mouth-Butt-Arms-Legs" because you can totally see spots in other places, too.

HFMD is commonly mistaken for other things. Often, parents worry about chicken pox. Remember—chicken pox is itchy and tender. HFMD is not. Folks also mistake these for bug bites—again, not itchy like bug bites are.

The mouth sores hurt. They're typically the main complication I see with HFMD—they sometimes hurt so much that kids don't want to eat or drink. The eating I don't mind -but it's important that they drink. Load up on popsicles. All my sugar rules go out the door when a kiddo has HFMD. Sometimes if it's really bad we will prescribe a mouthwash for the pain.

It'll go away on its own. This can typically take seven to five days for most kids. The spots may last for weeks as they face and—get this—a few weeks later, the skin can peel off the palms and soles, and finger and toenails may peel off! Such a bizarre little virus. Kids do just fine with it, and a HFMD diagnosis is no reason to panic, I promise.

Croup

I'll never forget my first personal experience with croup. I was at a Taylor Swift concert (the *1989* tour!) and my mom, who had my toddler son, Jack, called me at 10 p.m.. This was highly unusual.

"He's breathing very loudly, and I'm not sure what's wrong with him." At that point, *over the sounds of a stadium full of screaming fans*, I heard my son trying to breathe. And it scared the *shit* out of me. It was something called stridor; it was new, and it was terrifying. And this was his first (of many) bouts of croup. He was eventually fine, and yes, I missed the last few songs of the night, but just trust me on this one—I know how scary croup can be.

The best way to think about croup is that it's a cold that has parked its inflammation in the one of the worst possible spots in the body.

That spot is in the upper area of our respiratory system, around the voice box and the top of the windpipe. This is why the main first symptoms are often a sudden barking "seal" cough and a change in voice. These babies can rapidly get very hoarse and fussy. I think their throat really hurts with croup, too. They can experience high fevers and a runny nose, and sometimes they have high-pitched breathing sounds we call *stridor*. This gets worse when they get upset or agitated. Babies hear themselves cough and struggle, and I think these new sounds scare them as much as their parents do.

Most babies do just fine and can be taken care of at home. Suction of the snot, pain-reducing medications like acetaminophen and ibuprofen, and steamy showers are my first recommendations. You have to try to keep them as calm as possible. I often joke that all the rules go out the window with croup. Sugary treat, playing with mommy's coveted phone, new toy, whatever—keep them happy and try to keep the breathing steady and calm. We put Jack in a warm steamy shower and let him play with toys in there for a while. Cool fluids and popsicles also helped.

I worry about a baby with croup if:

- The breathing sounds high-pitched even when they're calm;
- They make noisy, high-pitched breathing sounds when breathing *both* in and out;
- They struggle to swallow and are drooling a lot;
- They are using their chest and stomach muscles to breathe for more than five minutes without calming down;
- They breathe at a faster rate than usual for more than five minutes;
- They can't drink enough to pee every six to eight hours.

In cases where any of this is happening, I recommend you see a doctor as soon as possible in the urgent care or ER. Sometimes we need to do a special breathing treatment to help them out—a treatment called *racemic epinephrine*. And sometimes kids with croup need steroids to calm down the swelling in the airway. Rarely, some kids need to be observed overnight in the hospital until they are more comfortable, and their breathing struggles resolve.

19

Movin' and Groovin'

I'll never forget the first—and only—time a baby fell off one of my clinic exam tables.

I had just finished seeing my little nine-month-old patient for her checkup, and she was doing great. Her dad had brought her in, and he was a bit overwhelmed. It was partially my fault—we give parents a lot of forms to sign and fill out at my office—and his sweet baby was newly and very mobile now. He juggled the paperwork and the screaming, bucking, thrashing, flailing infant like a real pro.

But a minute or two after I walked out of the room—we suddenly heard screaming of the baby (and grown man) variety.

She had launched herself right off the exam table while he scrambled to grab her clothes.

Everyone was *fine*, thank goodness. Just a little shaken up. Dad and I were more than kid, for sure!

It's pretty cool when your baby starts to move, and watching her develop a little independence is such a special part of parenting. It's also terrifying, right? But know that life certainly can get a little easier here in some ways. When babies start to sit on their own, you can keep that car seat in the car—sitting them in the grocery store cart is so much fun! And the restaurant high chair is an easy bonus, too. Let's chat about some other movement milestones, and what you should be seeing around the later parts of the first year.

What Types of Big Movements Should My Baby Start Doing?

In the back of the book, you'll find a list of all the things I hope to start seeing developmentally by each month of age. In the first four months of life, you'll notice that babies aren't doing too much as far as big body movements. You'll generally start to see less chaotic flailing of the arms and legs over time and more head-lifting and leg-straightening as you hold them up to sit and stand.

Between four and six months, I like to see babies start holding their head up consistently (no more floppy newborn head hangin' around) and start rolling over when placed on the belly and back. Sometimes they prefer to only flip over in one direction, and that's okay at first. I'd like them to bear weight on their legs when you prop them upright.

Between six and nine months of age, I'd like to start seeing infants gain more strength and coordination in the muscles of the core, shoulders, torso, and hips. This generally means starting to sit while propped up on their arms, sitting stably without help, and starting to move across the floor. Rolling both directions should be easier by now.

By nine to ten months, they should be able to sit on their own, move into a crawling position, then pop back up into sitting again. I want to see them start pulling up to stand alongside furniture or while holding your hands, and even start to take a few steps along the couch, while holding on (cruising).

Most babies start to master the art of crawling around nine months, but please know that *not all babies crawl*. If they can find some other way to get across the rug, and it works, they may just stick to that routine until they start walking. This includes movements like impressively quick army crawling, one-legged forward thrusts, lots of rolling, and butt-scooting. If this is their preferred method, that's okay. It's just a transitional stage before the real fun begins: walking. If you have any questions about the way your baby moves across the floor, just ask your doc!

Is There Some Variability in How and When Babies Start to Move?

Abso-freakin'-lutely.

I can think of a lot of scenarios where I have not seen infants meet all the movement milestones we like to see at their age. Was your baby born prematurely? That can play a big role in when they start to move. The earlier in gestation your baby is born, the longer it may take for him to develop the strength and tone to do things like sit and crawl. Body type can also play a role. I sometimes find that long, lean babies tend to start moving a little sooner than chubbier, shorter babies (lots of exceptions here of course). I suspect it's the difference in their muscle mass/body weight ratio.

And honestly, personality plays a role, too. Some babies are *frantic* to work for toys and have a strong pull toward curiosity. Other babies are less motivated, or may find themselves interested in an object, but not enough to start quickly exercising to get to it.

All types of development in infants—gross motor, fine motor, social, verbal—is variable. We pediatricians are trained to identify the outliers—the ones who sit a few standard deviations from the norm—and may recommend physical therapy if a child seems to be pretty behind in these movements. Honestly, my friend—therapy never hurt anyone, and I've never turned down a request for physical therapy if a parent wants help with encouraging their child to move.

What Are Some Ways I Can Encourage My Baby to Start Sitting and Moving More?

To encourage sitting, try placing your baby in your lap on the floor and putting toys on the floor in front of you, or hold one out maybe a foot or so away. The goal is for your baby to reach out to grab a toy and use their core muscles to return to upright again. It's a workout!

It may take some time to get enough strength to do this. Sometimes just sitting in a "tripod" or "prop sitting" stance is great work—this is where you prop her arms down on the ground slightly in front of her to let her support herself upright on three points.

Another fun trick to encourage sitting and strengthen the core is to place her in a long, narrow diaper box. Put pillows or blankets and a few toys in front of and behind her, and watch her learn how to balance herself upright!

To help them with rolling over, reaching for toys, and crawling, try to do a lot of tummy time each day. Prop her in different positions—sides and stomach. Arms in, arms out, legs in, legs out. She may get a little pissed off about it, but that's okay from time to time. Being frustrated with their position can be motivating for babies. Put their favorite toys juuuuust out of reach, or roll a ball away from her. Tuck her knees under her tummy so she can get a sense of what it feels like to lift that belly up (and may try it herself in the future).

To encourage standing, put super-loved items on the edge of the couch cushion. This may motivate her to at least pop up for a look upright on her knees! Assist her with standing often—initially pulling her up gently yourself with both hands, and then letting her slowly learn how to push up onto her feet. Propping her up on her knees from time to time can also encourage her to try to reach higher.

As I mentioned earlier, if your baby seems to be behind and you want help with learning how and when to encourage certain movements, don't hesitate to ask your pediatrician if they can refer you to an occupational or physical therapist. Our OT and PT friends are full of tips, tricks, and knowledge in this department.

Bouncers and Walkers (A Personal Story)

My daughter Abby had some developmental delays when she was an infant.

By the time she was ten months old, she could not crawl with her belly off the floor, pull up to stand, bear weight on her legs for more than a few seconds, or shift from sitting to crawling to sitting again—common movements we like to see at this age. She had delays in what we call "gross motor development"—or, the development of the "big movements."

As I mentioned earlier, lots of things can contribute to delays. Sometimes it's just genetics. As for body size, Abby was a chunky potato, so this may have played a role. And like I mentioned before, a baby's temperament and personality can also lead to delays. Some kids want to go go go . . . and some are completely fine with sitting still and working with what's in the close vicinity. Abby certainly fit into this latter scenario.

Anyway, I believe a big player in Abby's delays was the amount of time she spent in her favorite jumpers.

Baby jumpers, bouncers, and activity centers (they're all basically the same thing) are stationary devices that allow a child to stand and bounce prior to developing those skills naturally. Kids love them because they're fun and stimulating—most have toys and games attached—and they get to see more of the room and things going on around them while being upright. Parents love them because, let's face it—they're a quick and safe option for a break.

Baby walkers are similar—except they are on wheels, so babies can bounce/pull themselves around the house. I have never owned one of these because they come with plenty of safety risks—children can fall down stairs, tip over, touch a hot stove, get pushed by siblings, pinch fingers, and slam into walls in these devices, and as fun as they seem, they're not a good idea. 0/10, Do Not Recommend.

Around four to five months, we started putting Abby in a jumper and she was thrilled! Finally, she could be propped up and see everyone! She could control her body enough to bounce and loved it. We were happy, too, because we were constantly chasing her two-year-old brother around, and it was nice to have a safe place to plop her down while that happened. Admittedly, it became a habit. When we'd read books, Abby would be propped up to be able to see the pictures. When we'd sing songs and play music with her big brother . . . Abby would get to howl and jump along in the bouncer. When we had to deal with brother's two-year-old tantrums, in she went. Emptying groceries? Bouncer. Going to the bathroom? Bouncer. Cooking dinner? Boom. Folding laundry? Ker-splat. She was probably in them a total of forty-five to sixty minutes a day.

Looking back, she was in the bouncer way too much. Learn from my mistakes, friends. Yes, pediatricians make mistakes. Physical therapists have been warning parents for years about the problems with bouncers. And the more I've practiced, the more I've realized that too much time in these things can be detrimental to the development of some kids.

Bouncers hinder a baby's ability to explore and move. And that pull to explore is so important. Also, look at your baby in her bouncer. See how she's on her tiptoes? This is a typical position, and leads to the majority of the strength being recruited from her calves and thighs. What is not strengthened is her hip, gluteal, pelvic, and core muscles—and these are the ones that help children crawl and eventually walk. The hips are spread unnaturally wide by a piece of stiff fabric. They often lock their knees, especially the younger babies. Babies can't see their feet or the ground in these devices either—and thus cannot coordinate their body well in them. Their upper bodies are also thrust forward—taking all the pressure/weight off their gluteal and hip muscles. The very muscles they need to strengthen.

The same things happen in walkers—babies are pulling themselves along while most of their weight is supported, and this works out and coordinates all the wrong muscles. They also can't see the ground or their feet. "Walkers" are a true oxymoron here—they lead to delays in walking naturally.

So, what do I recommend to parents now? Well . . . go buy a bouncer! They're great! But—use them in moderation. Use it only for very short periods of time—maybe fifteen minutes here and there, once or twice a day—twenty or thirty minutes a day, max.

And avoid baby walkers in general. I am not convinced they're safe or worth the money.

My little potato? Well, after giving away all her bouncers and putting her on the floor for the majority of the day, she was moving in no time. She, like most of us, just needed a little . . . frustration and motivation.

When Will Walking Happen?

It's a myth that babies should be walking around the age of twelve months. I honestly find such variation here. Some babies are walking around nine months, and some not until eighteen months (like my own kid). Both are considered normal as long as progress is seen over time and there are no red flags along the way. After eighteen months, if they're not walking independently, I like to get the help of a physical therapist.

Independent standing is something I like to see around anywhere from nine to fifteen months. A trick that can lead to independent standing is asking your baby to hold objects for you while they're walking along the furniture. Whoopsie! No hands left to hold the couch!

Once we've got independent standing down, the next step to learn is . . . steps! One tool that I think worked great for my kids was a push walker. These are the little things they stand behind and hold onto while learning to put one foot in front of another. I think they're great for helping babies learn how to shift their weight as they take steps, while stabilizing them and keeping them upright. You totally don't have to buy one of these, though—the same help can be found with an overturned laundry basket, or that cardboard box!

When your baby does start walking, don't expect that walk to look like yours and mine. There's a lot of waddling, wide-gait standing, and side-to-side stepping you'll see at first. Also, there are lots of funny arm movements to help with balance. I also sometimes see in-toeing or a "bowlegged" appearance to the walk before things straighten out over time. Clumsiness is to be expected, at least at first and with each growth spurt they have.

Now . . . how do we make your home safe for a newly moving baby?

20

Baby-Proofing, A to Z

Is your kid officially moving?

Well, shit's about to get real.

Here's a quick run-down of things to think about when it comes to home safety. This list is by no means complete, but I wanted to get your brain juices flowing on where and what to focus your energy. Because your baby will *absolutely* try to find as many ways as possible to get hurt. You've never been as afraid of silence as when your home suddenly enters it with a mobile child on the loose.

- A: *Alcohol* needs to be stored up high, or inside a cabinet with locks. We don't need any drunk babies around here.
- B: *Bathtub* temperature can be accidentally turned up too hot by either the baby or the parent. Set your water heater to max out at 120 degrees Fahrenheit to prevent burns.
- C: *Crib mattresses* need to be lowered to the lowest setting once a baby starts experimenting with pulling up to stand.
- D: *Detectors* for smoke and carbon monoxide are a must.
- E: *Electrical cords* should be bundled or hidden so babies can't chew on them or wrap them around their body parts.

F: *Free-standing furniture* needs to be anchored to the wall. When little people start pulling up on things like bookcases or dressers, the furniture may fall down on them. This is a huge cause of skull and rib fractures. Buy those anchors!

G: *Glasses and glass dishes* should be kept up high in cupboards or locked up.

H: *Hearths* need fireplace screens and cover the sharp brick corners if needed.

I: *Install baby gates.* I know they're unsightly, annoying, and bulky. But trust me—those stairs are *fun*, and once your baby can start crawling, you will understand why.

J: *Jutting furniture and fireplace corners* can be covered in foam cushions if they are in risky areas.

K: *Knob covers* for doors—or even better, look up something called a "Door Monkey©."

L: *Lamps* can be tipped over or shattered. Try to tuck away the tall skinny ones and put the short ones out of reach.

M: *Medications* should be kept high up in cupboards or locked up. Babies *love* to taste test those tiny pills.

N: *Nursery changing table* falls are actually *super* common when changing a wiggly baby. I've seen a few skull fractures! You may want to invest in a table that has a guardrail, safety straps, and a changing mat with a concave middle.

O: *Outlets* need to be covered. The baby will find them, and will enjoy sticking an item (or a finger) in them.

P: *Pb (lead)* risks. Lead gets into the home in many ways. One common way is when family members who work at construction sites (or in-home remodeling) track lead dust into the home. The fine dust gets on the floor or toys, and babies put these things in their mouths. Try to barricade/tarp off any home renovation projects where paint or walls are coming down, and if you work in construction zones, take off your shoes before you go into the house. Lead can also enter a baby's body if they're exposed to or chew on imported goods from other countries.

(*Bonus P: POOL FENCE! Any and all bodies of water should have a pool fence installed in homes with young children!*)

Q: "*Quality drawer*" is what I call a kitchen drawer full of Tupperware, wooden spoons, and pots and pans to bang and throw and experiment with so that the baby's attention can be held away from the other more dangerous areas of the kitchen. Try it!

R: *Ranges (Stovetops)* deserve a lot of attention—try to cook on the back burners, and cover the knobs.

S: *Safe for guns*: always, always keep your guns locked up in a gun safe.

T: *Toilet seat locks*. Just trust me on this one.

U: *Unplug* kitchen appliances, portable heaters, and fans when you're not using them. Little hands get into little places.

V: *Vitamins*—Easily accessible children's vitamins are a significant cause of ER visits for infants. The gummies look and taste like candies. Lock 'em up.

W: *Window blinds* can be deadly, if you can believe it. Window cords in particular can wrap around a baby's neck and strangle them. Try to find cordless window coverings.

(*Bonus W: WATER BEADS can also be deadly. They can swell in the body and lead to choking and internal injury. Throw them out! I would not have these in the home.*)

X: *Toxic substances* like cleaning liquids, antifreeze, and bleach need to be put up high, or locked in cabinets.

Y: *You* should know that *button batteries* can be deadly if swallowed—and little babies love to put tiny things like this in their mouths. Hide/put up all button batteries (I even refused to allow toys that required button batteries for fear they'd fall out while my babies were playing with them).

Z: *Zones of safety*, which I also dub "baby jails," are a great way to get things done across a room while knowing your kid is safe in a baby-proofed area. Use a playpen or series of connected baby gates/fencing to make one of these safe zones.

21

Taking Care of Teeth

There's this discussion thread on Reddit somewhere that I read a few years ago that I remember being very profound and thought-provoking. The title of it was, "What is Something You Wish You Could Tell Yourself Twenty Years Ago?" In this thread, folks discussed lots of very important and poignant thoughts. "I wish I could have told myself to take that risk." "I wish I spoke to my father more." "I wish I could have told myself to avoid that relationship." The number one answer, with almost ten thousand votes? "I wish I could go back and tell myself to take better care of my teeth."

It made me chuckle at the time. But seriously, the health of our teeth is something we probably all take for granted at some point or another, right? Many parents may not realize that baby teeth need as much love and care as big-people teeth. This is a great age to start forming some good habits. Let's run through a few basics of care for those chompers.

Is There Any Mouth or Gum Care I Need to Do Before the First Tooth Comes In?

Tooth care actually starts before the teeth erupt from the gums. Use a damp, clean cloth to wipe down the gums once or twice a day after a meal.

When Will the First Tooth Come In? Which One Will It Be?

Most of the time, the first tooth pops in between ages six and twelve months. That being said, I've seen kids born with teeth (they're called *natal teeth*), and I know plenty of kids that didn't get a first tooth until well after age one!

Generally, the first teeth I see erupt are the two bottom front teeth, also known as the lower central incisors. The top two central front teeth typically come in next. There are lots of exceptions here.

Do I Need to Brush My Baby's First Teeth?

Yes, you do need to brush your baby's teeth when they start to come in! Baby teeth are actually more susceptible to decay than adult teeth,[1] because they have thinner layers of something called *enamel*, which protects the tooth.

Brushing twice a day is best. Try to use a small, soft-bristled toothbrush and aim toward where the tooth meets the gum. Gently brush in small circles around the tooth. This gets more fun with time, as your sweet infant slowly morphs into a psychotic angry flailing Tyrannosaurus rex.

Which Toothpaste Should I Use?

Fluoride toothpaste and fluoride treatments are the best way to prevent teeth from getting cavities.[2] Fluoride is naturally found everywhere—in soil, water, animals, and plants. It works by putting calcium and phosphate into our enamel, to make it harder. As a result, it reduces cavities and prevents tooth decay and loss. Using fluoride toothpaste—a *very tiny* amount of it, causes a lot more prevention and protection of human teeth than harm. Using a "rice grain-sized smear" is generally what we recommend when you brush your baby's teeth.

I find social media to be sometimes loud and misinformed about fluoride. Fluoride is in many of our drinking water systems, supplemented in small amounts as a means of community prevention. It is also naturally found in almost all water on Earth, including ocean water, at higher concentrations than most city water. It is in our teas, our sodas, and our natural juices.

Fluorosis, or too-high levels of fluoride in the body, causes white spots on the teeth and, in some rare cases tooth pitting. The internet really likes to blame fluoride in our water sources for a condition called skeletal fluorosis, but generally this is only seen in situations where a huge amounts of fluoride ingested or inhaled for a chronic period of time. There is some thought that high levels of fluoride may affect bone and brain cells, or cause certain cancers, but again, the research I've read doesn't support this as being a common occurrence at all.[3-5] Also—the levels that have been studied are *super* high, and unattainable with day-to-day typical toothpaste and fluoridated water use. Just my two cents.

When Should My Baby See a Dentist?

Generally, around one year of age. Sometimes sooner if a baby has a tooth issue or is born with a natal tooth. "Within six months of the first tooth" is another recommendation I have heard from our dental friends.

What Is "Bottle Rot"?

You've probably heard your pediatrician ask you not to let your baby go to bed with a bottle. This is because of the bad tooth decay we see in some babies who are allowed to do this, which we have lovingly coined *bottle rot*. The sugars in milk, formula, juices, and sodas feed the bacteria in the mouth. As the baby falls asleep, the milk sits on the teeth for long periods of time. This leads to widespread tooth decay (you can find some pictures online—yeesh). Prevent this by (1) brushing the teeth after the last evening bottle and (2) not letting your baby hold his bottle to fall asleep.

22

The Top 10 Weirdest Baby Things That Parents (Understandably) Worry About

Despite giving up most of my twenties for my medical education, I swear there are some parent questions I get that *no amount of training* could have prepared me for. They are hilarious, thought-provoking, and important causes of parental stress that I never knew I'd get asked about so often. I wrote this list on social media a few years ago, and thought it'd be fun to share with you here.

10. Snot Color

Ah, snot color. It seems to be the nose's true indicator of how sick your child actually is, right? For decades we have held onto the idea that green or yellow snot means bad, and clear means good. I'm here to tell you that studies (and lots of experience) show me that snot color isn't necessarily a good guide for knowing if your kid has a bacterial versus a viral infection.[1] Remember, bacteria need antibiotics to get better, and viruses do not. And most of the snot I see, no matter what the color, is caused by a virus.

It doesn't mean green boogers don't make me pause—but honestly, for me, the "big picture" is the most important part. Baby getting over a cold with some new green boogers here and there? No worries. Baby who has been sick for weeks, who now has lots of green boogers, fussiness, and a new fever? Different story.

When normal colds start to dry up and go away, it's completely normal to see green and yellow boogers come out of your kid's nose. Maybe even red, if a little blood—a true stoplight of snot experiences. There are cells in snot—nostril cells, skin cells, immune cells. When the clear watery drainage at the beginning of a cold starts to dry up and contain less water, it's normal to start to see the presence of those cells—and the snot color changes.

9. Earwax Color/Texture/Amount

Parents really worry about earwax, when truly it's one of the most ingenious things our body makes.

Earwax lines our ear canals and is super protective. It keeps dust, bugs, and water from reaching the eardrum. It has antibiotic properties, if you can believe it, which prevent ear canal infections. It's made in the canal, and naturally circulates around, eventually moving to the outer ear and coming out.

It can be dry or wet. It can be all sorts of colors—white, yellow, orange, tan, brown, and black. And yes, some babies make a lot of it. The best way to deal with earwax is to leave it alone. If a little bit comes out of the ear, wipe it away. If there's too much in there, and I can't get a good look inside, I'll gently clean it out myself. We also have warm water irrigation tools we can use in the office to clean things out if things get wild in there.

8. Teeth Grinding

I'll never forget the night my baby's room monitor kept going off because of a weird clicking sound. It freaked me out. What the hell was that weird noise? Well, it turns out, it was him clicking and grinding his new teeth together. The minute babies get one or two teeth on top, to match the one or two on the bottom, they like to experiment with the feeling of rubbing them together. And yes, it can be *loud*. And it generally doesn't cause any harm to the teeth.

7. Popping Joints ("Things Crack When I Pick Her Up!")

It's totally normal for joints in your baby's shoulder and spine bones to feel like they are popping a bit here and there when you pick her up. Those bones are growing rapidly, and things like synovial fluid and ligaments shift in joints sometimes. If your baby isn't screaming in pain, I promise you didn't hurt her!

Feel free to bring it up with your doctor if you're worried. The joint I tend to pay special attention to here is the hip joint.

6. Wonky Crawling

As I mentioned earlier in the book, crawling is actually a milestone that a few babies never reach—they move straight into walking. But some babies, once they figure out the ability to move, have the goofiest crawls you've ever seen. One leg tucked under. One arm leading the way. Dragging some body parts here to there. Foregoing arms and legs altogether and butt-scooting. I have seen it all.

Once a baby learns how to get from Point A to Point B effectively and quickly, why would they change that to reach the classic hands-and-knees-on-ground position? It's completely okay for their crawl to look a little wonky if nothing else seems amiss. As long as they can move and use their arms and legs equally in other situations, with equal strength and coordination, you're good. You can always ask your pediatrician to check this out if you're worried.

5. Bow Leggedness in Newborns

Many parents really worry about how bow-legged their baby's lower legs look when they're born and in the months following. Babies are squished in the uterus—and they have to be folded into themselves a certain way to fit in there. The hips are crunched up, and the knees are crunched up, and the shins have to lay across each other on the stomach. This leads to curved-looking, "C"-shaped lower legs.

This "bowlegged" appearance is completely normal! And it is necessary so that the baby can fit in the uterus. And it will straighten out over time. By "time" I mean months, in most cases. Most bowed legs straighten out as children start walking. Always talk with your pediatrician if you're worried about bowleggedness in your baby. We are always on the watch for a condition called *clubfoot* here, along with more rare orthopedic conditions like *rickets* or *Blount's Disease*.

4. Ear Pulling

All babies pull on their ears at some point or another. Sometimes, it's because a tooth is coming in, and they feel it in the jaw area—which can radiate to the ear. Sometimes, it's because the ear hurts. I tend to think about this if the baby has been a lot fussier lately and has a cold or fever.

The *vast majority* of the time? Babies have just, well, *found* their ears, and like to play with them. They have these hands—these cool new grabbing utensils—and they can grab all the things now! Including—"what's this? What's this weird thing on my head? Whoa. Squishie. Funsies. And I can poke a finger in it? Bonus. Let me do this constantly so I can freak out my parents." Some babies do it all the time without thinking about it, like a girl twirling her hair.

If your baby isn't acting sick, hasn't had a cold, doesn't have drainage coming out of the ear, hasn't been fussier, and hasn't had a fever—that ear pulling is probably no big deal.

3. Poop Smell

Whoooeeee, I get this question a lot. A lot of parents worry their baby's poop smells "too bad." Or that the farts smell bad. Or that the poop or fart smell has changed. The smell of stools and gas is dependent on two main things: the normal bacteria that are living in the baby's gut (and there are a lot of them), and the food your baby is eating.

A sudden change in the poop smell can happen for a few reasons. Sometimes, a "tummy bug" might be the cause. These mild infections can cause a change in the smell, texture, and appearance of the poop. New medications (especially antibiotics) can also cause changes in the smell of poops.

2. Toenails

Baby toenails can be really freakin' weird. Some of them are completely flat and almost look like they're growing into the skin of the toe folds. Some of them flip up on the sides and have "wings." Some of them are weird colors or textures. Please know that the way your baby's toenails may look now is not indicative of how their toenails will look as they grow older! Toes and nails change a lot with growth.

If you notice any redness or tenderness on the sides of the toenails, there may be a tiny ingrown nail there, and it may need to be checked out by the doctor. Otherwise, just know that newborn toenails are absolutely strange—and this pediatrician gets asked about them daily.

1. Penis Color

Drumroll, please: the most common and unexpected question that I get asked about is penis color. This cracks me up. Not because the parents are worried—but because baby penises really *can* be weird. Most newborn penises are pink, peach, or brown and match the skin of the rest of the body. But some penises and penis heads are blue, yellowish, red, brown, or even purple. If it looks a little weird, but your baby seems happy and content, it's okay to ask the doctor about it the next time you see her!

Honorable Mention: Belly Button Color

Sometimes, the skin inside baby belly buttons is darker than the surrounding skin. Generally a darker brown or even black. You can scrub and scrub and it may not change. It ain't comin' off with alcohol or soap and water, folks.

23

Moving into Toddlerhood (Good Luck and Godspeed)

If you've made it this far, you probably haven't drowned in a pool of fear and frustration (or pee, poop, or drool). Your baby survived his first year. *You* survived his first year. Congratulations, you badass.

As your little one transitions into the cute, angry, drunk dictator that we generally refer to as a toddler, you may start to see some changes in his personality.

At the end of your baby's first year, your small roommate will now sort of resemble a moody teenager. He wants more independence. He can move more, and with movement comes freedom and adventures. He's getting a little better (or worse?) at communicating what he needs. He's developing some pretty strong opinions, and expressing those opinions with some pretty strong mood swings (let's face it: we call them tantrums in teenagers, too).

It's honestly a really fun time. I was always astounded to realize my baby suddenly understood me a little when I talked to him. And then willingly chose not to listen—ha! He was learning how to solve problems and accomplish his little movement and play goals with ease. And seeing him explore and test and create messes was delightful and exhausting.

Don't feel nervous if you don't quite know what comes next. There are a lot of changes that happen at the twelve-month mark. Milk transitions happen, food preferences start to vary, sleep may become a shitshow, and surprise behaviors may come out of nowhere. Trust the process and learn as you go—I did—and know that sometimes everything and sometimes nothing that anyone blabs online may apply to you and your kid.

Walk softly, and carry a big snack.

Pediatricians know that surviving your first year is a huge accomplishment, and please don't hesitate to ask us anything about the near or far future at this stage, no matter how silly it seems. We understand that the idea of your baby turning into a proper little human may be a little daunting. In fact, there will be no question you can't ask us that we haven't already heard before (remember the penis color section?).

* * *

I am the pediatrician for most of my friends' children.

It's an honor and a privilege to be their doctor. Not trying to be cheesy—it really is an amazing feeling to be trusted with the most precious thing in their lives. And watching these sweet kids grow and thrive has been great, but watching my *friends* turn into parents has been the greater wonder for me.

The wild party girl? She had her first child, and now dotes every molecule of attention on raising her daughter in the most peaceful of environments. The Type A, somewhat neurotic friend had his first baby and became a parent who suddenly went with the flow of things, accepting all the ups and downs with ease. My intense professional bestie had her first baby, and suddenly all the pressing demands of work took a very distant backseat. I had a front-row seat, and I watched all of them ease into parenthood so naturally.

I was a bit envious.

I wasn't that parent. I was sloppy. I was scared. Medical degree be damned; I had no idea what I was getting myself into when I gave birth to my first kid. Later on, I looked back at the mistakes I made in the first year of my baby's life, and I cringed. I saw the ease with which my friends slid into parenthood—and realized I felt like I had slammed into a brick wall. I loved my baby with a fierce intensity, but mourned the loss of the person I used to be and the life I used to have.

I'm a little easier on myself now that my kids are older. That scared and lost person? She did her damned best. The mistakes were so small in retrospect and completely forgivable. My kids thrived and had all their physical and emotional needs met, dammit, and I loved them as best I could despite the fear. My worries and experiences were valid, even though I was nervous to voice them at the time. And I'm grateful my life now consists of everything I want and need it to be (by having the ability to take some time for myself . . . and to write a certain book).

If your transition into parenthood was a comfortable and beautiful transition, I am genuinely delighted for you! It is a gift to be at peace with such intense and beautiful change. If you stumbled and hiccuped a little bit, like I did, please know that I am delighted for you, too.

Because there is nothing like being a little lost in order to find yourself.

Development Roll Call

Months 1–12

In this Appendix, I will walk you through some of the basic and normal developmental steps I tend to see at each age if a baby is born term (after thirty-seven weeks gestation).

This list is not complete by any means—but is meant to be used as a quick-reference guide.

All babies are different and can develop these skills at different times. Premature babies often hit these milestones later than their term peers. Always consult your pediatrician if you're worried your baby isn't meeting his or her developmental goals.

Month 1

- Big (Gross) Motor: jerky arm thrusts, quivers of arms and legs, head flops backward if unsupported, may startle with fast movements or sudden noises.
- Little (Fine) Motor: holds hands in fists, grasps things (like your finger or their own hair—ouch!).
- Speech: cries for all general needs/wants.
- Sensory (Sights, Smells, Hearing, and Touch): eyes wander and sometimes cross, tend to spend more time gazing at high-contrast (black-and-white) objects than other patterns,

startles with loud noises or sudden movements; hearing is fully developed, can recognize familiar voices, can recognize the smell of mother's breastmilk.

Month 2

- Big Motor: moves both arms and legs equally, holds head up for a few seconds when on tummy.
- Little Motor: opens and closes hands, will often hold hands in fists
- Speech: starts to make cooing sounds when spoken to
- Social: calms down when picked up, enjoys being talked to, and sometimes smiles when you smile
- Sensory: looks at a toy for several seconds and studies your face

Month 3

- Big Motor: can raise head and upper chest when lying on stomach, kicks, and stretches legs, pushes down when feet are placed on a surface
- Little Motor: brings hands to mouth, takes swipes at dangling objects with hands, grasps and shakes objects in hands
- Speech: often makes cooing sounds and babbling sounds, and sometimes can imitate your pitch and tone
- Social: can imitate some movements and facial movements, social smiles, and enjoys being played with
- Sensory: can study objects for several seconds, follow moving objects, and watch faces

Month 4

- Big Motor: brings hands to mouth, can hold head up without support, bears weight on legs when held up, starts rolling movements
- Little Motor: holds a toy when it is placed in the hand, brings objects to the mouth
- Speech: may copy your sounds, giggles, lots of "ooh" and "aah" sounds, and may start "blowing raspberries"
- Social: freakin' cute spontaneous smiles, mimicking your facial movements
- Sensory: eyes can start tracking you across the room, get excited/open mouth when they see a bottle, eyes focus on things without going cross-eyed

Month 5

- Big Motor: rolling over (sometimes with direction preference), holds head up at least ninety degrees when on belly, sits up with support
- Little Motor: starting to reach out for toys and grabbing them, hands in mouth a lot
- Speech: blowing raspberries, chuckling when you try to make them laugh, and may start squealing noises
- Social: may start to show fear of strangers, enjoys mimicking your sounds, and may respond to your emotions
- Sensory (Sights, Smells, Hearing, and Touch): making eye contact with you, explores everything with mouth, patterns and shapes are interesting to look at

Month 6

- Big Motor: rolls from back to tummy and tummy to back, sits up while self-supporting with hands (tripod sitting), puts feet in mouth, and working to get to toys
- Little Motor: can pass an object from hand to hand, reach for objects and grasp them, and put things in the mouth to explore them
- Speech: shrieking, practicing with voice volume, giggling, and babbling
- Social: recognizes familiar people, likes to look at himself in the mirror, and may show fear of strangers
- Sensory: easy eye contact with you, explores everything with the mouth

Month 7

- Big Motor: rolls over in both directions, sits up independently, puts arms out to balance while sitting, may bounce up and down when held up
- Little Motor: reach out for objects with one hand, and transfer objects from hand to hand
- Speech: more consonant sounds ("ba ba ba")
- Social: responds to another's emotions, recognizing familiar faces
- Sensory: explores different parts of a toy, may find partially hidden objects, and puts things in the mouth

Month 8

- Big Motor: gets from tummy to sitting position, sits steadily without support, scooting around on tummy, and supports full weight when standing
- Little Motor: three-finger grasp, transfers objects hand to hand easily
- Speech: consonant babbling (like b's, m's, and d's)
- Social: may turn head when name is called, may start responding to "no," responds to emotions of others, may start to develop a fear of strangers
- Sensory: starts to find hidden objects and puts things in the mouth

Month 9

- Big Motor: crawling (though not all babies crawl), pulling up to stand along furniture, cruising (walking along the furniture)
- Little Motor: pincer grasp (picks things up with thumb and finger), hits two objects together.
- Speech: making lots of different consonant sounds strung together ("mamama," "babababa"), starts responding to "no"
- Social: may turn head when name is called, responds to emotions of others, may start to develop fear of strangers, smiles/laughs with "peekaboo"
- Sensory: can find fully hidden objects, puts things in the mouth often

Month 10

- Big Motor: pull up to a standing position, sit back down from a standing position, cruise the furniture, and fast crawling (though some babies never crawl)
- Little Motor: pincer grasp, can hand an object to another person when asked
- Speech: lots of consonant babbling, may start to understand "no," and may turn and look when name is called
- Social: may start having some separation anxiety
- Sensory: lots of exploration with hands and mouth

Month 11

- Big Motor: can pull up to stand, cruise the furniture quickly, may take steps holding onto a finger or hand (or walk independently), fast crawling (though some babies never crawl)
- Little Motor: precise pincer grasp, hands objects to another person, can place small objects (like raisins) in a cup, and can pull off socks
- Speech: may start to understand words like "no" and "come here," may turn and look when their name is called
- Social: may clap, wave bye-bye, blow a kiss, and may start having some separation anxiety (like crying when you leave the room)
- Sensory: lots of exploring through touch—banging, throwing, dropping, and pushing!

Month 12

- Big Motor: may take steps holding onto a finger or hand (or walk independently), stand independently near furniture
- Little Motor: precise pincer grasp, feeds himself, hands objects to another person, pokes things with index finger, turns over containers to dump contents out, drinks from a cup
- Speech: may say "Mama" and "Dada" appropriately, may understand words like "no" and "come here," and will look when name is called
- Social: may wave goodbye, mimic clapping, blow a kiss, may have separation anxiety (crying when you leave the room), shows affection for familiar people
- Sensory: exploring objects through banging, throwing, and pushing

Acknowledgments

No one writes a book alone. Especially when the author happens to be a full-time working mom.

Thank you to my husband, Drew, for picking up the slack each and every time I muttered the words, "I've gotta go work on the book." I think the majority of 2024 was spent with my face staring at a computer screen, and you never asked me to step away.

Thank you to my parents, Linda and Samir, who from day one told me I could do and be anything I wanted—and have always been my biggest cheerleaders. I'm so lucky to have you as parents. Not all kids get to experience the unwavering help, encouragement, and devotion you two have shown me. I am forever grateful. Now I'm crying.

There were several smarter, more doctorly doctors who read parts of my book and gave me excellent feedback and an encouraging pat on the back—Drs. Alice Phillips, Alyson Zulfer, Andrea Wadley, and Millard Tierce, thank you from the bottom of my heart. Lauren Hudson, thank you for reading my sleep chapter and for letting me know it wasn't too harsh. Sleep (or lack of it) makes all of us sensitive, the author included. Love you, friend. Angela Guzzetta, you've been a dear friend for over half of my life now, and your input about this book was invaluable. Thank you for telling me you believed it was in the top 3% of books you've ever read, and thank you for being such a sweet and convincing liar.

Acknowledgments

Also, a big thanks to my partners at the office—Drs. Brad Mercer, Ramon Kinloch, and Eriel Hayes—and to all our office providers and staff (especially Veronica) for putting up with me polling you allllll the questions, begging for your input, and constantly having to hear about *the book*. Also, thanks for being really good friends and humans.

To the two text groups of beloved women that sustained my sanity and cheered me on throughout this process—The Lady Docs and my Dingledongs—you know who you are, and I love you lots.

THANK YOU to my patients and their families. I have learned about the thousands of beautiful and diverse ways to successfully raise a child from you, and I thank you for trusting me to be your doctor and for cheering me on while I WROTE A FREAKIN' BOOK!

To Christen Karniski and Rowman & Littlefield/Bloomsbury Publishing—thanks for giving this weird Texan doctor the chance to have a voice in the world. I appreciate all your guidance and help so much. I so admire what you do for the literary world every day.

Huge, gargantuan thanks to Carolyn Garza, the sweetest literary agent, who in 2023 dropped into my DMs on Instagram and said: "Hey boo, I read your fever post whenever my kids get sick. I think you'd write a great book. Let's do this," (or something to that effect). Thank you for believing in me, and for holding my hand throughout this whole 3+-year-long process.

And finally, thank you to my children, Jack and Abby. You two made me a mother, opening the door to a completely different dimension in life. It is a place that has astounded me and humbled me, and kicked my butt daily. I am so proud of the little people you are becoming. Thank you for forgiving my bad days (of which there have been plenty), and for showing me such unconditional love (despite the teen years which are quickly approaching). I love you with every molecule in my body. Now I'm crying again.

Notes

Chapter 1

1. Mitchell EA, Hutchison L, Stewart AW. The continuing decline in SIDS mortality. *Arch Dis Child.* 2007 Jul;92(7):625–6. doi: 10.1136/adc.2007.116194. Epub 2007 Apr 3. PMID: 17405855; PMCID: PMC2083749. https://www.ncbi.nlm.nih.gov/pmc/articles/PMC2083749/.

2. Auger N, Fraser WD, Smargiassi A, Kosatsky T. Ambient heat and sudden infant death: A case-crossover study spanning 30 years in Montreal, Canada. *Environ Health Perspect.* 2015 Jul;123(7):712–6. doi: 10.1289/ehp.1307960. Epub 2015 Mar 6. PMID: 25748025; PMCID: PMC4492261. https://pubmed.ncbi.nlm.nih.gov/25748025/.

3. Mitchell EA, Ford RP, Stewart AW, Taylor BJ, Becroft DM, Thompson JM, Scragg R, Hassall IB, Barry DM, Allen EM, et al. Smoking and the sudden infant death syndrome. *Pediatrics.* 1993 May;91(5):893–6. PMID: 8474808. https://pubmed.ncbi.nlm.nih.gov/8474808/.

Chapter 2

1. The Happiest Baby on the Block; Fully Revised and Updated Second Edition: The New Way to Calm Crying and Help Your Newborn Baby Sleep Longer by Harvey Karp, MD, Bantam 2015.

2. Smith RW, Colpitts M. Pacifiers and the reduced risk of sudden infant death syndrome. *Paediatr Child Health.* 2020 Jun;25(4):205–6. doi: 10.1093/pch/pxz054. Epub 2019 May 4. PMID: 32549734; PMCID: PMC7286729. https://pubmed.ncbi.nlm.nih.gov/32549734/.

Chapter 4

1. Altobelli E, Angeletti PM, Verrotti A, Petrocelli R. The impact of human milk on necrotizing enterocolitis: A systematic review and meta-analysis. *Nutrients*. 2020 May 6;12(5):1322. doi: 10.3390/nu12051322. PMID: 32384652; PMCID: PMC7284425. https://www.ncbi.nlm.nih.gov/pmc/articles/PMC7284425/.

2. Lee JS, Shin JI, Kim S, Choi YS, Shin YH, Hwang J, Shin JU, Koyanagi A, Jacob L, Smith L, Jeong HE, Noh Y, Oh IS, Rhee SY, Min C, Cho SH, Turner S, Fond G, Boyer L, Suh DI, Acharya KP, Shin JY, Lee SW, Yon DK. Breastfeeding and impact on childhood hospital admissions: A nationwide birth cohort in South Korea. *Nat Commun*. 2023 Sep 20;14(1):5819. doi: 10.1038/s41467-023-41516-y. PMID: 37730734; PMCID: PMC10511528. https://www.ncbi.nlm.nih.gov/pmc/articles/PMC10511528/.

3. Hossain S, Mihrshahi S. Exclusive breastfeeding and childhood morbidity: A narrative review. *Int J Environ Res Public Health*. 2022 Nov 10;19(22):14804. doi: 10.3390/ijerph192214804. PMID: 36429518; PMCID: PMC9691199. https://www.ncbi.nlm.nih.gov/pmc/articles/PMC9691199/.

4. Xue M, Dehaas E, Chaudhary N, O'Byrne P, Satia I, Kurmi OP. Breastfeeding and risk of childhood asthma: A systematic review and meta-analysis. *ERJ Open Res*. 2021 Dec 13;7(4):00504-2021. doi: 10.1183/23120541.00504-2021. PMID: 34912884; PMCID: PMC8666625. https://www.ncbi.nlm.nih.gov/pmc/articles/PMC8666625/.

5. Alotiby AA. The role of breastfeeding as a protective factor against the development of the immune-mediated diseases: A systematic review. *Front Pediatr*. 2023 Feb 16;11:1086999. doi: 10.3389/fped.2023.1086999. PMID: 36873649; PMCID: PMC9981158. https://www.ncbi.nlm.nih.gov/pmc/articles/PMC9981158/.

6. Polavarapu M, Klonoff-Cohen H, Joshi D, Kumar P, An R, Rosenblatt K. Development of a risk score to predict sudden infant death syndrome. *Int J Environ Res Public Health*. 2022 Aug 18;19(16):10270. doi: 10.3390/ijerph191610270. PMID: 36011906; PMCID: PMC9407916. https://www.ncbi.nlm.nih.gov/pmc/articles/PMC9407916/.

7. Kramer MS, Chalmers B, Hodnett ED, Sevkovskaya Z, Dzikovich I, Shapiro S, Collet JP, Vanilovich I, Mezen I, Ducruet T, Shishko G, Zubovich V, Mknuik D, Gluchanina E, Dombrovskiy V, Ustinovitch A, Kot T, Bogdanovich N, Ovchinikova L, Helsing E; PROBIT study

group (Promotion of Breastfeeding Intervention Trial). Promotion of Breastfeeding Intervention Trial (PROBIT): A randomized trial in the Republic of Belarus. *JAMA*. 2001 Jan 24–31;285(4):413–20. doi: 10.1001/jama.285.4.413. PMID: 11242425. https://www.ncbi.nlm.nih.gov/pmc/articles/PMC11018178/.

8   Mustafa M, Sarfraz S, Saleem G, Khan TA, Shahid D, Taj S, Amir N. Beyond milk and nurture: Breastfeeding's powerful impact on breast cancer. *Geburtshilfe Frauenheilkd*. 2024 Jun 13;84(6):541–54. doi: 10.1055/a-2313-0637. PMID: 38884025; PMCID: PMC11175834. https://www.ncbi.nlm.nih.gov/pmc/articles/PMC11175834/.

9   Obeagu EI, Obeagu GU. Exploring the profound link: Breastfeeding's impact on alleviating the burden of breast cancer—A review. *Medicine* (Baltimore). 2024 Apr 12;103(15):e37695. doi: 10.1097/MD.0000000000037695. PMID: 38608095; PMCID: PMC11018178. https://www.ncbi.nlm.nih.gov/pmc/articles/PMC11018178/.

10 Ajami M, Abdollahi M, Salehi F, Oldewage-Theron W, Jamshidi-Naeini Y. The Association between household socioeconomic status, breastfeeding, and infants' anthropometric indices. *Int J Prev Med*. 2018 Oct 12;9:89. doi: 10.4103/ijpvm.IJPVM_52_17. PMID: 30450172; PMCID: PMC6202780. https://journals.lww.com/ijom/fulltext/2018/09000/the_association_between_household_socioeconomic.85.aspx.

11 Renée Flacking, Kerstin Hedberg Nyqvist, Uwe Ewald, Effects of socioeconomic status on breastfeeding duration in mothers of preterm and term infants. *Eur. J. Public Health*. 2007 Dec 17;6:579–84. https://doi.org/10.1093/eurpub/ckm019.

12 Sampieri CL, Fragoso KG, Córdoba-Suárez D, Zenteno-Cuevas R, Montero H. Influence of skin-to-skin contact on breastfeeding: Results of the Mexican national survey of demographic dynamics, 2018. *Int Breastfeed J*. 2022 Jul 7;17(1):49. doi: 10.1186/s13006-022-00489-2. PMID: 35799253; PMCID: PMC9261042. https://pubmed.ncbi.nlm.nih.gov/35799253/.

13 Bedford R, Piccinini-Vallis H, Woolcott C. The relationship between skin-to-skin contact and rates of exclusive breastfeeding at four months among a group of mothers in Nova Scotia: A retrospective cohort study. *Can J Public Health*. 2022 Aug;113(4):589–97. doi: 10.17269/s41997-022-00627-7. Epub 2022 Apr 1. PMID: 35362936; PMCID: PMC9263019. https://pubmed.ncbi.nlm.nih.gov/35362936/.

14 Jaafar SH, Ho JJ, Jahanfar S, Angolkar M. Effect of restricted pacifier use in breastfeeding term infants for increasing duration of breastfeeding. CDSR. 2016;8. Art. No.: CD007202. DOI: 10.1002/14651858.CD007202.pub4. https://www.cochranelibrary.com/cdsr/doi/10.1002/14651858.CD007202.pub4/full.

15 Borowitz SM. What is tongue-tie and does it interfere with breastfeeding?—a brief review. *Front Pediatr.* 2023 Apr 25;11:1086942. doi: 10.3389/fped.2023.1086942. PMID: 37181430; PMCID: PMC10167863. https://www.ncbi.nlm.nih.gov/pmc/articles/PMC10167863/.

16 Visconti A, Hayes E, Ealy K, Scarborough DR. A systematic review: The effects of frenotomy on breastfeeding and speech in children with ankyloglossia. *Int J Speech Lang Pathol.* 2021 Aug;23(4):349–58. doi: 10.1080/17549507.2020.1849399. Epub 2021 Jan 27. PMID: 33501864. https://pubmed.ncbi.nlm.nih.gov/33501864/.

17 Wang J, Yang X, Hao S, Wang Y. The effect of ankyloglossia and tongue-tie division on speech articulation: A systematic review. *Int J Paediatr Dent.* 2022 Mar;32(2):144–56. doi: 10.1111/ipd.12802. Epub 2021 May 22. PMID: 33964037. https://pubmed.ncbi.nlm.nih.gov/33964037/.

Chapter 5

1 Jankiewicz M, van Lee L, Biesheuvel M, Brouwer-Brolsma EM, van der Zee L, Szajewska H. The effect of goat-milk-based infant formulas on growth and safety parameters: A systematic review and meta-analysis. *Nutrients.* 2023 Apr 27;15(9):2110. doi: 10.3390/nu15092110. PMID: 37432055; PMCID: PMC10181279. https://pmc.ncbi.nlm.nih.gov/articles/PMC10181279/.

2 DiMaggio DM, Du N, Scherer C, Brodlie S, Shabanova V, Belamarich P, Porto AF. Comparison of imported European and US infant formulas: Labeling, nutrient and safety concerns. *J Pediatr Gastroenterol Nutr.* 2019 Oct;69(4):480–6. doi: 10.1097/MPG.0000000000002395. PMID: 31107795. https://pubmed.ncbi.nlm.nih.gov/31107795/.

Chapter 6

1 Metcalf TJ, Irons TG, Sher LD, Young PC. Simethicone in the treatment of infant colic: A randomized, placebo-controlled, multicenter trial. *Pediatrics.* 1994 Jul;94(1):29–34. PMID: 8008533.

2   Biagioli E, Tarasco V, Lingua C, Moja L, Savino F. Pain-relieving agents for infantile colic. CDSR. 2016;9. Art. No.: CD009999. DOI: 10.1002/14651858.CD009999.pub2. Accessed 08 August 2024.

3   Jain K, Gunasekaran D, Venkatesh C, Soundararajan P. Gripe water administration in infants 1-6 months of age-a cross-sectional study. *J Clin Diagn Res*. 2015 Nov;9(11):SC06–8. doi: 10.7860/JCDR/2015/13727.6738. Epub 2015 Nov 1. PMID: 26673749; PMCID: PMC4668494.

4   Simonson J, Haglund K, Weber E, Fial A, Hanson L. Probiotics for the management of infantile colic: A systematic review. *MCN Am J Matern Child Nurs*. 2021 Mar-Apr 01;46(2):88–96. doi: 10.1097/NMC.0000000000000691. PMID: 33315632.

Chapter 7

1   Trikha A, Baillargeon JG, Kuo YF, Tan A, Pierson K, Sharma G, Wilkinson G, Bonds RS. Development of food allergies in patients with gastroesophageal reflux disease treated with gastric acid suppressive medications. *Pediatr Allergy Immunol*. 2013 Sep;24(6):582–8. doi: 10.1111/pai.12103. Epub 2013 Aug 2. PMID: 23905907; PMCID: PMC4528619. https://www.ncbi.nlm.nih.gov/pmc/articles/PMC4528619/.

2   Mitre E, Susi A, Kropp LE, Schwartz DJ, Gorman GH, Nylund CM. Association between use of acid-suppressive medications and antibiotics during infancy and allergic diseases in early childhood. *JAMA Pediatr*. 2018 Jun 4;172(6):e180315. doi: 10.1001/jamapediatrics.2018.0315. Epub 2018 Jun 4. PMID: 29610864; PMCID: PMC6137535. https://www.ncbi.nlm.nih.gov/pmc/articles/PMC6137535/.

3   Moon RY, Darnall RA, Feldman-Winter L, Goodstein MH, Hauck FR, & Task Force on Sudden Infant Death Syndrome. SIDS and other sleep-related infant deaths: Evidence base for 2016 updated recommendations for a safe infant sleeping environment. *Pediatrics* 2016 Nov;138(5): e20162940. 10.1542/peds.2016-2940 https://publications.aap.org/pediatrics/article/138/5/e20162938/60309/SIDS-and-Other-Sleep-Related-Infant-Deaths-Updated.

Chapter 10

1   Tikotzky, L. Postpartum maternal sleep, maternal depressive symptoms and self-perceived mother–infant emotional relationship. *BSM*. 2014;14(1):

5–22. https://doi.org/10.1080/15402002.2014.940111 https://www.tandfonline.com/doi/abs/10.1080/15402002.2014.940111.

2 McQuillan ME, Bates JE, Staples AD, Deater-Deckard K. Maternal stress, sleep, and parenting. *J Fam Psychol.* 2019 Apr;33(3):349–59. doi: 10.1037/fam0000516. Epub 2019 Feb 14. PMID: 30762410; PMCID: PMC6582939. https://www.ncbi.nlm.nih.gov/pmc/articles/PMC6582939/.

3 Merrill RM, Slavik KR. Relating parental stress with sleep disorders in parents and children. *PLoS One.* 2023 Jan 25;18(1):e0279476. doi: 10.1371/journal.pone.0279476. PMID: 36696403; PMCID: PMC9876271. https://www.ncbi.nlm.nih.gov/pmc/articles/PMC9876271/.

4 Jun Liu BSN, Yu Sun BSN, Xiaoxiao Fan BSN, Tianzi Zang BSN, Lu Han BSN, Julia Elise Slack BSN, Jinbing Bai PhD, Hong Chen BSN and Yanqun Liu PhD. Effects of psychosocial sleep interventions on improving infant sleep and maternal sleep and mood: A systematic review and meta-analysis. *Sleep Health.* 2023 Dec 01;9(5):662–71. https://www.sciencedirect.com/science/article/abs/pii/S2352721823001328.

5 Kalmbach DA, O'Brien LM, Pitts DS, Sagong C, Arnett LK, Harb NC, Cheng P, Drake CL. Mother-to-infant bonding is associated with maternal insomnia, snoring, cognitive arousal, and infant sleep problems and colic. *Behav Sleep Med.* 2022 Jul-Aug;20(4):393–409. doi: 10.1080/15402002.2021.1926249. Epub 2021 May 28. PMID: 34047659; PMCID: PMC8627527. https://www.ncbi.nlm.nih.gov/pmc/articles/PMC8627527/.

6 Eckerberg B. Treatment of sleep problems in families with young children: Effects of treatment on family well-being. *Acta Paediatr.* 2004 Jan;93(1):126–34. doi: 10.1080/08035250310007754. PMID: 14989452. https://pubmed.ncbi.nlm.nih.gov/14989452/.

7 Mindell JA, Kuhn B, Lewin DS, Meltzer LJ, Sadeh A. American academy of sleep medicine. Behavioral treatment of bedtime problems and night wakings in infants and young children. *Sleep.* 2006 Oct;29(10):1263–76. Erratum in: *Sleep.* 2006 Nov 1;29(11):1380. PMID: 17068979. https://pubmed.ncbi.nlm.nih.gov/17068979/.

8 Price AMH, Wake M, Ukoumunne OC, Hiscock H. Five-year follow-up of harms and benefits of behavioral infant sleep intervention: Randomized trial. *Pediatrics.* 2012;130(4): 643–51. https://publications.aap.org/pediatrics/article/130/4/643/30241/Five-Year-Follow-up-of-Harms-and-Benefits-of.

9 Hall WA, Hutton E, Brant RF. et al. A randomized controlled trial of an intervention for infants' behavioral sleep problems. *BMC Pediatr.* 2015;15:181. https://doi.org/10.1186/s12887-015-0492-7.

10 Sadeh A, De Marcas G, Guri Y, Berger A, Tikotzky L, Bar-Haim Y. (2015). Infant sleep predicts attention regulation and behavior problems at 3–4 years of age. *Dev. Neuropsychol.* 2015;40(3): 122–37. https://doi.org/10.1080/87565641.2014.973498.

11 Cook F, Conway LJ, Giallo R, et al. Infant sleep and child mental health: A longitudinal investigation. *ADC.* 2020;105:655–60. https://adc.bmj.com/content/105/7/655.

12 Bilgin A, Wolke D. Parental use of 'cry it out' in infants: No adverse effects on attachment and behavioural development at 18 months. *J Child Psychol Psychiatry.* 2020 Nov;61(11):1184–93. doi: 10.1111/jcpp.13223. Epub 2020 Mar 10. PMID: 32155677. https://pubmed.ncbi.nlm.nih.gov/32155677/.

13 Giesbrecht GF, Letourneau N, Campbell T, Hart M, Thomas JC, Tomfohr-Madsen L, APrON Study Team. Parental use of "cry out" in a community sample during the first year of infant life. *J Dev Behav Pediatr.* 2020 Jun/Jul;41(5):379–87. doi: 10.1097/DBP.0000000000000791. PMID: 32097246. https://pubmed.ncbi.nlm.nih.gov/32097246/.

14 Paul IM, Hohman EE, Loken E, Savage JS, Anzman-Frasca S, Carper P, Marini ME, Birch LL. Mother-infant room-sharing and sleep outcomes in the INSIGHT study. *Pediatrics.* 2017 Jul;140(1):e20170122. doi: 10.1542/peds.2017-0122. Epub 2017 Jun 5. PMID: 28759407; PMCID: PMC5495531. https://pubmed.ncbi.nlm.nih.gov/28759407/.

Chapter 11

1 Hyvärinen L, Walthes R, Jacob N, Chaplin KN, Leonhardt M. Current understanding of what infants see. *Curr Ophthalmol Rep.* 2014;2(4):142–9. doi: 10.1007/s40135-014-0056-2. PMID: 25478306; PMCID: PMC4243010. https://pmc.ncbi.nlm.nih.gov/articles/PMC4243010/.

2 Stocks CO, Carson RA. Newborn and infant vision screening in primary care: A clinical review. *J Spec Pediatr Nurs.* 2024 Jan;29(1):e12421. doi: 10.1111/jspn.12421. PMID: 38284218. https://pubmed.ncbi.nlm.nih.gov/38284218/.

3   Bito LZ, Matheny A, Cruickshanks KJ, Nondahl DM, Carino OB. Eye color changes past early childhood. The Louisville Twin Study. *Arch Ophthalmol.* 1997 May;115(5):659–63. doi: 10.1001/archopht.1997.01100150661017. PMID: 9152135. https://pubmed.ncbi.nlm.nih.gov/9152135/.

4   Balk SJ, Bochner RE, Ramdhanie MA, Reilly BK, Council on Environmental Health and Climate Change, & Section on Otolaryngology–Head and Neck Surgery. Preventing excessive noise exposure in infants, children, and adolescents. *Pediatrics.* 2023 Nov 1;152(5):e2023063752. doi: 10.1542/peds.2023-063752. PMID: 37864407. https://pubmed.ncbi.nlm.nih.gov/37864407/.

5   Hugh SC, Wolter NE, Propst EJ, Gordon KA, Cushing SL, Papsin BC. Infant sleep machines and hazardous sound pressure levels. *Pediatrics.* 2014 Apr;133(4):677–81. doi: 10.1542/peds.2013-3617. Epub 2014 Mar 3. PMID: 24590753. https://pubmed.ncbi.nlm.nih.gov/24590753/.

6   Franks AM, Seaman C, Franks EK, Rollyson W, Davies T. Parental reading to infants improves language score: A rural family medicine intervention. *J Am Board Fam Med.* 2022 Dec 23;35(6):1156–62. doi: 10.3122/jabfm.2022.220064R2. Epub 2022 Nov 17. PMID: 36396412. https://pubmed.ncbi.nlm.nih.gov/36396412/.

7   Byers-Heinlein K, Lew-Williams C. Bilingualism in the early years: What the science says. *Learn Landsc.* 2013 Fall;7(1):95–112. PMID: 30288204; PMCID: PMC6168212. https://pmc.ncbi.nlm.nih.gov/articles/PMC6168212/.

Chapter 12

1   Plutzer K, Spencer AJ, Keirse MJ. How first-time mothers perceive and deal with teething symptoms: A randomized controlled trial. *Child Care Health Dev.* 2012 Mar;38(2):292–9. doi: 10.1111/j.1365-2214.2011.01215.x. Epub 2011 Mar 6. PMID: 21375564. https://pubmed.ncbi.nlm.nih.gov/21375564/.

2   Memarpour M, Soltanimehr E, Eskandarian T. Signs and symptoms associated with primary tooth eruption: A clinical trial of nonpharmacological remedies. *BMC Oral Health.* 2015 Jul 28;15:88. doi: 10.1186/s12903-015-0070-2. PMID: 26215351; PMCID: PMC4517507. https://pubmed.ncbi.nlm.nih.gov/26215351/.

3 A Nemezio M, Mh De Oliveira K, C Romualdo P, M Queiroz A, Wg Paula-E-Silva F, Ab Silva R, C Küchler E. Association between fever and primary tooth eruption: A systematic review and meta-analysis. *Int J Clin Pediatr Dent*. 2017 Jul-Sep;10(3):293–8. doi: 10.5005/jp-journals-10005-1453. Epub 2017 Feb 27. PMID: 29104392; PMCID: PMC5661046. https://pubmed.ncbi.nlm.nih.gov/29104392/.

4 Canto FMT, Costa Neto OC, Loureiro JM, Marañón-Vásquez GA, Ferreira DMTP, Maia LC, Pithon MM. Efficacy of treatments used to relieve signs and symptoms associated with teething: A systematic review. *Braz Oral Res*. 2022 May 2;36:e066. doi: 10.1590/1807-3107bor-2022.vol36.0066. PMID: 36507753. https://pubmed.ncbi.nlm.nih.gov/36507753/.

5 DI Pierro F, Bertuccioli A, Donato G, Spada C. Retrospective analysis of the effects of a hyaluronic-based gum gel to counteract signs and symptoms of teething in infants. *Minerva Pediatr* (Torino). 2022 Apr;74(2):101–6. doi: 10.23736/S2724-5276.21.06550-2. Epub 2021 Sep 13. PMID: 34515447. https://pubmed.ncbi.nlm.nih.gov/34515447/.

6 Nissen MD, Lau ETL, Cabot PJ, Steadman KJ. Baltic amber teething necklaces: Could succinic acid leaching from beads provide anti-inflammatory effects? *BMC Complement Altern Med*. 2019 Jul 5;19(1):162. doi: 10.1186/s12906-019-2574-9. PMID: 31277614; PMCID: PMC6612214. https://pubmed.ncbi.nlm.nih.gov/26215351/.

7 de Azevedo MMF, de Araújo CS, Fernandes-Freitas LB, Soviero VM, Valente AP, Kelly da Silva Fidalgo T. Unjustified use of amber necklaces for teething symptoms alleviation: Succinic acid release underperforms compared with natural skin bacteria production. *Int J Paediatr Dent*. 2024 Jul 19. doi: 10.1111/ipd.13240. Epub ahead of print. PMID: 39031911. https://pubmed.ncbi.nlm.nih.gov/39031911/.

Chapter 13

1 Schaal B, Marlier L, Soussignan R. Human foetuses learn odours from their pregnant mother's diet. *Chem Senses*. 2000 Dec;25(6):729–37. doi: 10.1093/chemse/25.6.729. PMID: 11114151. https://pubmed.ncbi.nlm.nih.gov/11114151/.

2 Mennella JA, Jagnow CP, Beauchamp GK. Prenatal and postnatal flavor learning by human infants. *Pediatrics*. 2001 Jun;107(6):E88. doi: 10.1542/

peds.107.6.e88. PMID: 11389286; PMCID: PMC1351272. https://pubmed.ncbi.nlm.nih.gov/11389286/.

3. Remy E, Issanchou S, Chabanet C, Nicklaus S. Repeated exposure of infants at complementary feeding to a vegetable puree increases acceptance as effectively as flavor-flavor learning and more effectively than flavor-nutrient learning. *J Nutr.* 2013 Jul;143(7):1194–200. doi: 10.3945/jn.113.175646. Epub 2013 May 22. PMID: 23700337. https://pubmed.ncbi.nlm.nih.gov/23700337/.

4. Ventura AK, Worobey J. Early influences on the development of food preferences. *Curr Biol.* 2013 May 6;23(9):R401–8. doi: 10.1016/j.cub.2013.02.037. PMID: 23660363. https://pubmed.ncbi.nlm.nih.gov/23660363/.

5. Tanzi MG, Gabay MP. Association between honey consumption and infant botulism. *Pharmacotherapy.* 2002 Nov;22(11):1479–83. doi: 10.1592/phco.22.16.1479.33696. PMID: 12432974. https://pubmed.ncbi.nlm.nih.gov/12432974/.

6. Arnon SS, Midura TF, Damus K, Thompson B, Wood RM, Chin J. Honey and other environmental risk factors for infant botulism. *J Pediatr.* 1979 Feb;94(2):331–6. doi: 10.1016/s0022-3476(79)80863-x. PMID: 368301. https://pubmed.ncbi.nlm.nih.gov/368301/.

7. Du Toit G, Roberts G, Sayre PH, Bahnson HT, Radulovic S, Santos AF, et al. Randomized trial of peanut consumption in infants at risk for peanut allergy. *N Engl J Med.* 2015;372:803–13. https://www.nejm.org/doi/full/10.1056/NEJMoa1414850.

8. Yakaboski E, Robinson LB, Arroyo A, Espinola JA, Geller RJ, Sullivan AF, Rudders SA, Camargo CA. Early introduction of food allergens and risk of developing food allergy. *Nutrients.* 2021 Jul 5;13(7):2318. doi: 10.3390/nu13072318. PMID: 34371828; PMCID: PMC8308770. https://pubmed.ncbi.nlm.nih.gov/34371828/.

9. Trogen B, Jacobs S, Nowak-Wegrzyn A. Early introduction of allergenic foods and the prevention of food allergy. *Nutrients.* 2022 Jun 21;14(13):2565. doi: 10.3390/nu14132565. PMID: 35807745; PMCID: PMC9268235. https://www.ncbi.nlm.nih.gov/pmc/articles/PMC9268235/.

10. Martinón-Torres N, Carreira N, Picáns-Leis R, Pérez-Ferreirós A, Kalén A, Leis R. Baby-led weaning: What role does it play in obesity risk during the first years? A systematic review. *Nutrients.* 2021 Mar 21;13(3):1009. doi:

11 D'Auria, E., Bergamini, M., Staiano, A. et al. Baby-led weaning: What a systematic review of the literature adds on. *Ital J Pediatr.* 2018;44:49. https://doi.org/10.1186/s13052-018-0487-8.

12 Bocquet A, Brancato S, Turck D, Chalumeau M, Darmaun D, De Luca A, Feillet F, Frelut ML, Guimber D, Lapillonne A, Linglart A, Peretti N, Rozé JC, Simeoni U, Briend A, Dupont C, Chouraqui JP, Committee on Nutrition of the French Society of Pediatrics (CNSFP). "Baby-led weaning"—Progress in infant feeding or risky trend? *Arch Pediatr.* 2022 Oct;29(7):516–25. doi: 10.1016/j.arcped.2022.08.012. Epub 2022 Sep 13. PMID: 36109286. https://pubmed.ncbi.nlm.nih.gov/36109286/.

13 Gomez MS, Novaes APT, Silva JPD, Guerra LM, Possobon RF. Baby-led weaning, an overview of the new approach to food introduction: Integrative literature review. *Rev Paul Pediatr.* 2020 Jan 13;38:e2018084. doi: 10.1590/1984-0462/2020/38/2018084. PMID: 31939505; PMCID: PMC6958549. https://www.ncbi.nlm.nih.gov/pmc/articles/PMC6958549/.

Chapter 14

1 Warren C, Nimmagadda SR, Gupta R, Levin M. The epidemiology of food allergy in adults. *Ann Allergy Asthma Immunol.* 2023 Mar;130(3):276–87. doi: 10.1016/j.anai.2022.11.026. Epub 2022 Dec 9. PMID: 36509408. https://pubmed.ncbi.nlm.nih.gov/36509408/.

2 Peters RL, Soriano VX, Allen KJ, Tang MLK, Perrett KP, Lowe AJ, Wijesuriya R, Parker KM, Loke P, Dharmage SC, Koplin JJ. The prevalence of IgE-mediated food allergy and other allergic diseases in the first 10 years: The population-based, longitudinal healthnuts study. *J Allergy Clin Immunol Pract.* 2024 Jul;12(7):1819–30.e3. doi: 10.1016/j.jaip.2024.03.015. Epub 2024 Apr 8. PMID: 38597846.

3 Duckett SA, Bartman M, Roten RA. Choking. [Updated 2022 Sep 19]. In: StatPearls [Internet]. Treasure Island (FL): StatPearls Publishing; 2024 Jan. Available from: https://www.ncbi.nlm.nih.gov/books/NBK499941/.

4 Dunne CL, Peden AE, Queiroga AC, Gomez Gonzalez C, Valesco B, Szpilman D. A systematic review on the effectiveness of anti-choking suction devices and identification of research gaps. *Resuscitation.* 2020 Aug;153:219–

26. doi: 10.1016/j.resuscitation.2020.02.021. Epub 2020 Feb 27. PMID: 32114068. https://pubmed.ncbi.nlm.nih.gov/32114068/.

Chapter 15

1   Kubb C, Foran HM. Online health information seeking by parents for their children: Systematic review and agenda for further research. *J Med Internet Res.* 2020 Aug 25;22(8):e19985. doi: 10.2196/19985. PMID: 32840484; PMCID: PMC7479585. https://www.ncbi.nlm.nih.gov/pmc/articles/PMC7479585/.

2   Tan SS, Goonawardene N. Internet health information seeking and the patient-physician relationship: A systematic review. *J Med Internet Res.* 2017 Jan 19;19(1):e9. doi: 10.2196/jmir.5729. PMID: 28104579; PMCID: PMC5290294. https://pubmed.ncbi.nlm.nih.gov/28104579/.

Chapter 16

1   Moraes-Pinto MI, Suano-Souza F, Aranda CS. Immune system: Development and acquisition of immunological competence. *J Pediatr (Rio J).* 2021 Mar-Apr;97 Suppl 1(Suppl 1):S59–S66. doi: 10.1016/j.jped.2020.10.006. Epub 2020 Nov 9. PMID: 33181111; PMCID: PMC9432342. https://www.ncbi.nlm.nih.gov/pmc/articles/PMC9432342/.

2   Basha S, Surendran N, Pichichero M. Immune responses in neonates. *Expert Rev Clin Immunol.* 2014 Sep;10(9):1171–84. doi: 10.1586/1744666X.2014.942288. Epub 2014 Aug 4. PMID: 25088080; PMCID: PMC4407563. https://www.ncbi.nlm.nih.gov/pmc/articles/PMC4407563/.

3   Belkaid Y, Hand TW. Role of the microbiota in immunity and inflammation. *Cell.* 2014 Mar 27;157(1):121–41. doi: 10.1016/j.cell.2014.03.011. PMID: 24679531; PMCID: PMC4056765. https://www.ncbi.nlm.nih.gov/pmc/articles/PMC4056765/.

4   Altveş S, Yildiz HK, Vural HC. Interaction of the microbiota with the human body in health and diseases. *Biosci Microbiota Food Health.* 2020;39(2):23–32. doi: 10.12938/bmfh.19-023. Epub 2019 Dec 25. PMID: 32328397;

PMCID: PMC7162693. https://www.ncbi.nlm.nih.gov/pmc/articles/PMC7162693/.

5 Klein NC, Cunha BA. Treatment of fever. *Infectious Disease Clinics of North America*, 1996;10(1):211–16. doi: 10.1016/S0891-5520(05)70295-6. https://www.sciencedirect.com/science/article/pii/S0891552005702956?via%3Dihub#bib7.

6 Earn DJ, Andrews PW, Bolker BM. Population-level effects of suppressing fever. *Proc Biol Sci*. 2014 Jan 22;281(1778):20132570. doi: 10.1098/rspb.2013.2570. PMID: 24452021; PMCID: PMC3906934. https://pubmed.ncbi.nlm.nih.gov/24452021/.

7 Calder PC. Nutrition, immunity and COVID-19. *BMJ Nutr Prev Health*. 2020 May 20;3(1):74–92. doi: 10.1136/bmjnph-2020-000085. PMID: 33230497; PMCID: PMC7295866. https://pubmed.ncbi.nlm.nih.gov/33230497/.

8 Collins N, Belkaid Y. Control of immunity via nutritional interventions. *Immunity*. 2022 Feb 8;55(2):210–23. doi: 10.1016/j.immuni.2022.01.004. PMID: 35139351. https://pubmed.ncbi.nlm.nih.gov/35139351/. Lee GY, Han SN. The role of vitamin E in immunity. *Nutrients*. 2018 Nov 1;10(11):1614. doi: 10.3390/nu10111614. PMID: 30388871; PMCID: PMC6266234. https://pubmed.ncbi.nlm.nih.gov/30388871/.

Chapter 17

1 Facciolà A, Visalli G, Laganà A, Di Pietro A. An overview of vaccine adjuvants: Current evidence and future perspectives. *Vaccines* (Basel). 2022 May 22;10(5):819. doi: 10.3390/vaccines10050819. PMID: 35632575; PMCID: PMC9147349. https://www.ncbi.nlm.nih.gov/pmc/articles/PMC9147349/.

2 Apostólico Jde S, Lunardelli VA, Coirada FC, Boscardin SB, Rosa DS. Adjuvants: Classification, modus operandi, and licensing. *J Immunol Res*. 2016;2016:1459394. doi: 10.1155/2016/1459394. Epub 2016 May 4. PMID: 27274998; PMCID: PMC4870346. https://www.ncbi.nlm.nih.gov/pmc/articles/PMC4870346/.

3 Zhang C, Liu Y, Zhao H, Wang G. Global patterns and trends in total burden of hepatitis B from 1990 to 2019 and predictions to 2030. *Clin Epidemiol*. 2022 Dec 14;14:1519–33. doi: 10.2147/CLEP.S389853. PMID:

36540899; PMCID: PMC9760077. https://pmc.ncbi.nlm.nih.gov/articles/PMC9760077/.

4 Marulappa VG, Manjunath R, Mahesh Babu N, Maligegowda L. A ten year retrospective study on adult tetanus at the Epidemic Disease (ED) hospital, Mysore in Southern India: A review of 512 cases. *J Clin Diagn Res*. 2012 Oct;6(8):1377–80. doi: 10.7860/JCDR/2012/4137.2363. PMID: 23205351; PMCID: PMC3471487. https://pmc.ncbi.nlm.nih.gov/articles/PMC3471487.

5 Kandeil W, van den Ende C, Bunge EM, Jenkins VA, Ceregido MA, Guignard A. A systematic review of the burden of pertussis disease in infants and the effectiveness of maternal immunization against pertussis. *Expert Rev. Vaccines*. 2020;19(7):621–38. https://doi.org/10.1080/14760584.2020.1791092.

6 Pavia M, Bianco A, Nobile CG, et al. Efficacy of pneumococcal vaccination in children younger than 24 months: A meta-analysis. 2009. In: Database of Abstracts of Reviews of Effects (DARE): Quality-assessed Reviews [Internet]. York (UK): Centre for Reviews and Dissemination (UK); 1995-. https://www.ncbi.nlm.nih.gov/books/NBK78004/.

7 Hood N, Flannery B, Gaglani M, Beeram M, Wernli K, Jackson ML, Martin ET, Monto AS, Zimmerman R, Raviotta J, Belongia EA, McLean HQ, Kim S, Patel MM, Chung JR. Influenza vaccine effectiveness among children: 2011–2020. *Pediatrics*. 2023 Apr 1;151(4):e2022059922. doi: 10.1542/peds.2022-059922. PMID: 36960655; PMCID: PMC10071433. https://www.ncbi.nlm.nih.gov/pmc/articles/PMC10071433/.

8 Tenforde MW, Weber ZA, Yang DH, DeSilva MB, Dascomb K, Irving SA, Naleway AL, Gaglani M, Fireman B, Lewis N, Zerbo O, Goddard K, Timbol J, Hansen JR, Grisel N, Arndorfer J, McEvoy CE, Essien IJ, Rao S, Grannis SJ, Kharbanda AB, Natarajan K, Ong TC, Embi PJ, Ball SW, Dunne MM, Kirshner L, Wiegand RE, Dickerson M, Patel P, Ray C, Flannery B, Garg S, Adams K, Klein NP. Influenza vaccine effectiveness against influenza a-associated emergency department, urgent care, and hospitalization encounters among US adults, 2022–2023. *J Infect Dis*. 2024 Jul 25;230(1):141–51. doi: 10.1093/infdis/jiad542. PMID: 39052725; PMCID: PMC11306194. https://pubmed.ncbi.nlm.nih.gov/39052725/.

9 Albalawi ARS, Alhassun JAS, Almarshud RK, Almejali HA, Alharbi SM, Shaybah AM, Alshehab ZMA, Alzahrani SM, Abomelha LS, Almalki AA, Alkhurayyif AO, Alalawi MS, Alnass AJ, Alzibali KF, Alabdulrahim JM. Unlocking the power of influenza vaccines for pediatric population:

A narrative review. *Cureus*. 2024 Feb 28;16(2):e55119. doi: 10.7759/cureus.55119. PMID: 38558642; PMCID: PMC10979318. https://www.ncbi.nlm.nih.gov/pmc/articles/PMC10979318/.

10 Shang M, Blanton L, Brammer L, Olsen SJ, Fry AM. Influenza-associated pediatric deaths in the United States, 2010–2016. *Pediatrics*. 2018 Apr;141(4):e20172918. doi: 10.1542/peds.2017-2918. Epub 2018 Feb 12. PMID: 29440502. https://pubmed.ncbi.nlm.nih.gov/29440502/.

11 Hobbs CV, Woodworth K, Young CC, Jackson AM, Newhams MM, Dapul H, Maamari M, Hall MW, Maddux AB, Singh AR, Schuster JE, Rowan CM, Fitzgerald JC, Irby K, Kong M, Mack EH, Staat MA, Cvijanovich NZ, Bembea MM, Coates BM, Halasa NB, Walker TC, McLaughlin GE, Babbitt CJ, Nofziger RA, Loftis LL, Bradford TT, Campbell AP, Patel MM, Randolph AG, for the Overcoming COVID-19 Investigators. Frequency, characteristics and complications of COVID-19 in hospitalized infants. *Pediatr Infect Dis J*. 2022 Mar 1;41(3):e81–6. doi: 10.1097/INF.0000000000003435. PMID: 34955519; PMCID: PMC8828316. https://pubmed.ncbi.nlm.nih.gov/34955519/.

12 Flaxman S, Whittaker C, Semenova E, et al. Assessment of COVID-19 as the underlying cause of death among children and young people aged 0 to 19 years in the US. *JAMA Netw Open*. 2023;6(1):e2253590. doi:10.1001/jamanetworkopen.2022.53590. https://jamanetwork.com/journals/jamanetworkopen/fullarticle/2800816.

13 Klein NP, Demarco M, Fleming-Dutra KE, Stockwell MS, Kharbanda AB, Gaglani M, Rao S, Lewis N, Irving SA, Hartmann E, Natarajan K, Dalton AF, Zerbo O, DeSilva MB, Konatham D, Stenehjem E, Rowley EAK, Ong TC, Grannis SJ, Sloan-Aagard C, Han J, Verani JR, Raiyani C, Dascomb K, Reese SE, Barron MA, Fadel WF, Naleway AL, Nanez J, Dickerson M, Goddard K, Murthy K, Grisel N, Weber ZA, Dixon BE, Patel P, Fireman B, Arndorfer J, Valvi NR, Griggs EP, Hallowell C, Embi PJ, Ball SW, Thompson MG, Tenforde MW, Link-Gelles R. Effectiveness of BNT162b2 COVID-19 vaccination in children and adolescents. *Pediatrics*. 2023 May 1;151(5):e2022060894. doi: 10.1542/peds.2022-060894. PMID: 37026401. https://pubmed.ncbi.nlm.nih.gov/37026401/.

14 Razzaghi H, Forrest CB, Hirabayashi K, Wu Q, Allen AJ, Rao S, Chen Y, Bunnell HT, Chrischilles EA, Cowell LG, Cummins MR, Hanauer DA, Higginbotham M, Horne BD, Horowitz CR, Jhaveri R, Kim S, Mishkin A, Muszynski JA, Naggie S, Pajor, N. M., Paranjape, A., Schwenk, H. T., Sills, M. R., Tedla, Y. G., Williams, D. A., & Bailey, L. C.; RECOVER

CONSORTIUM. Vaccine effectiveness against long COVID in children. *Pediatrics.* 2024 April;153(4): e2023064446. 10.1542/peds.2023-064446. https://publications.aap.org/pediatrics/article/153/4/e2023064446/196419/Vaccine-Effectiveness-Against-Long-COVID-in.

15 Tsai MH, Chiu CY. Allergic reactions to vaccines in children: From constituents to specific vaccines. *Biomedicines.* 2023 Feb 18;11(2):620. doi: 10.3390/biomedicines11020620. PMID: 36831156; PMCID: PMC9953196. https://www.ncbi.nlm.nih.gov/pmc/articles/PMC9953196/.

16 Cheng DR, Perrett KP, Choo S, Danchin M, Buttery JP, Crawford NW. Pediatric anaphylactic adverse events following immunization in Victoria, Australia from 2007 to 2013. *Vaccine.* 2015 Mar 24;33(13):1602–7. doi: 10.1016/j.vaccine.2015.02.008. Epub 2015 Feb 16. PMID: 25698493. https://pubmed.ncbi.nlm.nih.gov/25698493/.

Chapter 18

1 King HH, Mai J, Morelli Haskell MA, Wolf K, Sweeney M. Effects of osteopathic manipulative treatment on children with plagiocephaly in the context of current pediatric practice: a retrospective chart review study. *J Osteopath Med.* 2023 Nov 24;124(4):171–7. doi: 10.1515/jom-2023-0168. PMID: 37999741. https://pubmed.ncbi.nlm.nih.gov/37999741/.

2 Bagagiolo D, Priolo CG, Favre EM, Pangallo A, Didio A, Sbarbaro M, Borro T, Daccò S, Manzoni P, Farina D. A randomized controlled trial of osteopathic manipulative therapy to reduce cranial asymmetries in young infants with nonsynostotic plagiocephaly. *Am J Perinatol.* 2022 Dec;39(S 01):S52–62. doi: 10.1055/s-0042-1758723. Epub 2022 Nov 30. PMID: 36451623. https://pubmed.ncbi.nlm.nih.gov/36451623/.

3 Del Vecchio MT, Doerr LE, Gaughan JP. The use of albuterol in young infants hospitalized with acute RSV bronchiolitis. *Interdiscip Perspect Infect Dis.* 2012;2012:585901. doi: 10.1155/2012/585901. Epub 2012 Aug 26. PMID: 22966227; PMCID: PMC3433131. https://pmc.ncbi.nlm.nih.gov/articles/PMC3433131/.

4 Drysdale SB, Cathie K, Flamein F, Knuf M, Collins AM, Hill HC, Kaiser F, Cohen R, Pinquier D, Felter CT, Vassilouthis NC, Jin J, Bangert M, Mari K, Nteene R, Wague S, Roberts M, Tissières P, Royal S, Faust SN, HARMONIE Study Group. Nirsevimab for prevention of hospitalizations due to RSV

in infants. *N Engl J Med.* 2023 Dec 28;389(26):2425–35. doi: 10.1056/NEJMoa2309189. PMID: 38157500. https://pubmed.ncbi.nlm.nih.gov/38157500/.

5   GBD 2017 Influenza Collaborators. Mortality, morbidity, and hospitalisations due to influenza lower respiratory tract infections, 2017: An analysis for the Global Burden of Disease Study 2017. *Lancet Respir Med.* 2019 Jan;7(1):69–89. doi: 10.1016/S2213-2600(18)30496-X. Epub 2018 Dec 12. PMID: 30553848; PMCID: PMC6302221. https://pubmed.ncbi.nlm.nih.gov/30553848/.

6   Feldstein LR, Britton A, Grant L, Wiegand R, Ruffin J, Babu TM, Briggs Hagen M, Burgess JL, Caban-Martinez AJ, Chu HY, Ellingson KD, Englund JA, Hegmann KT, Jeddy Z, Lauring AS, Lutrick K, Martin ET, Mathenge C, Meece J, Midgley CM, Monto AS, Newes-Adeyi G, Odame-Bamfo L, Olsho LEW, Phillips AL, Rai RP, Saydah S, Smith N, Steinhardt L, Tyner H, Vandermeer M, Vaughan M, Yoon SK, Gaglani M, Naleway AL. Effectiveness of bivalent mRNA COVID-19 vaccines in preventing SARS-CoV-2 infection in children and adolescents aged 5 to 17 years. *JAMA.* 2024 Feb 6;331(5):408–16. doi: 10.1001/jama.2023.27022. PMID: 38319331; PMCID: PMC10848053. https://pubmed.ncbi.nlm.nih.gov/38319331/.

7   Yousaf AR, Mak J, Gwynn L, Lutrick K, Bloodworth RF, Rai RP, Jeddy Z, LeClair LB, Edwards LJ, Olsho LEW, Newes-Adeyi G, Dalton AF, Caban-Martinez AJ, Gaglani M, Yoon SK, Hegmann KT, Phillips AL, Burgess JL, Ellingson KD, Rivers P, Meece JK, Feldstein LR, Tyner HL, Naleway A, Campbell AP, Britton A, Saydah S. COVID-19 vaccination and odds of post-COVID-19 condition symptoms in children aged 5 to 17 years. *JAMA Netw Open.* 2025 Feb 3;8(2):e2459672. doi: 10.1001/jamanetworkopen.2024.59672. PMID: 39992656; PMCID: PMC11851240. https://pmc.ncbi.nlm.nih.gov/articles/PMC11851240/.

Chapter 21

1   Brecher EA, Lewis CW. Infant oral health. *Pediatr Clin North Am.* 2018 Oct;65(5):909–21. doi: 10.1016/j.pcl.2018.05.016. PMID: 30213353. https://pubmed.ncbi.nlm.nih.gov/30213353/.

2   Lewis CW. Fluoride and dental caries prevention in children. *Pediatr Rev.* 2014 Jan;35(1):3–15. doi: 10.1542/pir.35-1-3. PMID: 24385561. https://pubmed.ncbi.nlm.nih.gov/24385561/.

3   Kim FM, Hayes C, Williams PL, Whitford GM, Joshipura KJ, Hoover RN, Douglass CW, National Osteosarcoma Etiology Group. An assessment of bone fluoride and osteosarcoma. *J Dent Res*. 2011 Oct;90(10):1171-6. doi: 10.1177/0022034511418828. Epub 2011 Jul 28. PMID: 21799046; PMCID: PMC3173011. https://pubmed.ncbi.nlm.nih.gov/21799046/.

4   Blakey K, Feltbower RG, Parslow RC, James PW, Gómez Pozo B, Stiller C, Vincent TJ, Norman P, McKinney PA, Murphy MF, Craft AW, McNally RJ. Is fluoride a risk factor for bone cancer? Small area analysis of osteosarcoma and Ewing sarcoma diagnosed among 0-49-year-olds in Great Britain, 1980-2005. *Int J Epidemiol*. 2014 Feb;43(1):224-34. doi: 10.1093/ije/dyt259. Epub 2014 Jan 14. PMID: 24425828; PMCID: PMC3937980. https://pubmed.ncbi.nlm.nih.gov/24425828/.

5   Archer NP, Napier TS, Villanacci JF. Fluoride exposure in public drinking water and childhood and adolescent osteosarcoma in Texas. *Cancer Causes Control*. 2016 Jul;27(7):863-8. doi: 10.1007/s10552-016-0759-9. Epub 2016 May 17. PMID: 27189068. https://pubmed.ncbi.nlm.nih.gov/27189068/.

Chapter 22

1   Altiner A, Wilm S, Däubener W, Bormann C, Pentzek M, Abholz HH, Scherer M. Sputum color for diagnosis of a bacterial infection in patients with acute cough. *Scand J Prim Health Care*. 2009;27(2):70-3. doi: 10.1080/02813430902759663. PMID: 19242860; PMCID: PMC3410464. https://pubmed.ncbi.nlm.nih.gov/19242860/.

Further Reading

Chapter 1

Moon RY, Carlin RF, Hand I, TASK FORCE ON SUDDEN INFANT DEATH SYNDROME and THE COMMITTEE ON FETUS AND NEWBORN. Evidence base for 2022 updated recommendations for a safe infant sleeping environment to reduce the risk of sleep-related infant deaths. *Pediatrics*. 2022 Jul 1;150(1):e2022057991. doi: 10.1542/peds.2022-057991. PMID: 35921639. https://pubmed.ncbi.nlm.nih.gov/35921639/.

Chapter 2

The Happiest Baby on the Block; Fully Revised and Updated Second Edition: The New Way to Calm Crying and Help Your Newborn Baby Sleep Longer by Harvey Karp, MD, Bantam 2015.

Chapter 3

It's Not Yeast: Retrospective Cohort Study of Lactating Women with Persistent Nipple and Breast Pain. https://pubmed.ncbi.nlm.nih.gov/33305975/.

ABM protocol for Mastitis. https://www.bfmed.org/assets/ABM%20Protocol%20%2336.pdf.

Chow S, Chow R, Popovic M, Lam H, Merrick J, Ventegodt S, Milakovic M, Lam M, Popovic M, Chow E, Popovic J. The use of nipple shields: A review. *Front Public Health*. 2015 Oct 16;3:236. doi: 10.3389/fpubh.2015.00236. PMID: 26528467; PMCID: PMC4607874. https://www.ncbi.nlm.nih.gov/pmc/articles/PMC4607874/.

Chapter 12

Sood S, Sood M. Teething: Myths and acts. *J Clin Pediatr Dent*. 2010 Fall;35(1):9–13. doi: 10.17796/jcpd.35.1.u146773636772101. PMID: 21189758. https://pubmed.ncbi.nlm.nih.gov/21189758/, https://oss.jocpd.com/files/article/20220727-829/pdf/JOCPD35.1.9.pdf.

Fessler DM, Abrams ET. Infant mouthing behavior: The immunocalibration hypothesis. *Med Hypotheses*. 2004;63(6):925–32. doi: 10.1016/j.mehy.2004.08.004. PMID: 15504558. https://pubmed.ncbi.nlm.nih.gov/15504558/.

Chapter 13

Borowitz SM. First bites-why, when, and what solid foods to feed infants. *Front Pediatr*. 2021 Mar 26;9:654171. doi: 10.3389/fped.2021.654171. PMID: 33842413; PMCID: PMC8032951. https://www.ncbi.nlm.nih.gov/pmc/articles/PMC8032951/.

Addendum guidelines for the prevention of peanut allergy in the United States: Report of the National Institute of Allergy and Infectious Diseases–sponsored expert panelTogias, Alkis et al. *Annals of Allergy, Asthma & Immunology*, 118(2): 166–173.e7 https://www.annallergy.org/article/S1081-1206(16)31164-4/abstract.

Chapter 17

Madsen KM, Hviid A, Vestergaard M, Schendel D, Wohlfahrt J, Thorsen P, Olsen J, Melbye M. A population-based study of measles, mumps, and rubella vaccination and autism. *N Engl J Med*. 2002 Nov 7;347(19):1477–82. doi: 10.1056/NEJMoa021134. PMID: 12421889. https://pubmed.ncbi.nlm.nih.gov/12421889/.

Black C, Kaye JA, Jick H. Relation of childhood gastrointestinal disorders to autism: Nested case-control study using data from the UK General Practice Research Database. *BMJ*. 2002 Aug 24;325(7361):419-21. doi: 10.1136/bmj.325.7361.419. PMID: 12193358; PMCID: PMC119436. https://www.ncbi.nlm.nih.gov/pmc/articles/PMC119436/.

Uno Y, Uchiyama T, Kurosawa M, Aleksic B, Ozaki N. Early exposure to the combined measles-mumps-rubella vaccine and thimerosal-containing vaccines and risk of autism spectrum disorder. *Vaccine*. 2015 May 15;33(21):2511–6. doi: 10.1016/j.vaccine.2014.12.036. Epub 2015 Jan 3. PMID: 25562790. https://pubmed.ncbi.nlm.nih.gov/25562790/.

Jain A, Marshall J, Buikema A, Bancroft T, Kelly JP, Newschaffer CJ. Autism occurrence by MMR vaccine status among US children with older siblings with and without autism. *JAMA*. 2015 Apr 21;313(15):1534–40. doi: 10.1001/jama.2015.3077. Erratum in: JAMA. 2016 Jan 12;315(2):204. doi: 10.1001/jama.2015.17754. PMID: 25898051. https://pubmed.ncbi.nlm.nih.gov/25898051/.

Taylor LE, Swerdfeger AL, Eslick GD. Vaccines are not associated with autism: An evidence-based meta-analysis of case-control and cohort studies. *Vaccine*. 2014 Jun 17;32(29):3623–9. doi: 10.1016/j.vaccine.2014.04.085. Epub 2014 May 9. PMID: 24814559. https://pubmed.ncbi.nlm.nih.gov/24814559/.

Mrozek-Budzyn D, Kiełtyka A, Majewska R. Lack of association between measles-mumps-rubella vaccination and autism in children: A case-control study. *Pediatr Infect Dis J*. 2010 May;29(5):397–400. doi: 10.1097/INF.0b013e3181c40a8a. PMID: 19952979. https://pubmed.ncbi.nlm.nih.gov/19952979/.

Hornig M, Briese T, Buie T, Bauman ML, Lauwers G, Siemetzki U, Hummel K, Rota PA, Bellini WJ, O'Leary JJ, Sheils O, Alden E, Pickering L, Lipkin WI. Lack of association between measles virus vaccine and autism with enteropathy: A case-control study. *PLoS One*. 2008 Sep 4;3(9):e3140. doi: 10.1371/journal.pone.0003140. PMID: 18769550; PMCID: PMC2526159. https://pubmed.ncbi.nlm.nih.gov/18769550/.

Uchiyama T, Kurosawa M, Inaba Y. MMR-vaccine and regression in autism spectrum disorders: Negative results presented from Japan. *J Autism Dev Disord*. 2007 Feb;37(2):210–7. doi: 10.1007/s10803-006-0157-3. PMID: 16865547. https://pubmed.ncbi.nlm.nih.gov/16865547/.

Klein KC, Diehl EB. Relationship between MMR vaccine and autism. *Ann Pharmacother*. 2004 Jul-Aug;38(7-8):1297–300. doi: 10.1345/aph.1D293. Epub 2004 Jun 1. PMID: 15173555. https://pubmed.ncbi.nlm.nih.gov/15173555/.

Offit PA, Jew RK. Addressing parents' concerns: Do vaccines contain harmful preservatives, adjuvants, additives, or residuals? *Pediatrics*. 2003 Dec;112(6 Pt 1):1394–7. doi: 10.1542/peds.112.6.1394. PMID: 14654615. https://pubmed.ncbi.nlm.nih.gov/14654615/.

Index

acrocyanosis   44, 45
acute gastroenteritis   97, 208
adjuvant   179
alcohol consumption and
    breastfeeding   60
aluminum   179
amber teething necklaces   136–7
American Academy of Pediatrics
    (AAP)   15, 59, 75
amino acid-based formulas   69
anaphylaxis   153, 187, 205
ankyloglossia   61–2
antibodies   168–9, 178
antigen   178
arms of newborns   44–5
ascorbic acid   144
Auditory Brainstem Response (ABR)
    testing   128
autism   185–6

baby acne   192–3
Baby-Led Weaning (BLW)   141,
    146–8
baby-proofing   225–8
baby squeaks   125–30
barfing   144–5
Barr, Ronald G.   78
bathing routine, newborns   30–1

belly button   42
    color   238
    stuff   197–8
belly of newborns   41–2
beta carotene   159
bicycle legs   80–1
bilirubin   38
blocked tear duct   57
bottle rot   231–2
bottle warmers   29
bouncers   221–3
bow leggedness in newborns   236
brachycephaly   34
breast milk
    biologically beneficial option   49
    clues about coming in   53–4
    mixing formula and   59
    producing   48
    "protective" nature of   50
breastfeed/breastfeeding
    and alcohol consumption   60
    and bad feelings   62–4
    and cancer   50
    and data   49–51
    emotional stress   48
    first few days of   52–3
    good nursing latch   55–6
    holding a baby while   54–5

learning to   51–2
pacifiers   60–1
pain   56–7
parenting experience   47–66
  in public   55
  time one should   59
burping   98–9
butt pops   29

calmoseptine   194
care of teeth   229–32. *See also* teething
  bottle rot   231–2
  mouth/gum care   229
  toothpaste   230–1
carotenemia   159
CDC vaccine   185
cephalohematomas   34
cerebrospinal fluid (CSF)   176
cerumen   37
chest of newborns   40–1
childhood survival rates   180
choking   157–8
clubfoot   45
common colds   200–3
common medical ailments   189–216
  baby acne   192–3
  belly button stuff   197–8
  common colds   200–3
  Covid 19   211–12
  cradle cap   193
  croup   214–16
  diaper rashes   193–5
  drool rashes   200
  ear infections   203–4
  eczema   198–200
  eye goo/pink eye   189–91
  fever   195–7
  flat head (plagiocephaly)   191–2
  flu (Influenza)   209–11
  Hand, Foot, and Mouth Disease (HFMD)   213–14
  hives   205–6
  Respiratory Syncytial Virus (RSV)   206–8
  roseola   212–13
  tummy bugs (throwing up and diarrhea)   208–9
  viral rashes   204–5
constipation   96–7
Consumer Product and Safety Commission Recall Search Page   17
coughing   144–5
Covid-19   162, 184, 211–12
Cow Milk Protein Allergy. *See* Milk and Soy Protein Intolerance (MSPI)
cowpox   176
cow's milk-based infant formulas   68
cradle cap   35, 193
cradle position   54
crawling   218–20
Cribsheet (Oster)   51
Crigler massage   190
cross-cradle position   54
croup   214–16
cry it out/Extinction method   118, 122
crying   25
  fake   25
  Period of PURPLE Crying   77–83

DEET   105–6
deformational plagiocephaly   191
delayed teething   132
development roll call   243–9
developmental dysplasia of the hip   42
diaper dermatitis   193–4
diaper rashes   193–5

diarrhea   97–8
diphtheria   180
disseminated primary
    varicella   183
dream feeds   120
drool rashes   200
dysphagia   156
Dysphoric Milk Ejection Reflex
    (D-MER)   63–4

ear infections   203–4
ear pulling   236–7
ears of newborns   35–7
earwax color/texture/amount   234–5
eating habits   11–12, 19–22
Eat-Play-Sleep routine   116–17
eczema   198–200
Elecare   83
emotional stress, and
    breastfeeding   48
encephalitis/Guillain Barre
    Syndrome   182–3
Enfamil Nutramigen   83
entertainment for newborns   31–2
epiglottitis   181
Epstein pearls   37
erythema toxicum   39
eustachian tubes   203
eyes
    color   127
    goo/pink eye   189–91
    of newborns   35–7

Facebook   47, 85, 161
fake crying   25
fatigue   26
feet of newborns   44–5
Ferber Method   118
Ferber, Richard   118
fever   170–2, 195–7
fingers of newborns   45–6

flat head (plagiocephaly)   191–2
flu (influenza)   183–4, 209–11
fontanelles   34
food allergies   152–4
food protein-induced enterocolitis
    syndrome (FPIES)   142, 145,
    154–5
foods   139–49
    Baby-Led Weaning (BLW)   141,
        146–8
    barfing   144–5
    coughing   144–5
    eight to twelve months   143
    four to five months   140–1
    gagging   144–5
    juice   148
    making or buying   143–4
    one to two meals a day   141–2
    peanut allergy   145–6
    poop changes   148–9
    recommendations for starting
        new   140–3
    sippy cups (open cups)   148
    six to seven months   141–2
    three meals a day   143
    water   148
    zero to one meal a day   140–1
football hold   54
formula
    choosing   67–70
    milk and breast milk   59
    mixing   71–3
    mixing machines   29
    ordering from Europe   74–5
    temperature   73
    transition from breast milk
        to   74
    using toddler   75
four to seven months   101–7
    changes in   103–4
    entertaining   104–5

going outside   105–6
toys worth the money   106–7
Four-Month Sleep Regression   121–2
frenulums   37
fully hydrolyzed/hypoallergenic formulas   69
fussiness
   causes in newborns   25–7
   fatigue   26
   hunger   26
   mimicking the womb   27–8
   pain   27
   positioning   28–9
   technology   29–30

gagging   144–5
gastroesophageal reflux (GER)   86
Gastroesophageal Reflux Disease (GERD)   86
goat milk formulas   69
good nursing latch   55–6
Gradual Extinction method. *See* Ferber Method

Haemophilus influenzae   176
Haemophilus influenzae type B (Hib)   176, 181
hair of newborns   35
Hand, Foot, and Mouth Disease (HFMD)   213–14
hands of newborns   44–5
Happiest Baby on the Block, The (Karp)   27
"Happy Potato Stage"   101–7
head of newborns
   brachycephaly   34
   cephalohematomas   34
   fontanelles   34
   plagiocephaly   34
   sutures   33

hearing   125–30
hemangiomas   39
hepatitis   183
Hepatitis B (HBV)   180
high-risk infants   146
hips of newborns   42
hives   205–6
hormone therapy   64
hunger   26
hydrocele   43
hymenal tag   44

immune amnesia   182
immune system   167–73, 179, 186
   antibodies   168–9
   lymph nodes   170
   vaccination   172
   vitamins/supplements   172
incarcerated umbilical hernia   198
induced breastfeeding   64
infant dyschezia   95
infant sound machines (white noise machines)   129
Instagram   4, 48, 161, 251
Intensive Care Unit (ICU)   176

jaundice   36, 38
Jenner, Edward   176
juice   148

Karp, Harvey   27
   Happiest Baby on the Block, The   27

lacrimal duct massage   36
lacrimal duct stenosis   36, 190
lactation consultants (LCs)   53
lactose intolerance   155–6
laid-back position   54
language
   development in first year   129–30

exposing baby to more than
  one 130
lanugo 38
"lazy eye" 127
Learning Early about Peanut Allergy
  (LEAP) trials 145
legs of newborns 44–5
lymph nodes 35, 170

make noises while sleeping 111–12
mastitis 57
Matrix, The 177
measles 182–3
measles-mumps-rubella vaccine
  (MMR) 186
meconium 94
medication for reflux 88–9
milia 36, 39
Milk and Soy Protein Intolerance
  (MSPI) 82–3, 155
  and reflux 90
Moro reflex 44
mottled look 38
mouth of newborns 35–7
mouthing 103, 132
movements and growth 217–24
  bouncers and walkers 221–3
  encourage sitting 220–1
  types of 218–19
  variability in 219
  walking 223–4
mumps 183

nap schedules 114
natal teeth 132
National Center on Shaken Baby
  Syndrome 78
neck of newborns 40–1
Neocate 83
neomycin 179
neonatal acne 39

nevus simplex 36–7
newborn body
  vs. adult body 33
  arms 44–5
  belly 41–2
  chest 40–1
  ears 35–7
  eyes 35–7
  feet 44–5
  fingers 45–6
  hair 35
  hands 44–5
  head 33–5
  hips 42
  legs 44–5
  mouth 35–7
  neck 40–1
  penises 42–4
  skin 37–40
  toes 45–6
  vaginas 42–4
Newborn Notes from a
  Pediatrician 20–2
newborn poops
  burping 98–9
  colors 95
  constipation 96–7
  dark and sticky 94
  diarrhea 97–8
  farts 99
  orange or pink spots in newborn's
    diaper 98
  supposed to look like 95
new mothers
  hydration 9
  napping/sitting area 10
  pointers for 9–10
  temporary diaper-changing
    stations 10
newborns/new babies
  antibodies 168–9

bathing routine   30–1
bow leggedness in   236
causes of fussiness in   25–7
crying   25
eating habits   11–12, 19–22
entertainment   31–2
experiencing reflux   86
going out with   13–15
good sleep practices   18–19
hearing, protection   128–9
learning personality of   24
safe sleep environment   15–17
skin turning yellow   158–9
timeline for meeting people   12–13
Nexium   88
nighttime sleep success   114–16
nipple shields   57
Nirsevimab   208
nursing. *See* breastfeed/breastfeeding

online/social media   161–5
Osteopathic Manipulative Treatment (OMT)   192
Oster, Emily   51
otitis externa   203
otitis media   203
Otoacoustic Emissions (OAE) testing   128

pacifiers   29, 60–1
pain
    breastfeed/breastfeeding   56–7
    fussiness   27
Parent Imposter Syndrome   5
partially hydrolyzed formulas   69
peanut allergy   145–6
penis color   238
penises of newborns   42–4
Pepcid   88
Period of PURPLE Crying   77–83

causes of   79–80
Milk and Soy Protein Intolerance (MSPI)   82–3
things that are worrisome   81–2
typical things seen during   80
periodic breathing   40–1
personality of newborns   24
pertussis (whooping cough)   181
plagiocephaly   34
plugged ducts   57
pneumococcal disease (Streptococcus pneumoniae)   182
pneumonias   173
polio   176, 182
polydactyly   46
poop
    changes   148–9
    smell   237
popping joints   235
positioning, and fussiness   28–9
Prevacid   88
Pseudostrabismus   127
pumping, breast milk   58
pyloric stenosis   90

randomized control trials (RCTs)   165
reflux   85–91
    babies experiencing   86
    causes of   86
    formulas   70
    medication for   88–9
    and Milk and Soy Protein Intolerance (MSPI)   90
    some signs of   87
    things to do about baby's   87–8
Respiratory Syncytial Virus (RSV)   206–8
roseola   212–13
rotavirus   182
ruptured tympanic membrane   204

safe sleep environment
    new babies 15–17
    pointers 16–17
schedule/routine
    Eat-Play-Sleep 116–17
    sleep 113–14
scrotum 42–3
seborrheic dermatitis 193. *See also* cradle cap
sepsis 173
sickness 172–3
side-lying position 54
sight 125–30
Similac Alimentum 83
sippy cups (open cups) 148
skin of newborns
    bilirubin 38
    erythema toxicum 39
    hemangiomas 39
    jaundice 38
    lanugo 38
    milia 39
    mottled look 38
    neonatal acne 39
skin-to-skin contact 52
sleep 109–24
    baby sleeping in own room 123–4
    Eat-Play-Sleep routine 116–17
    four months 121–2
    Four-Month Sleep Regression 121–2
    good sleep practices 18–19
    hiccups 123
    importance for babies 111
    make noises while sleeping 111–12
    nap schedules 114
    new babies 15–17
    new babies clothes for 18
    nighttime sleep success 114–16
    overtired 113
    quick tips by age 120–3
    safe sleep environment 15–17
    schedule or routine 113–14
    six months and older 122–3
    six weeks to three months 120
    sleep training 117–19
    training 117–19
    wake times 112–13
smallpox 176
smart bassinets 30
smegma 43
snot color 233–4
social media. *See* online/social media
Solve Your Child's Sleep Problems (Ferber) 118
sound machines 29
soy formulas 69
special formulas 70
stabilizers 179
sterilizing practices 73
streptomycin 179
subacute sclerosing panencephalitis (SSPE) 182
Sudden Infant Death Syndrome (SIDS) death 15, 50
sundowning 80
sunscreen 105–6
sutures 33
swaddles 18
systematic reviews 165

teeth grinding 235
teething 131–7
    Baltic amber teething necklaces 136–7
    symptoms 133–5
tetanus 180–1
TikTok 161–2, 164
toddlerhood 239–41

toenails 237–8
toes of newborns 45–6
tongue tie (ankyloglossia) 61–2
torticollis 191
toys 106–7
troubles with swallowing 156–7
tummy bugs (throwing up and diarrhea) 208–9

ultra-processed foods 144
umbilical granuloma 198
umbilical hernia 197
umbilicus 41, 197

vaccines/vaccination 172, 175–88
   and autism 185–6
   childhood survival rates 180
   defined 177–8
   against diseases 179–84
   Haemophilus influenzae type b (Hib) 176
   harmful ingredients in 178–9
   injuries 187
   side effects of 186–7
   spread out 184–5
vaginas of newborns 42–4
varicella-zoster (chicken pox, shingles) 183
vibrating baby chairs 30
viral rashes 204–5
vision problems
   cross-eyed babies 126–7

eye color 127
   lazy eye 127
   red flags for 126
Vitamin D 64
vitamins/supplements 172

Wadley, Andrea 48–9
wake times 112–13
walkers 221–3
water 148
weirdest baby things 233–8
   belly button color 238
   bow leggedness in newborns 236
   ear pulling 236–7
   earwax color/texture/amount 234–5
   penis color 238
   poop smell 237
   popping joints 235
   snot color 233–4
   teeth grinding 235
   toenails 237–8
   wonky crawling 235–6
womb 27–8
wonky crawling 235–6
World Health Organization (WHO) 59

xiphoid process 40

YouTube 181, 190

About the Author

Diane Arnaout, MD, FAAP, is a mom and general pediatrician in Fort Worth, Texas. She has been practicing medicine for over fifteen years and writing on social media as an educator for more than ten of those years.

Each day in her exam rooms, she learns what parents worry about the most when it comes to their kids, and she enjoys calming their fears by writing and teaching both in-person and online. Over time, she has built an online following and has been featured in numerous television interviews and international news sites about common childhood topics, stories, and ailments.

She is married to her version of Mr. Darcy and has two wonderful kids. She has a cat named Joe. In her free time, she enjoys yoga, reading, painting, attending concerts (while pretending she's twenty-two again), and playing her drumset badly.